AF226137

Fifteen Critical Insights For Business Owners Over Fifty

Leander Jackie Grogan

groganbooks.com

Publishing Services Worldwide

Printed in the United States of America
First Printing: April, 2021
ISBN-978-1-5136-8108-5

Dedication

This book is dedicated to Chuck Conley, Managing Partner of Workforce Innovations and legendary human resources and organizational consultant, nationally recognized for developing cutting-edge business strategies, transforming cultures, and aligning major corporations with their core values and profit objectives. Without his deep insights and wonderful firsthand experiences, this book would not be possible... Thank you, Chuck!

Leander Jackie Grogan

About the Author

Leander Jackie Grogan

Award-Winning Author

Twenty years as a seasoned marketing consultant and content creator specializing in sequential mapping, SOP compliance, and transformation of complex technical concepts into simple, digestible brochures, manuals, and videos is a dream career within itself. And yet, Grogan's savvy marketing expertise and innovative approach to problem-solving have always been driven by his passion for writing, his fascination with the transformative power of written words.

Grogan is the author of nine fiction and nonfiction books, distributed in eleven countries and five different languages. He has won numerous local and national awards in creative writing for radio, print, and the web. Besides having authored a number of nonfiction articles in national magazines such as AdWeek and Jet, his business bestseller, What's Wrong With Your Small Business Team, has changed the dynamics of evaluating human capital (people) in small business environments.

What does all of this mean to you? It means your author has been around the block a time or two. He understands what it means to be over fifty with a fast clock ticking inside your head. You don't have time to waste. You need an excellent communicator, succinct guidance, and a solid plan of action without the gibberish of "tech talk" from some wet-behind-the-ears YouTube guru trying to sound important.

That's what you need to give your business a solid foundation after the monstrous game-changer we know as COVID-19. That's what you're going to get with **Fifteen Critical Insights For Business Owners Over Fifty.**

Silver Microphone National Award

Houston Association of Radio Broadcasters Award

Who's Who In Advertising

Matrix Award

Matrix Best Of Category Award

CEBA National Award - New York

Crystal Communicator Award of Excellence

TABLE OF CONTENTS

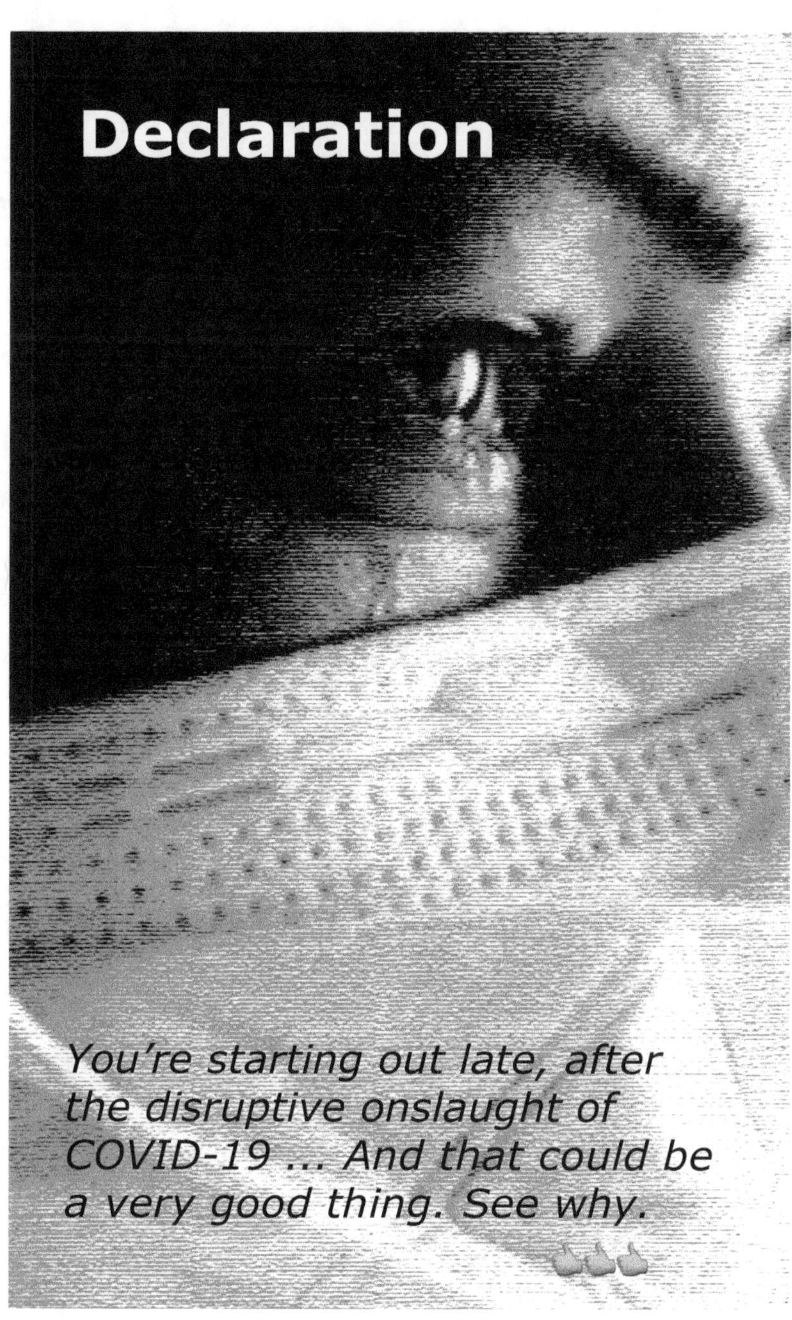

Declaration
You're starting out late, after the disruptive onslaught of COVID-19 ... And that could be a very good thing. See why.

So You're Over Fifty and Want To Become A Successful Entrepreneur.

*T*here are basically two ways you arrived at this point ... **Push or Pull**. Either, in the aftermath of COVID-19, some organization, engrossed in restructuring, downsizing, or payroll reduction, **pushed** you out of the door. Or, a lifelong yearning to follow your passion and pursue a more meaningful lifestyle that pays what you're worth and gives you more control over your life, **pulled** you into action.

Either way, before you call in the lawyers, bookkeepers, and marketing consultants, your first move involves a huge, invisible, often trivialized step that will ultimately empower or sabotage your entire journey. No. It is not your choice of markets or partners or goods or services. **Rather, it is the recognition and acceptance of the need to transform your mind.**

For years (unless you worked for a company like Google, Southwest Airlines, or GE ... unique cultures, hungry for employee-generated feedback and innovation), you've operated under a system of **action-oriented rewards.** On a daily basis, often relinquishing your opinion and biting your tongue, you carried out certain premeditated actions to please your boss and secure your job. This could have been something as trivial as getting back from lunch precisely on time, or laughing at the district manager's stale jokes, or attending the CEO's annual company picnic.

These were survival techniques that kept a target off your back and food on your table. But, as a business owner, these techniques will be of little value. A thousand self-realization books by successful entrepreneurs will tell you it's imperative to flush that whole mindset down the drain. From this moment on, actions (alone) are not relevant unless they contribute to the stated goals and objectives of your organization.

Getting up at the crack of dawn; Arriving at your restaurant at 5:00 AM are actions that means nothing if the meat truck comes by at 4:30 AM.

Mama might be proud of you, answering the call of the alarm clock. Your "actions", however, simply mean you're going to lose customers because you've run out of meat.

As a new business owner, your actions are tied to a new standard of accountability. **Don't tell me what you did. Tell me what you accomplished toward the end goal.** This becomes your daily "mirror-view" confession, your new standard of performance.

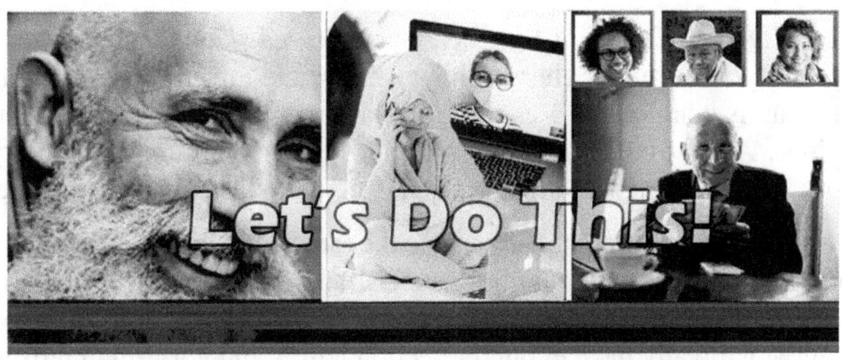

What Are Your Chances For Success?

Let's dispel the doom and gloom about starting a business when you're over fifty. Let's be honest. Let's reach into the shadows to drag all of the real and imagined enemies into the light.

Some challenges are inescapable. Others mask themselves as enemies, but in reality, are tools of empowerment to give you the edge. Take out a pen and poster. So you might be reminded each day, write down this new reality and pin it to a prominent spot on the wall. You're the commanding general now, with the fate of your future resting squarely on YOUR shoulders. In this war, it is your duty to identify each adversary, both internally and externally, and especially the ones that abide inside your head. At this point, you're not trying to craft strategies to conquer these enemies. You are simply identifying them for future dismantling.

Just so you understand the harsh reality of your poster on the wall, you may find that early on, **your spouse is the enemy.** Each day, he or she reminds you of all of the reasons you're going to fail. Constantly, she laments about the fallacy of investing your precious severance pay in a pipe dream. She bombards you with articles about new companies moving to the area, desperately in need of your expertise. She speculates out loud about the monthly bills, and how living expenses are going up while your income is going down.

Don't be too hard on her. She's scared. Hell, you're scared too. But you have the wherewithal to know, the government stimulus program is temporary. Resulting inflation will eat a hole in your savings. AND, if they haven't already dumped you and your hefty Baby Boomer salary into the *farewell cradle*, it's just a matter of time.

And what about those "new to the area companies"? At fifty and counting, with the uncertainty of new strains of COVID-19, looming in the distance, none of them are eager to hire you. She doesn't know it, but you already have enough rejection letters and not-a-fit emails to keep the Christmas fireplace going until New Year's Day.

We're going to fix it (Chapter 15). But for now, she's the enemy. The poster on the wall is a reminder not to sugarcoat this unpleasant reality. She belongs on the list, along with your smoking habit, outrageous, resource-sucking BMW car note, and reckless tendency to forgo data-driven research to rely on your uninformed gut.

In this book, we will examine all of these enemies. Prep work for a would-be entrepreneur is demanding, sacrificial, and brutally honest. EASY does not have a boarding pass on your rocket ship to the stars. Get ready for a soul-searching ride.

Let's identify a few, if not all, of the enemies with which you should immediately expect to contend.

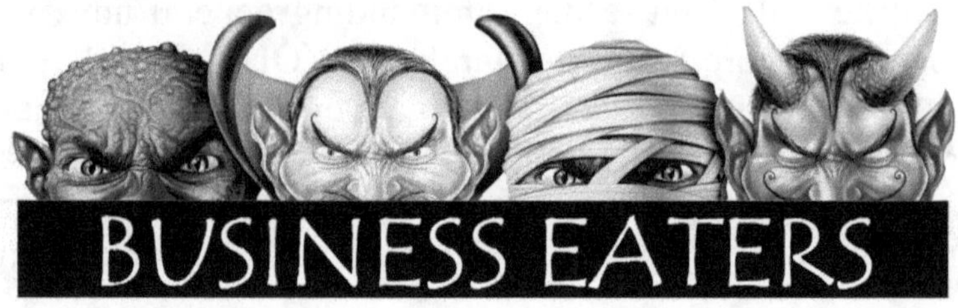

List of Enemies:

1. You're going to have less energy than a caffeine-crazed twenty-year-old on Modafinil.

Clinical studies (Ergography) report a universal trend among midlife and older adults. We tend to feeling less energized, accompanied by increased difficulty in focusing and sustaining mental alertness. This is due in part to *Circadian* changes, that is to say, changing biological rhythms that often cause us to fall asleep early and wake up more frequently during the middle of the night. This reduces critical deep sleep restoration phases our mind and body require. Thus, we awaken the next day feeling drained, sluggish, and unable to focus.

Working in tandem against us is the normal depreciation of our physical body. By our late 60s, we lose roughly one-third of our muscle mass, which translates into decreased endurance and increased fatigue. Somebody better sit next to the old guy at the conference table after 3:00 P.M. Kick him, elbow him, whatever you have to do.

Finally, during our late 50s, the brain, itself, undergoes both physical and chemical-related changes, including shrinkage in the frontal lobe and hippocampus, and a reduction in levels of serotonin which helps with mood, sleep, and nervous system communications.

Upon starting a business, you'll need to be sharper, more energized, and more in tune with your daily environment. With so many inevitable crises to manage, you don't need your critical mental and physical faculties running for the hills.

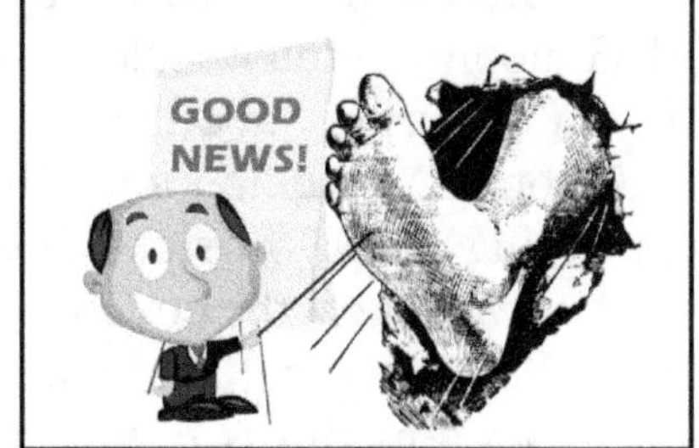

You can stomp all of these age-related enemies into the ground or, at least, make them nonfactors in your march

toward victory. Diet, exercise, weight training, a "mandatory" thirty-minute walk each day are proven, effective, unfaltering weapons against lingering fatigue and the foggy-brain syndrome of old age. Being mentally engaged as an entrepreneur, learning something new each day, will dramatically transform your ability to focus, while simultaneously creating new neural pathways in the brain. **You're going to get smarter whether you like it or not.**

Don't let anyone tell you you're too old to manage this war. You have powerful weapons at your disposal. In this *one* strategic area, you can immediately start to change the dynamics and probabilities for success by simply committing to a new regimen of mental and physical toughness. Buy the book by the nation's sleep guru, ***Shawn Stevenson, called Sleep Smarter.*** It's a life-changer. Then, find  the site for ***Helen Dennis***, a nationally recognized leader on issues of aging, and ***Wellness Mama's*** online health food recipes. Follow their instructions explicitly. Add new over-fifty wellness coaches as you go. An exceptional one for over-fifty training is **bobandbrad.com.**

Your skin is the largest organ in your body. Roughly 60% of the solutions you apply to your outer skin end up inside your body. Stop using soaps, shampoos, and body washes that contain deadly toxins such as sulfates, parabens, polyethylene glycol, triclosan, and methylisothiazolinone. Start "reading" each label. You're sick and you don't know why. Get off the slow road to the graveyard.

Invest in a smart step-watch, ECG/ EKG monitor, gluten tester, fitness band, and home exercise bike. If you're serious about this entrepreneurial journey, you don't need someone kicking and elbowing you at the conference table, explaining how you slept through the contract offer. Start here. Start now. Get off the couch. Haul those big red steaks to the Food Bank. Your personal health and mental cognition are critical. **You can't run a business if you're walking around in a fog.**

2. You're going to have a shorter runway to make mistakes and recover.

UBER launched in 2009 and will finally become profitable in 2021. Peloton, a leading seller of high-end home exercise bikes and equipment, launched in 2012. The company has been losing roughly $200 million a year. Pinterest, founded in 2010, with a current valuation of $12.6 billion, is still losing $41 million a quarter. You, on the other hand, with a new gray hair punching out of an old socket each week, can't wait a decade to turn a profit.

This problem is not insurmountable. You'll have to work harder and smarter. Just like Amazon and Apple, you'll have to minimize your mistakes using data-driven decision-making tools. In this book (Chapter 13), we'll show you how. Just be aware there is a relentless clock ticking on your future. Unlike the young 30ish founders of UBER, it's not on your side.

3. Your life's journey has made you more cautious (pessimistic) than a young, naïve sky-walker who believes anything is possible. You will constantly have to fight a fatal tendency to limit experimentation and dismiss your best ideas before anyone else has the chance.

Perception is reality, that is to say, your beliefs might be totally incorrect, lacking the slightest iota of evidential proof. Nevertheless, they represent your framework of reality. Hillary Clinton's supporters say Donald Trump stole the election. Donald Trump's supporters say Joe Biden stole the election. If a time machine could take you back to age four, and your parents told you to go to bed early because Santa Claus was coming with lots of presents on his sleigh, you'd believe it. You'd retire without a fuss.

Because negative experiences impact us more profoundly, we tend to remember bad things more than good. Clinical research, charting the trajectory of the Optimism Index, indicates pessimism bias is more common among women than men. It also occurs more frequently in people who experience clinical depression. If we aren't careful, the cumulative effect of experiencing disappointment and defeat will turn us into entrepreneurial visionaries who always expect the worst of our visions to come to pass.

That's a very encumbered, counter-productive mindset. In this fourth quarter march toward victory, you don't have much time. You don't have much money. And now, you don't have much faith in your ability to invoke a positive return on your effort. That's no way to win a war. Seventy percent of this battle is mental. Twenty percent is physical. Ten percent is what some people refer to as good fortunes, blessings, or luck. If you control the first two, you'll get your fair share of the third.

4. Because of your limited familiarity with technology, many promising business opportunities will not be available to you.

What the heck is 5G or Blockchain or Hyper-automation or Incognito browsing? What do these bizarre terms mean to the 76-million mainframe, punch-card generation Baby Boomers in today's confusing technolog- ically driven marketplace?

Back in the old days, there were no personal computers. For most Baby Boomers, technology has been an inescapable nightmare. The Pew Research Center found that 77% of older Americans need someone to assist them with learning new technologies. Roughly

92% of Baby Boomers feel that technology has a negative effect on face-to-face communications. People don't talk to each other anymore.

Generally speaking, old age and technology don't mix. The inevitable learning curve, fear of failure, potential loss of privacy, threat of scams, and constant millennial berating make for a toxic brew. If the business opportunity is in technology, unless you're an exception to the rule (we talk about the resilient, self-taught, shape-shifter exceptions in Chapter 5), you're going to miss out. No worries. With so many other non-tech opportunities available to the diligent, persevering entrepreneur of any age, **you're still very much in the game.**

5. If you dip into your life savings and fail, there is little or no time to replenish the funds before age-related medical costs start to accumulate.

This is no surprise. The older we get, the more trips we make to the doctor, the more medical costs we incur. Preservation of our health is key.

There is, however, a deeper aspect to this health-conscious transition from wage income and personal savings to entrepreneurial revenue. And that is the mentality of debt. The government stimulus program won't last forever ... shouldn't last forever. Unless your rich uncle left you a bundle to start your own business, you're going to have to go into debt.

Yes, Baby Boomers have the highest retirement savings with an average of $152,000. They also possess more than half (54%) of all US household wealth. But these rosy numbers most often belong to affluent, cream-of-the-crop Baby Boomer households that make $350,000 or more, annually.

Since COVID-19, roughly nine million Americans have fallen into poverty. If you've been making the once-coveted, six-figure income of $100,000, and you're over fifty, with systemic age discrimination, the cost of healthcare rising, and the Social Security fund, projected to run out in 2030, you're probably headed for financial trouble.

Let's be perfectly honest about the new normalcy in which we live. Volatility in the marketplace is not going away. The fears and uncertainty of COVID-19 will linger for many years, perhaps, decades, disrupting normal buying patterns and creating huge spikes and dips in the economy's historical performance. **In this unpredictable environment, you CANNOT bootstrap your way to success.** Roughly, 76% of all businesses fail due to insufficient working capital. You're going to need financing (Chapter 15 - Debt) to increase your flexibility, cover your rookie mistakes, and preserve your personal savings for the age-related medical hardships to come.

6. Because you're over fifty, hiring Generation X and Millennial employees is going to be a nightmare.

The generation gap is real. Gen Xers (born 1965-1980) grew up with minimal adult supervision and thinking patterns free of conventional boundaries. They are well-educated, technologically adept, and demand independence and a sense of work-life balance. **They will never be the workaholic you are.** Millennials (born 1981-1997) are technology masters. Their brains are wired for virtual team-related interaction. They aren't afraid to question authority because they see the supervisor as an equal contributor. The dictatorial, command-down structure to which Baby Boomers are accustomed, will send Millennials flying out of the door.

You might be tempted to hire people who look, think, and act like you. But this would be a monumental mistake. You need the skill-sets and diversity these two generations bring to the table. **You can't build a solid team without them.** Thus, you'll need a reputable hiring agency that understands these generational nuances and can send you candidates that meet your specific needs.

There you have it, at least, some of it. This list of enemies gives you an overview of the major obstacles to anticipate in the early going.

Still there? GREAT! Let's move on to the weapons that over-fifty entrepreneurs intrinsically possess to give them an advantage and stomp their enemies into the ground.

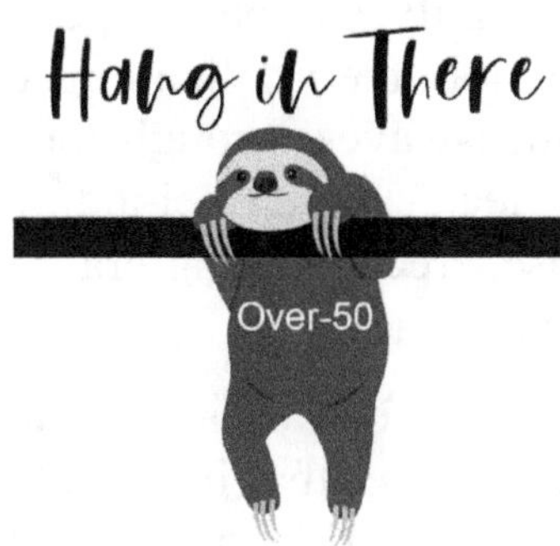

Weapons That Give You The Edge

As a new business owner over fifty, you might think you're operating at a disadvantage. You've come into the marketplace late, while everyone else is soaring into the stratosphere, light years ahead.

This is a popular misconception, not that you're late, but that the timing puts you at a disadvantage. Let's dispel this notion right now. **Contrary to the normal fears and skepticism that accompany a major, life-changing transition such as business ownership, you're in a good place, a very good place.** Let's talk about the reasons this is true.

Chances are you're old enough to remember or have read about the Russian satellite called *Sputnik*. In 1957, the Soviet Union launched the first technologically advanced artificial satellite into space. It was ten times the size of the first planned U.S. satellite, which was not scheduled to be launched until the following year. The U.S. military and scientific communities were caught off guard. During this highly combative period of atomic weapons and cold war aggression, the implications of Soviet technological superiority sent shock-waves through the American public. The United States had clearly fallen behind. This gloomy discovery ushered in an intense, free-spending era we reflect upon today as the international "space race".

If we were to fast-forward a mere decade after this chilling wake-up call, we'd discover that in the late '60s, with the help of imported scientists from Nazi Germany and unlimited government funding, the United States took a giant leap ahead, culminating its efforts with the Apollo lunar-landing program that put the first man on the moon.

In other words, the United States entered late but won the race.

Toyota entered the SUV market very late but is now number #1, ahead of Ford Explorer and Chevy Tahoe. Zantac (though plagued by lawsuits) entered late but is now the best-selling ulcer-relief drug in the world.

Allow this fact to settle into the deep crevices of your over-fifty mind. **Late means nothing if you employ the right strategies and resources.** In most instances, *late* offers the strategic advantage of avoiding costly mistakes that previous entrepreneurs have already made.

Here's the second reason to discard your skepticism. It may be more compelling than the first. It goes by the name of COVID-19.

Let's give some legs to our opening statement:

You're starting out late, after the disruptive onslaught of COVID-19 ... And that could be a very good thing. See why.

Oddly enough, we begin our discussion with a story about dust mites. Let's say you moved into a new office space intended to serve as headquarters for your new enterprise. A few weeks later, you and your small team begin to experience the same mysterious discomfort. Your skin feels itchy and scaly, as if fire ants were roaming beneath your pores. Days later, you all begin to see red welts on your face, neck, and arms. These welts turn into bumps that look like pimples. The pimples quickly spread to form a painful, itchy rash.

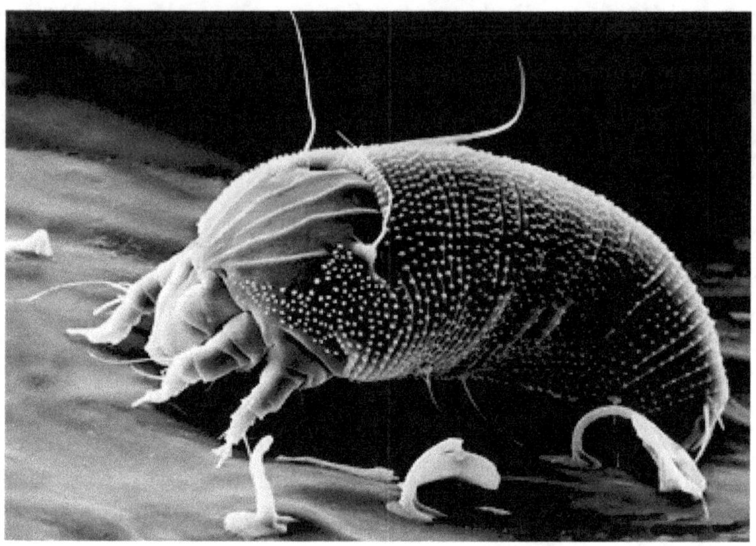

You call in an exterminator who pinpoints the problem. **You have dust mites.** These pesky creatures are invisible to the human eye. They don't actually bite. But their small bodies and feces become airborne, causing severe allergic reactions, often requiring medical treatment.

NOW, let's rewind.

Let's climb into your time machine and back-pedal this story to three months earlier. You're out and about, scouting the city for a commercial office space to house your new business. Standing on the sidewalk in front of a building, you see a well-dressed, briefcase-in-hand, probable tenant walk out. You stop him to ask about the building.

Here's what he says: *"The building is fine, good location, great view of downtown, and very secure. But we have a recurring problem with dust mites. I've had a couple of good employees quit because of them. We've called in several exterminating companies. But somehow, the little pesky bastards keep coming back. Right now, we're considering breaking our lease and moving somewhere else."*

Holy, moly, guacamole, McGillicuddy!!!
(Those are my little grandchildren's magic words to
make things disappear or transform into a new reality.)

This is huge!

Let's thoroughly examine the difference your time
machine has made. All of the other tenants are **"there already"**,
inside the building, claiming their space ahead of you. They
have those familiar headaches of moving furniture, transferring
phones, deploying networks and security systems, managing
signage, assigning parking, and meeting their new neighbor
all behind them. You are the new kid on the block, facing all
of those challenges, learning curves, and missteps the existing
tenants have already overcome.

AND YET... you have the upper hand. You know the dust
mites are inside, waiting. You can't see them with your physical
eyes. But you CAN see them with your visionary eyes, your trusted
deciphers of cause-and-effect that predict major disruptions in
daily operations and valuable, rash-bedeviled employees, walking
out on you. You haven't signed a lease. Your rent money is still
in the bank. Because you CAN see what the existing tenants
COULDN'T see, you have options they don't have. Arriving at the
building late has turned out to be a very good thing.

**Let's apply this analogy to the catastrophic new normal
the worldwide coronavirus (COVID-19) has created.**

With 21 million jobs lost, an unemployment rate, hovering
above14%, the highest since the Great Depression, and over
100,000 stores, factories, and small businesses closed, we have our
pick of industries completely devastated by COVID-19 ... **hotel
industry, travel industry, sports and performing arts industry,
amusement parks, casinos, restaurants, and bars, etc**. Let's
keep things simple with America's universal pastime of eating out.

COVID-19 hit the dine-in restaurants and bars industry with staggering repercussions. From massive reductions in restaurant reservation and bar drinking tabs, followed by food suppliers, dumping tons of milk, smashing eggs, and burying cows and hogs, to the daily spoilage of high-end meats and exotic delicacies, to the layoff of cooks, waitresses, and food truck drivers, to the closing of slaughterhouses and food distribution centers, the devastation is unprecedented. The whole restaurant supply chain runs on a just-in-time order and delivery system perfected over decades. Stakeholders cannot simply roll up the system and roll out another one in its place. A huge backlog of food, moving through the supply chain, will never make it to the designated restaurants and bars. The glut on the supply side will continue to drive prices down.

COVID-19 has driven consumers away from restaurants and into grocery stores. Except, many consumers have altered their buying patterns and are no longer going inside. Between February and March of 2020, downloads for the grocery delivery app **Instacart** increased 215 percent. **Walmart's** grocery app spiked 49%. The pandemic has created a *new normal* in which people still need food, but don't want to go out into an infected world to get it. The miracle vaccine has turned out to be a painfully slow remedy. Any routine that minimizes the risk of contracting the coronavirus seems worth a try.

People who do venture out buy in bulk, which means the grocery store manager has to figure out how to avoid spoilage on one hand, and empty shelves on the other. Too many empty shelves send a message to skittish consumers that the store is not prepared, perhaps, not even following the proper health protocols. Invariably, shoppers stop coming at all.

If you're starting your business and sitting there with five franchise proposals in front of you ... Wendy's, Baskin-Robbins, Fuddruckers Hamburgers, Denny's, and Applebee's, dump all of them into the trash. You can't see COVID-19 with your physical eyes. But you can see the *new normal* its devastation has created. You can see what existing franchise owners couldn't see ... empty seats, sporadic food truck deliveries, and employees, afraid to come to work. Your money is still in the bank. You have options they don't have. All of the previously learned protocols to give them the edge are out the window. Arriving at the restaurant portal *late* has turned out to be a very good thing.

Let's Examine A Few Other Reasons You Have The Edge:

2. Multiple studies have concluded a 50-plus-year-old founder is almost two times more likely to achieve sustained growth and longevity than a 30-year-old founder.

This simply means, although a 30-year-old founder might initially be more nimble and innovative, the chances are, he or she is not going to last. The SBA estimates that 20% of all small businesses fail the first year; 55% are gone by year 5. The number of over-fifty owned businesses still standing after year five is twice that of 30-year-old owned businesses. The longevity of a business depends on more than fast feet and an innovative idea.

3. A 50-plus-year-old founder has more extensive experience in key processes of management, marketing, and finance.

Your years of exposure to the nuts and bolts of key areas of business operations have had a cumulative effect on the breadth and depth of your knowledge base. **You know things you don't know you know** ... interpersonal strategies, cohesion of purpose, nuances of averages and extremes, and decision-making apparatuses to which most 30-year-olds have not been exposed. Time has given you an arsenal of insights on the connectivity of functions (management, marketing, finance, human capital, technology, etc.) the 30-year-olds have yet to acquire.

4. You have developed a deep network of business contacts and potential sources of capital.

In 1997, Microsoft stepped in with a pithily $150 million investment to save Apple from bankruptcy. Sometimes, a few dollars to stretch out your runway can make all the difference in the world.

YOU NEED CAPITAL. Sometimes, when the banks say no, friends and family say yes ... that is to say, if you've treated them fairly and given them the confidence to believe in you. The legendary California hedge-fund

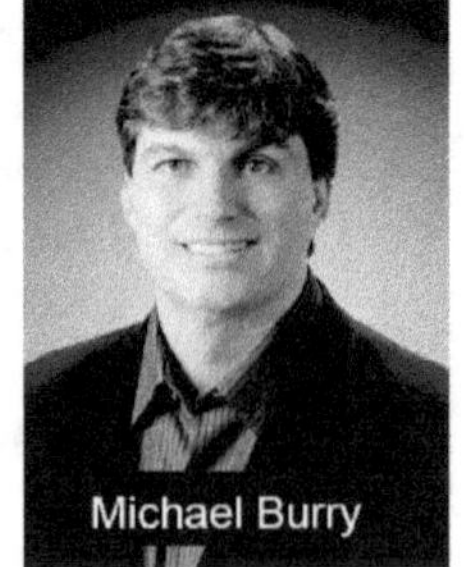

manager, Dr. Michael Burry, started his business with a small loan from his mother and siblings. At the end of the toxic subprime derivatives crash in 2008, he had racked up a cool $725 million for his investors and $100 million for himself.

5. You have developed a lifelong mastery of uncertainty and unexpected chaos due to global greed and resource mismanagement.

You lived through OPEC's oil embargo crisis, the Savings and Loan collapse, the national food poisoning scare, the 911 World Trade Center attack and subprime derivatives recession. **More than any other generation since WWII, you're hardened for war**. You understand crisis management. More importantly, you're too old to be rattled or frustrated by it. In times of uncertainty,

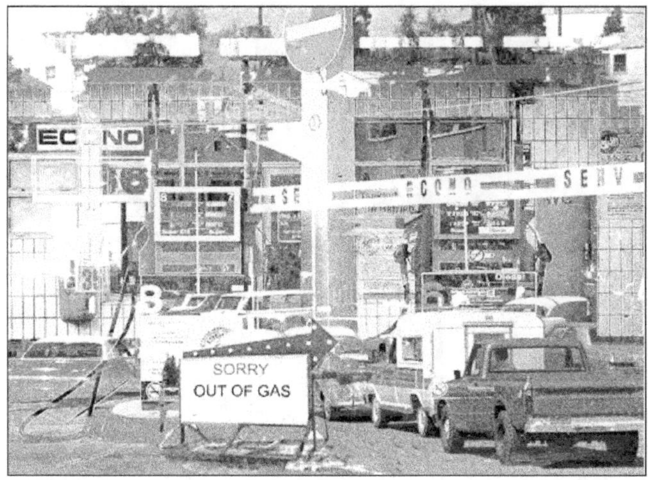

you've learned to keep a steady hand.

There are other reasons having to do with the wisdom and composure that, over the long haul, life has forced-fed into you. But for now, feast on these built-in advantages you have, but may never have considered before this important juncture in life. Know that the great pendulum of commerce has graciously swung your way.

Now, let's get going. It's time to become the successful entrepreneur for which you have unconsciously been preparing all these years.

BABY STEPS

*I*nsight #1 seems so intuitive. And yet, most startup entrepreneurs overlook it and fail. We have already talked about your first assignment ... **Embarking upon that critical journey to transform your action-oriented mindset into an entrepreneurial mindset.** It doesn't matter if you went to work on time one hundred days in a row. The question is: **What did you accomplish while you were there?**

This process is ongoing, but not indefinite. At some point, you'll realize you've crossed over that vast ocean of corporate politics, peer rivalries, and ego-driven decision-making to a new land in which productivity and accomplishment define your reality. For now, however, it's time to take the first step in formulating the framework of your business model and industry focus.

Back in high school, they would say, *"this is heavy, man."* So let's break it down into three baby steps.

Step One: Identify what you like. 

You might call this your *passion probe*. But it's a bit more complicated than that. It's a complex process of peeling back the layers of invisible influences and self-induced, roll-with-the-punches acclamations that have led you down a lifelong road of pretense and compromise. **You have pleased others for so long, you may have totally lost touch with those things that please you.** Your true passions are there. But you'll have to dig them out of the rubble. You'll have to discover them all over again.

Let's take a deep dive into the realm of human consciousness. Since this is vitally important to your journey of self-realization and re-discovery, we do not want to leave a single stone unturned.

Let's begin with a universal admission. **No one understands the mind in its totality.** We don't even know if the mind and the brain are the same. We don't know if consciousness exists outside the human skull. What we do know is the mind is a very powerful mechanism. It can perform over 1,000,000,000,000,000 operations per seconds, far superior to any computer on earth. Thousands of algorithms run, simultaneously, inside our human apparatus, often referred to in scientific terms as the homeostatic impulse.

Without thinking about it, this homeostatic impulse keeps our heart rate between 60 and 100 beats per minute, our body core temperature between 97°F and 99°F, and regulates to millisecond precision our critical body systems ... integumentary, muscular, skeletal, nervous, circulatory, lymphatic, respiratory, and so on. All of this complex horsepower is controlled by the subconscious mind. Roughly 96% of our existence runs on automatic, which means only 4% is allocated to logic and free will.

Most of the time, everything runs without a hitch. There is, however, one major problem with the system. **With all of its dazzling horsepower and magnificent functionality, the subconscious mind cannot distinguish between fantasy and reality.** Clinical studies have confirmed this puzzling phenomenon over and over again.

Think about it this way. When you have a bad dream, you awaken in a state of terror. Your heart is racing; your mouth is dry; your body is trembling from head to toe.

It was just a dream, a terrifying fantasy. The vampire wasn't

real. But your subconscious doesn't know that. Within the isolated, bio-electromagnetic cavities of darkness, there are no eyes to see, or ears to hear. Your brain releases all kinds of fight-or-flight hormones to help you navigate the danger and keep you alive. Ironically, it was your brain that originated the dream in the first place.

Your brain is built to regulate your physical self. But it tries to regulate your mental self as well. Your mind is constantly filtering stimuli in and out, bringing to your attention information that affirms your preexisting beliefs. This is known in psychology as "confirmation bias." I saw five people speeding on the freeway, so I'm going to speed too. Forget the 40 drivers we passed obeying the speed limit. This is regulated blindness, a systematic creation of reality, presenting you with repeated thoughts and impulses that mirror concepts you have accepted in the past. The subconscious is focused on your well-being and peace of mind. And this is where the rubber meets the road.

> **FOR THE SAKE OF YOUR SUCCESS, HAPPINESS, WHOLENESS, AND HEALING, YOUR SUBCONSCIOUS WILL TELL YOU A LIE.**

In codependency counseling sessions with women who, for many years, had been abused, roughly half of the victims stated their husband or boyfriend loved them intensely and uncontrollably. That was the reason he was beating the hell out of them. That was the compensating truth the subconscious mind offered up to keep the victims from going insane.

The subconscious mind wants us to be happy, content, and continuously affirming the importance of our own existence. It will readily release happy dopamine hormones when we gamble or shop or kiss our spouse. It will release tons of Cortisol stress hormones when we try to go against previously held beliefs.

Tomatoes contain lectins, a carb-binding protein that sticks to cell membranes in the digestive tract and causes all kinds of gastric issues. Lectins in kidney beans can mimic food poisoning.

Eating tomatoes excessively can lead to kidney stones, acid reflux, and solanine-driven joint pains.

BUT I LOVE TOMATOES. My grandmother used to put them on our big, juicy, homemade hamburgers. My mother put fresh tomatoes on our salads. And ... I read an article by a doctor on the internet that says none of these "harmful tomato" claims are scientifically proven.

I don't have to tell you. **My subconscious mind is not going to go against the sacred memories of my childhood.** It's going to direct me to the more trustworthy truth submitted by the doctor on the internet.

When you try to peel back the layers of invisible influences and self-induced acclamations, your subconscious mind will resist. It takes a bit of work to bypass your practiced preferences and crowd-pleasing habits to rediscover your true passions. But you can do it. Start with a simple eyeball question.

What visual images or reading materials effortlessly draw you away from your intended task? 

Let's say you're scrolling Facebook, searching for an upcoming birthday event to which your friend invited you a few days ago. You end up clicking on a cute little puppy that takes you to a page about a dog kennel club and its efforts to rescue abused animals from the streets. You already have two dogs. You also plan to replace the cat that died a few months ago. For a small donation to support the overcrowded kennel, they'll send you a shiny new dog collar (two if you increase your donation).

You immediately call a close friend, another dog owner because many of your friends are pet owners. You ask her to join you in supporting the kennel.

... Stop before your subconscious mind wakes up to remind you that your uncle was a CPA, your mother was a math teacher, and you were brought into this world to juggle numbers.

You have a passion for animals (and humanitarian causes). Write it down. Also, write down the $300 you made last summer when your neighbors went on vacation and left their parrot with you. Also, think back to your childhood days when you made friends with the big neighborhood German Shepherd, the one all the other kids were afraid of.

We've identified at least one of your passions ... **You love animals.** While we have your subconscious on the ropes, let's move this unfiltered, re-discovered endearment to the front of the line.

Step Two: Identify what you do well, either intuitively or by choice?

Why is it, when the family goes on trips, you do most of the driving? Why do you have to pre-program the Am/Fm radio buttons and GPS system for everyone else? Why is it you were the only one who took cookies to the new family that moved in down the street? Most of your neighbors didn't even notice their arrival.

Several things are apparent.

First, you are alert, focused, and willing to drive in familiar and unfamiliar territory. Being over fifty, this speaks well of your motor skills and ability to concentrate while being bombarded by visual and audible distractions. Secondly, you are NOT totally disconnected from the world of technology, which is often the case for older entrepreneurs. You possess the basic aptitude to learn as you go. Thirdly, you have good social skills and empathy for others. This is a precious facet of human capital that will open many doors, especially running a business that requires daily customer interaction.

In this dry run, we have some basic information about you. Let's look at the direction in which the process has taken us thus far.

You may have heard of the *Golden Circle*. It's a meaningful metric that helps with career clarity. It merges the things you like with the things at which you are naturally gifted. In doing so, it attempts to identify a general career path that's best for you.

Here is a random example highlighting the skills of a medical professional. These same compatibility test could've been applied to any individual and any industry.

Inside this *Golden Circle* is a (nurse) career option that perfectly matches the individual with this combination of preferences and skills. Obviously, it's not the only option. But it's high on the list.

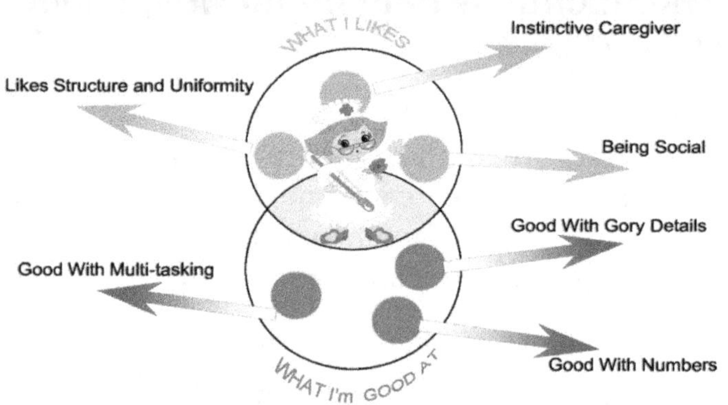

The key here is to identify a career that goes beyond earning a paycheck. If money is the only incentive for choosing a career option, you will most often find yourself miserable, even dreading the mere thought of going to work. **Money cannot overcome a life wasted, day in and day out, doing something you really don't want to do.**

IMPORTANT SIDE NOTE:

What you're naturally good at does not preclude what you CAN be good at. Everyone remembers the legendary Bo Jackson, perhaps, the greatest athlete of all times. As a new entrepreneur, it would be well worth your time to view the entire ESPN video on Jackson's incredible career. There are many lessons  you may learn about hard work, discipline, and individual integrity. The bottom line is most limits we face are self-imposed. Given the hard work and determination, we can accomplish almost anything we desire.

Let's look at your Golden Circle.

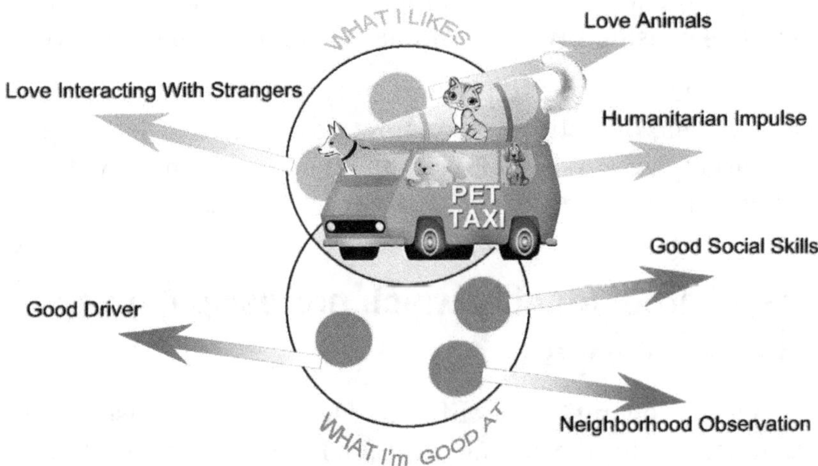

You love animals. When we pair your "likes" with your "skills", several familiar business models come to mind. Besides the primary "Pet Taxi" option above, we could also throw in pet sitting, pet training, pet boutique, and pet show consulting. AND ... if you have yet to read Stephen King's scary supernatural thriller, we could even throw in ownership of a pet cemetery. You're in the right field. Which row do you want to plow? You get the idea.

Before we get to the final question in our baby-step selection process, there is one thing to remember. Until the curtain opens and you walk out onto the stage, you won't know for sure. The latter chapters of this book introduce you to a sophisticated business owner assessment tool called **OVER 50 ENTREPRENEURIAL ASSESSMENTQ9.** Its powerful algorithms specifically identify correlations between your "likes" and "dislikes" and current entrepreneurial opportunities in the marketplace. Even then, you won't know **(with absolute certainty)** where your ever-evolving journey will take you.

Most businesses start out one way, then pivot to something else. Motorola no longer makes pagers. Hewlett Packard no longer sells digital cameras. Dick's Sporting Goods no longer sells guns. CVS no longer sells tobacco and tobacco-related products. The U.S. Department of the Treasury no longer sells paper savings bonds (thus causing my grandmother to roll over in her grave).

Inevitably, you will pivot in and out of niches, products and services, goals, objectives, and strategies based on the dynamics of the marketplace. As we move to the final question, stay flexible. You'll have a bit more time in Chapter 14 to tweak the results.

3. Step Three: Identify which profession(s) you would do for free?

Okay, operating a FREE 24-hour Jazzercise-tanning-massage service for the bunnies at Hugh Hefner's Playboy Mansion is not available at this time. Let's take that one off the table.

The legendary pop singer, Luther Vandross, once said

he was glad they paid him to sing. Deep down in his heart, he had made a commitment. He would never abandon his lifelong passion. If no one paid him a dime, he would still sing for free.

Let's examine a scenario in which you have $1 million in the bank and all your expenses paid for the next few years. What would you do with your time? If you started a business, what type of business would it be and what would be your role?

In the early days of Apple Computer, team members worked for free. Some (but not all) received stock options, basically, worthless paper until the company went public. Those employees gambled their time on a long-shot payoff that offered no guarantees.

And yet, neither cofounder Jobs nor Wozniak ever mentioned having to go out and run down employees, or beg them to come to work. Eagerly, they showed up each day because they loved what they were doing. Some days, they never went home. Everyone spoke of the excitement, uncertainty, and grand prospect of changing the world.

If you had that debt-free, tax-free million dollars in the bank, hoping to experience the same level of purpose and personal reward, what business would you pursue? Without the heavy lifting of analytics and profit potential, which product or service niche would you intuitively embrace?

You might start a construction company building houses for the homeless, or a missing person's website focusing on victims of human trafficking, or invest your time and money in a startup biotech company with a promising product to eliminate cigarette addiction. These are all noble causes with the potential to deliver a tremendous sense of purpose and personal reward.

Now, let's take away the $1 million safety net smugly deposited in the bank vault. How much would the loss of this financial guarantee impact your decision-making? For one glorious moment, you peeled back the restrictions of your subconscious mind. You dared to reconnect with those things that offered meaning and purpose. Now, without the money, how much would your list of potential business options change? Would you still sing for free?

Yes, in a capitalistic system, if you're going to survive, profit is a necessity. But most successful entrepreneurs attribute their sustainability to finding a business they love, a business in which they would work for free. They make the necessary sacrifices, fight through the hard time and gut-wrenching moments because they want to preserve and extend the huge sense of purpose and personal reward the business offers.

With \$20 or \$30 million in their personal bank account, why are these people still working on weekends? Why are they on the phone with the creative team in the middle of the night? At some point, optimally, at the very beginning of the journey, profit becomes a mere secondary reward. You're not working for the money. You're working for the sense  of purpose the business offers in return.

We will devote a full chapter to choosing a business model using an assessment of your personal profile, hardcore analytics, and fact-based decision-making. But for now, especially if you're over fifty with your runway growing shorter each day, all successful roads lead through your heart.

Ponder these simple baby steps and then take the leap. Remember, the race has already begun. The 30-year-olds are already scratching and digging and searching for pay-dirt on the other side.

CHOOSING YOUR BUSINESS

*I*nsight #2 represents the "logic" or "rationale" side of Chapter 1. First, choose with your heart. Then determine if fact-based logic supports your decision. If, over the years, corporate bureaucracy and office politics have not trampled your individual passions into extinction, you have some idea of what you want to do. Following the baby steps in Chapter 1, you have rediscovered those things for which you have a natural affinity. For instance, you may naturally choose a seat near the front, step back to allow others to go first, fix gadgets without reading the directions, and possess the uncanny ability to remember everyone's name in the room. On the other hand, you may not care who's in the room at all.

Starting to see who you really are.

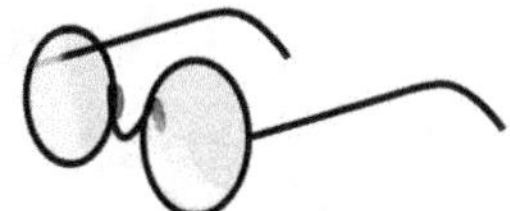

Hopefully, fingers crossed, knock on wood, you have begun to see yourself in a more realistic light. Not that you've changed, but rather, embraced the self-awareness that emerges from deliberately breaking the restrictive bonds of your subconscious mind and peeling away the lifelong layers of pretense and compromise. Your sense of observation has heightened. You've started to remember little things about yourself that, over the years, you had unknowingly suppressed.

This is a good thing. After all, you're starting a business with only one employee, one CEO with the destiny of the company in your hands. Who better should know the strengths, weaknesses, and natural inclinations of that CEO than you?

In this chapter, we get down to the business of business, the hardcore analytics that support or reject the choice(s) you've made 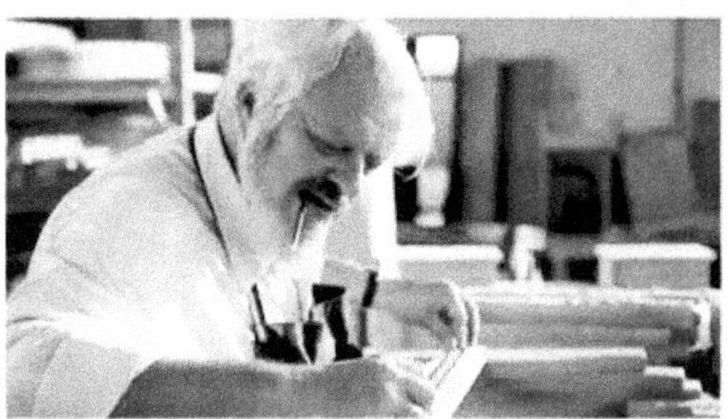 with your heart. You might wonder why this part is so difficult for most would-be business owners. The reason is simple and universal. Most entrepreneurs want to get on with the task and not the business that surrounds the task. Painters want to paint. Cooks want to cook. Mechanics want to tear down the motor and put it back together again. No self-respecting ghost hunter/ spiritual house cleanser wants to spend his time down at the courthouse, combing through records to see if his business name is still available. There are creepy voices to silence, demons to send back to hell.

The problem is, if you plan to be successful, this phase of the selection process is unavoidable. You have to know whether your business concept is feasible, and whether it has a fighting chance.

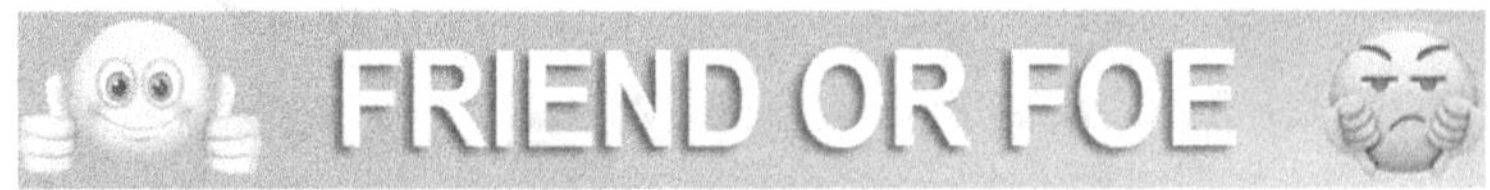

Let's dive in. Let's begin with the FRIEND OR FOE litmus test. Each revelation will either support or reject the choice(s) you initially made with your heart. This is not difficult. All you're doing is taking the free and widely available information other researchers have gathered to apply to your particular situation. If you've ever heard someone talk about the wisdom of the crowd, this is what they meant.

The Wisdom Of The Crowd

No matter the business you choose, understanding this concept is vital. Read this section as often as necessary to grasp its vast and ever-evolving application to your products and services. Your success depends on understanding the needs of your customers. You will act, and they will react, and you will react, and so on. Your customers will throw curve balls and respond with misdirection you won't initially understand. But this concept will shed some light. It will help you understand.

The wisdom of the crowd is a byproduct of rational action theory, a model for understanding individual decision-making based on the social, political, and economic options available to all individuals. The basic premise of rational action theory is that group social behavior results from the  behavior of individual actors, each of whom is making individual decisions that affect the whole. We can observe this process in the wisdom of the crowd syndrome. The drivers in front of you flip on their signal light and move into the left lane. Visually, unable to observe the reason for their collective effort to change lanes, but believing your lane is impeded, you predictably and instinctively move to the left lane too. The wisdom of the crowd influences your personal preferences. Rational action theory examines the association and interconnectivity of these individual choices.

Felix Kjellberg, better known as PewDiePie, is one of the top influencers in the world. He has 80.6 million followers on YouTube, 15.3 million on Instagram, and 7.4 million page likes on Facebook. He allegedly earns $12 million a year telling his content-hungry followers which products are good and which are not. Since they mimic his choices, selling them his limited-edition apparel line is easy as Pie.

Stay with me here. This is an important component in understanding rational action theory's influence on your future products and services, and the psychological nuances associated with the wisdom of the crowd.

These millions of followers are part of a chain reaction. As with the super influencer Kardashian girls, rubbing their precious posteriors with Pureleef Butt & Body Plumping Cream (What mere mortal would question their supreme wisdom on plump butts...), when PewDiePie wears a new $600 hoodie, millions of his followers buy that same hoodie, which causes their friends to buy it, and so on. They don't intuitively "know" the hoodie

is cool. But if PewDiePie is wearing it, and their best friends are wearing it, it must be cool.

You don't have to climb Mount Everest to know it's very high and very dangerous. You can extrapolate the official death count in comparison to other mountains and listen to the personal testimonies of hundreds of climbers who will confirm that it is very high and very dangerous. Most research sources on this subject are available for free.

But when it comes to gathering information to support your business choices, things take a slight turn ... really, a huge turn. Unlike the millions of followers who blindly accept their favorite influencer's endorsement as gospel, **you cannot afford to limit your sphere of influence to a single source.** You will still follow the wisdom of the crowd. But you will base your final decision on **many** crowds, **many** expert opinions, a diverse flow of multifaceted streams of information about you and your potential business choice.

Think about it this way. If you were an alien, dropping in from outer space, and wanted to know whether President Obama really deserved the Nobel Peace Prize, you wouldn't base your final decision on interviews from past presidents of the NAACP. If you want to know whether President Trump was unfairly overlooked by the Nobel Peace Prize Committee, you wouldn't ask Fox News.

Discovering the true potential of your business idea requires a broad, unbiased, sometimes raw and unpopular body of information far beyond the shallow advice of a single (PewDiePie) influencer.

TRUE OR FALSE ... Over two decades ago, did Al Gore concoct an alarmist outcry about global warming so he could get government funding and win the Nobel Prize?

YOU WILL HAVE TO DO SOME DIGGING...

Several respected Congressmen declared global warming to be a big hoax. You don't go to Al Gore's public relations firm, exclusively, to make sure he's right and the Congressmen are wrong. You will have to do some digging. As an entrepreneur, your mind must embrace a new prerequisite of rigid validation. There are charts, graphs, weather reports, melting ice caps, rising oceans, and jet stream calculations reflecting climate activity for 20 years. **The truth is there, if you really want to find it.**

How much information is enough?

Ultimately, you will have to ask yourself a question. How much digging is enough digging to create a sense of assurance and confidence in your final business ownership decision?

In keeping with our commitment to make this journey as painless as possible, let's narrow our focus to the objective at hand ... selecting a compatible business niche. You need to understand a few basic concepts about statistical analysis, but nothing to overwhelm you. There will be plenty of time for number-crunching craziness during the more complex phases of planning.

We would probably find the complex imagery needed to represent statistical analysis on the cover of a cognitive science book with physicist Stephen Hawkin pointing out sophisticated algorithms, predictive models, and fuzzy logic. But for our purposes, we will adopt a more practical definition. We are laser-focused on choosing a business niche. The Nobel Prize will have to come later.

Here is our FRIEND OR FOE definition.

Statistical analysis (sometimes called analytics or business intelligence) simply means the collection of data into meaningful categories to be analyzed for patterns that support or reject our business choices.

During the late 90s, Procter & Gamble used statistical analysis to reduce supply chain costs by $200 million a year. During the same period, Progressive Insurance gained an advantage over competitors by creating a sophisticated statistical cost analysis which allowed the company to offer coverage to drivers that other insurance companies turned away. In recent years, UPS used statistical analysis of customer preferences to reduce customer attrition by 20%. The process is huge, and for all practical purposes, indispensable to all businesses no matter their size or industry.

To perform a formal analysis of statistical data, you must first collect the data. But, again, how much data should you collect?

Obviously, the question leads back to the FRIEND OR FOE proposition ... How much digging is enough digging to create a sense of assurance and confidence in your final results? Which business niche is against you? And which is on your side?

We find the answer to these critical questions in a concept called the laws of large numbers. The law states that as a sample size grows, the accuracy of the results grows with it.

Insurance companies use the law of large numbers to estimate the losses a certain group of policyholders might create in the future. Their law states that as the number of actual policyholders increases, the more confident the insurance company can predict which groups (statistical profiles) have the greatest potential to create negative payouts that drive the company into the ground.

Size matters. Let's simplify the concept with this example.

If you have a combination of 5,000 red and green marbles in a bowl and you want to know how many are red without counting the entire bowl, you need to conduct a random sample of the combination. Each marble must have the same probability of being selected in your sample. The rule of large numbers states you need to choose at least 10% of the entire universe, or in this case, 500 marbles to get a reasonably trustworthy answer. HOWEVER, if the total universe of red and green marbles is a small number like100 or less, you must count the whole bowl because the universe of marbles is too small to sample accurately.

There's nothing mind-boggling here. If you want to know how many pet owners in Topeka, Kansas have the potential to buy your new artificial intelligence vibrating flea collar, you would first have to find out how many pet owners lived in Topeka, **your total universe**. Then, you would choose a sample size of at least 10% and segment with filters such as income and age.

There are two primary statistical methods used in data analysis. The first is **descriptive statistics**, which summarize data from a sample using indexes such as the mean or standard deviation. The second is **inferential statistics**, which draw conclusions from data that are subject to random variation, that is to say, observational errors and sampling variation.

 **... We are not going down the statistical sampling rabbit hole.**

We bring up the hardcore theory because you need to understand why you are **NOT** going to use this formal sampling method to validate your business choice.

First, you are just getting started. Chances are you cannot afford to hire a big, expensive research company to help you choose a business niche. **Today's statistical studies generally start at about $25,000.** According to the popular research firm, Market Connections, the price of a focus group study, depending on the number of groups, seniority of participants, narrowness of profession/expertise and location of groups would typically run upwards of $100,000. For the old-timers who remember the disastrous introduction of New Coke back in '85, the initial research study ran about $12 million.

Secondly, there are countless ways to mess up the statistical analysis process. Too many built-in biases; too much number-crunching; too many projections and extrapolations. Unless you've had some formal training in the discipline, your results are going to be flawed. Defining statistical analysis is a piece of cake. Executing the process is a disaster waiting to happen.

We have another way.

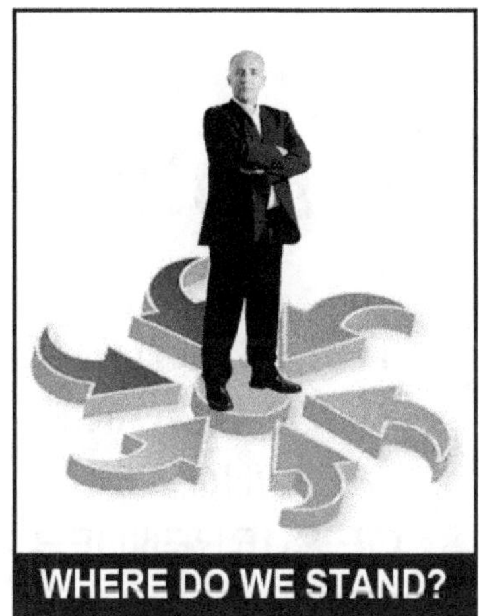

In the quest to validate your initial passions of the heart, all roads have brought you to this point. Where do you stand? What new truths have you absorbed thus far?

1 Assuming you've paused a moment to walk through your (Likes/Good at) *Golden Circle* exercise, you have a general idea of the business niche for which you are best suited. Like choosing a neighborhood, but, at this point, not the house. Nothing is engraved in stone.

2 You now know you cannot jump into an industry simply because you have a passion for it. Passion alone is not enough. You cannot succeed selling beepers if no one is buying beepers and all the odds are stacked against your passion for beepers ... same scenario for wagon wheel repairmen and switchboard operators.

3 You need to conduct some kind of rational, emotion-free, statistically-based research to determine if your choice of the heart has a fighting chance. To avoid the biased, self-serving recommendations from a few industry influencers, you need to do some formal statistical digging. This is tricky. Depending on your previous training and skill-set, research may represent a huge learning curve, not easily mastered without the help of an expert. Otherwise, your final results may be flawed.

4 You do not have a playbook for the *"new normal"* created by COVID-19. No one does. You will have to innovate, improvise, and extrapolate at unprecedented levels. You will have to become a master decision-maker on steroids and transform into a skywalker without a net.

NO!!!

THIS IS NOT THE
TIME TO RAISE
THE WHITE FLAG
OF SURRENDER.

This is the time to celebrate the beauty of having your own business and not being restricted by any bureaucratic modes of problem-solving. If there are solutions out there, and there are, you no longer have a short-sighted boss, standing in your way. You don't have to read through stacks of policies to determine which one prohibits you from executing your most radical, out-of-the-box solution. This is a glorious moment in your business history. **You have officially moved from action-oriented rewards to meaningful, goal-oriented accomplishments in real-time.**

Millions of entrepreneurs have been where you are right now. Their first instinct, that is to say, the most expedient solution that comes to mind, is to throw money at the problem. But since they don't have the money, they are forced to rise above the linear solution of finance to seek a more powerful tool, a more deep-rooted intervention, the bedrock of capitalism itself. **That tool is ... Innovation.**

Innovation has nothing to do with how many R&D dollars you have. When Apple came up with the Mac, IBM was spending at least 100 times more on R&D. It's not about money. It's about the people you have, how you're led, and how much you get it – **Steve Jobs.**

The real source of wealth and capital in this new era is not material things. It is the human mind, the human spirit, the human imagination, and our faith in the future – **Steve Forbes.**

Just as energy is the basis of life itself, and ideas the source of innovation, so is innovation the vital spark of all human change, improvement, and progress – **Ted Levitt.**

The Crucial, Indispensable Nature of Innovation

Innovation, whether forced or intended, produces benefits far beyond the problem itself. According to successful entrepreneurs such as Bill Gates and Michael Dell, innovation sets an important precedent (pattern of thinking) that liberates the confidence and ingenuity necessary to address future calamities. Creative juices from a million years of human evolution begin to flow, unleashing powerful improvisation most business owners didn't even know they possessed.

As **Nicolas Susco**, Founder of ElipseAgency, puts it, *"Creativity [innovation] is an essential tool for any entrepreneur. Creativity isn't just about coming up with ideas. It's about being able to adapt to new circumstances, navigate uncertainty, and find solutions as problems arise."*

You may recall from the Introduction, as an over-fifty entrepreneur, **navigating ambiguity and uncertainty** is a strategic advantage you hold over younger entrepreneurs. It's just a reminder you're in a good place. The great pendulum of commerce has again swung your way.

The type of creative thinking that produces innovation differs from other forms of thinking. The World Economic Forum has named creative thinking the 3rd most essential skill for the overall future of work, itself. It has the power to improve every other thinking model on the list.

Creative thinking reflects the ability to look at challenges from a fresh, uncommon perspective and find unusual solutions to apply. People who demonstrate this ability usually possess a rich imagination that allows them to envision things out of the ordinary. Fresh ideas may stem from looking at old ideas from a different perspective, and improving each iteration until a totally new product emerges. The evolutionary method of creativity reminds us every problem that has already been solved can be solved again in a better way. Successful architects, designers, and screenwriters use creative thinking throughout their daily routine. It's right brain thinking with a left brain twist.

Finally, creative thinking that produces innovation has the potential to foster unintended prosperity. In 1945, fiddling with a microwave-emitting magnetron, **Percy Spencer**, a Raytheon engineer, felt a strange sizzling sensation in his pants. He discovered, purely by chance, that a chocolate bar in his pocket had started to melt. From that unintended moment of serendipity came the modern **microwave oven**.

In 1928, while researching the effects of staphylococci, **Alexander Fleming** left behind some unclean Petri dishes in his lab and went away on vacation. When he returned, Fleming found that some kind of bacteria mold had inadvertently cleaned the dishes. After experimenting with the mold, Fleming identified the unusual compound that killed the bacteria. This discovery eventually led to the development of **penicillin**.

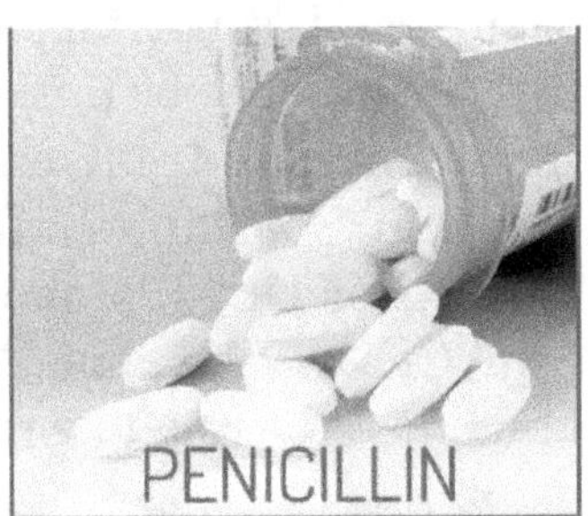

In 1942, while working on a totally unrelated precision gun project, **Dr. Harry Coover** of Eastman-Kodak Laboratories stumbled across a messy gooey substance he named cyanoacrylate. A full 16 years later, Coover realized the value of his discovery and started selling it as the indispensable product we know today ... **Super Glue**.

Creative thinking requires business owners to remove the traditional boundaries and venture into unknown territory. **Creativity flourishes within a mindset of pretending, imagining, wondering, and openly embracing the impossible.** The fewer roadblocks precipitated by discipline, rules, and linear progress, the better the chances for an incredible end product.

As an entrepreneur, you will always encounter problems to solve. But as long as you understand the power of creative thinking, a lack of finance will never relegate you to the sidelines. Facebook was once a little dinky college dorm app. The big boys at Blockbuster Video laughed **Reed Hastings** and his Netflix streaming idea out of the room. With the innovation that creative thinking brings, you're always one breakthrough away from running the table. **Think harder and smarter and know that money cannot keep you from your goal.**

We will talk about other modes of thinking in Chapters 9-10. But for now, it's time to get back to the problem at hand. You're trying to choose a business. You need to know if our *Golden Circle* selection has a fighting chance.

A BIG-TIME INNOVATIVE SOLUTION

You will be delighted to know there is a way to gather critical research insight without getting bogged down in formal statistical sampling. It's not that complicated. It will, however, require an investment of your time. **You might say you're trading time for money on the front end to save both time and money on the backend.** Sometimes referred to as the *macro-environmental forces* analysis or DESTEP model, we will call it our FRIEND OR FOE SMACKDOWN event. A tag team of environmental factors will climb into the ring to wrestle away your *Golden Circle* choices.

Don't worry. If the forces beat you down, you'll keep sending in new niche selections until you come out victorious. Remember, this is NOT a pointless, bureaucratic, role-playing exercise with your former boss. **This is the alternative to a big, expensive statistical research bill.** This is creative thinking, the fun side of owning your own business, your first freewheeling assault on a critical problem using your big stick of innovation and the confidence that money-matters will not get in your way.

HOW DOES THE SMACKDOWN EVENT WORK?

The primary objective of this SMACKDOWN event is to (1) present your *Golden Circle* choice as a concise, unambiguous value proposition, and (2) determine if the environmental forces support or reject your choice.

For example, let's say you're an old country boy with an affinity for ranching. **You've decided to become a senior citizen bull rider, the next George Foreman comeback on the national rodeo circuit.** You're going to rise above the fray, inspiring other seniors to stay active and pursue their dreams. The endorsement deals will pile up. Your old country boy grill will soon knock George's best-selling grill off the endorsement throne.

The problem is you have an injured leg from the Afghanistan War. The injury is only going to deteriorate with age, which means in the category of **physical environmental forces,** you're going to score very low marks. In addition, being over fifty, you're going to have trouble getting insurance. You can't join the rodeo circuit without being bonded. AND, when you throw in the cost of riding gear, traveling from city to city, room and board, and entry fees, the outlay of capital overwhelming. Most professional riders have corporate sponsors. You don't. In the **economic category**) you're going to get slammed to the mat.

By the time the SMACKDOWN tag-team bruisers are finished, you'll quickly realize your *Golden Circle* selection has been buried somewhere in the rodeo arena beneath a pile of bull manure.

Perhaps, you might look into breeding bulls, or creating a super bull health supplement, or hauling bulls in a special rodeo trailer equipped with computerized hydraulics that allow a single driver to load and unload bulls without assistance. You'd still be operating in the same niche, but pivoting to a product or service that offers the best fit for *you*. **Remember, you're not finished if the first round ends in defeat.** Macy's struck out the first five times before it evolved into the Macy's we know today. Hang tough! The initial agony of finding a compatible niche will eventually end with an old fashion Baby Boomer victory dance. You must, however, keep sending in your choices until you get a green light.

There are six different highly disruptive, hyperactive categories that will pass judgment on the business niche(s) you initially select. We treat these categories as SMACKDOWN opponents because, in all likelihood, **they harbor information that discourages the pursuit of your first few business choices.**

If you're health conscious and decide to open a fresh fruit stand, at least one or two of the categories will point out the (negative) low barrier to entry. **Anyone can open up a fruit stand across the street the very next day**. If their uncle owns a farm, they're going to beat you on price and freshness. On the other hand, if you decide to open up a nuclear plant, the **economic environmental forces** will quickly remind you that you don't have a billion dollars in the bank. The **political environmental forces** will add to the misery by pointing out the endless connections you'll need in Congress to get your plant approved.

Let's get this part straight. After all, to most would-be entrepreneurs, sincerely seeking a rewarding business opportunity, the SMACKDOWN process of getting slammed to the mat is counter-intuitive. You want to get on with your passion, your *Golden Circle* selection. But the categories appear to be designed to hold you back.

They are precisely designed to hold you back. 

Using this research technique, the head-to-head confrontation with these SMACKDOWN environmental forces is intended to **prevent you from making costly blunders that your heart would inadvertently overlook.** You meet a handsome prince that sweeps you off your feet. But when you run the background check, you find that his last three wives died of mysterious causes.

As much as your heart pounds with love and affection, you WANT the background check apparatus in place. So it is with these categories of environmental forces. You WANT your SMACKDOWN opponents to push you out of the ring until your business selection is so powerful, they willingly surrender the championship belt and join the team.

Meet Your SMACKDOWN Opponents...

 **ECONOMIC**

 **DEMOGRAPHIC**

 **TECHNOLOGICAL**

 **POLITICAL**

 **SOCIAL**

 **PHYSICAL**

These **FRIEND OR FOE** opponents are very important, so much so, that we will devote a chapter to your full comprehension of each. Don't worry. We will plug in the rating system and offer plenty of examples in the latter chapters.

But for now, remember, you don't have deep pockets for a full blow research study. This is your tried-and-true statistical analysis research alternative for making a prudent niche decision, staying on course, and saving precious time and resources on the back end of this critical selection process.

Here's a promise! By the time you reach Chapter 15, you'll be so happy you met these SMACKDOWN bruisers, you'll jump up from your desk and dance a timesaving, money-saving, resource-saving celebration jig.

ECONOMIC

Environmental Forces

Prepare to go toe-to-toe with the Economic Bruiser in Chapter 14 ...

*I*nsight #3 explains the crucial role economic forces play in choosing a business niche. Let's get a better feel for our opponent. Let's see if your choice-of-the-heart selection stands a fighting chance.

Still firmly committed (throughout this book) to simplicity and practicality over business school theory, let's briefly examine the meaning of economics in business. Business economics is a subset of the broad field of economic theory that focuses on quantitative methods of problem-solving. The keyword here is quantitative, which is just a big word for numbers. In dealing with this opponent, you can expect most challenges to be expressed in a numerical context and resolved with numerical solutions.

Surprisingly, you know more about economics than you realize. On any given day, thousands of news stories bombard our brains with bankruptcies, stock market crashes, union wage increases, Federal Reserve interest rate adjustments, retail price fluctuations, income tax loopholes for the wealthy, and most recently, the devastating losses caused by COVID-19. These daily revelations are mere drum majors in a perpetual, unavoidable numbers parade.

In the most rudimentary sense, we understand what these numbers mean. Depending on where we find ourselves within the scheme of the marketplace, we celebrate or complain, approve or denounce. Seldom, are we indifferent. In the long run, we know these numbers will have a direct impact upon our lives.

Key Performance Indicators (KPI)

In business, these numbers are critical to our survival strategies. As entrepreneurs, we live or die based on how well we interrupt and respond to their potential impact. If unemployment is down, wages are going up. A candidate

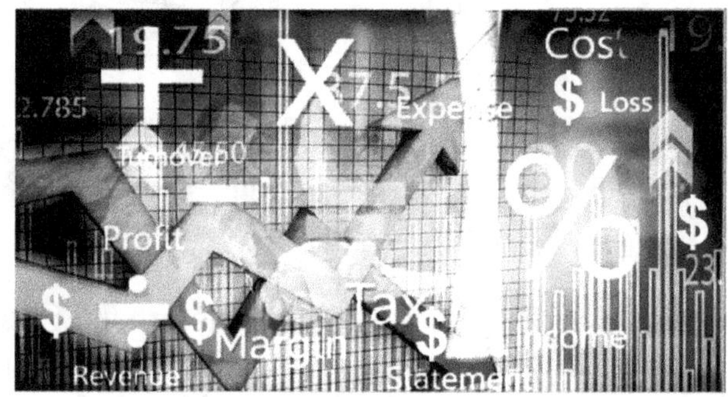

you hire today might demand more money today than in the soft economy a year ago. A house that listed for $500,000 might drop as much as $50,000 simply because the Feds lowered the interest rate by a few points.

There are key metrics (key performance indicators) that govern our decision-making. **Product acquisition costs, Operating margins, Return on equity, Cost of ad spent, Cost-per-click, Customer retention rate, and Net profit are just a few of the key performance indicators on which we rely.**

In choosing a business, we might be tempted to view these numbers in the narrow context of profit. But that would be a mistake. Profit is more than a number. It is a state of existence relative to the overall environment in which we exist. An 8% net profit by General Motors might be reason to celebrate. On the other hand, if Ford and Toyota netted 15% during the same period, that rosy 8% could signal approaching disaster.

> **Profit is defined as the amount of earnings realized (left over) when revenue exceeds expenses for a designated period of time.**

And yet, the official definition doesn't tell the full story. Profit could be:

♦ **Pure Profit -- Explicit Profit -- (FAT) Reasonable Profit**

♦ **Profit before corporate taxes**

♦ **Profit before a big legal settlement pushes the company into bankruptcy**

♦ **Profit before a super lucrative patent (like Lipitor) expires**

♦ **Profit before the auditors find all of the hidden lies**

In its heyday, Enron used creative accounting jargon, equity swaps, and misclassified offshore loans to create imaginary income and show a book profit that was never there. Goldman Sachs used similar unscrupulous tactics to conceal massive Greek debt. History teaches us that profit numbers are relative, and without the proper disclosure, can be conjured out of thin air.

If you're starting a business and focusing on the most profitable industry in which to take the plunge, remember that publicly disclosed, bottom-line profit numbers are connected to many other factors. Even if there is no fraud involved; even if all financial contingencies have been revealed, profit alone tells an incomplete story.

This chapter is about business economics and the true nature of profit. So let's take a deep dive.

Companies need positive cash flow and expanding sales to survive. Thus, a majority of companies focus on profit maximization rather than on shareholder value maximization.

Profit Maximization means operating in a manner in which decision-makers give priority to creating prices (input and output strategies) that lead to the highest attainable net profit. Over the years, this approach has gravitated toward the darker chambers of decision-making and become synonymous with *"This is capitalism. Do what you gotta do."*

Profit Maximization is a short-term approach with potentially deadly consequences. It undermines long-term planning, R&D, and innovation. It leans heavily on gimmicky sales marketing and promotions. It encourages abrupt cost-cutting and shedding valuable assets to produce deadline profits designed to keep investors at bay. In the end, it erodes long-term competitiveness by neglecting to invest in new market opportunities and squeezing the fragile (book value) life out of existing products and services.

You've heard the term, **"under pressure from stockholders"**.

♦ Naylor Company is under pressure from stockholders to increase net income.

♦ Under pressure from shareholders, BioCryst drops plan to merge with Idera.

♦ South Korean entertainment powerhouse SM Entertainment is under pressure to answer demands to improve shareholders' value.

♦ After a 38% decline in Bayer's share prices, the management of German conglomerate Bayer is under huge pressure to win back shareholders' trust.

Under pressure generally means stockholder's activist pressure on management to return more revenue to investors. Everybody has privy to the balance sheet. If a company like Apple is sitting on $200 billion in cash, shareholders want to know why some of that revenue can't find its way into their pockets.

Most companies are not sitting on that kind of cash pile. Thus, in an organization committed to maximizing profits, managers are always under pressure to hit their quarterly sales

numbers, and more importantly, projected dividend payouts to investors. That may mean closing stores, selling assets, canceling advertising campaigns, and laying off employees ... anything to reduce expenses before the quarter, anything to shine a favorable light on bottom-line profits. These are the short-term sacrifices that invariably hinder long-term growth.

Shareholder Value Maximization means operating in a manner in which shares will reflect a higher current and expected future value. Business owners adopt this approach when their primary objective is to increase earnings and share prices, and make the company as IPO-attractive as possible to current and future shareholders.

Through examining both definitions, you quickly realize **Profit Maximization** and **Shareholder Value Maximization** pursue similar (if not the same) objectives. Both want to grow the company and increase earnings. Both want the stock price to be an attractive lure for current and future investors.

The thing to remember is that these operating approaches pursue their objectives in different ways. Profit Maximization measures its effectiveness by the amount of profit coming in and dividends paid out. Shareholder Value Maximization measures its effectiveness by the company's overall strength in the marketplace, and more importantly, long-term potential to compete and prosper.

Let's look at a hypothetical example of both approaches in action.

For the sake of simplicity, let's say Uber is headquartered in Los Angeles. Mexico City won the bid for the Olympic Games. But because of a devastating earthquake, officials abruptly move the Games to Los Angeles. The last-minute scramble to accommodate millions of people descending upon the city reaches a frenzied pitch. In the midst of the chaos, Uber managers see an opportunity.

Following our simplistic approach, let's say Uber has a $3 million operating budget ... $1 million to pay employees; $1 million to pay the independent drivers; $1 million to support research and development. The entire operation is generating a 1-to-4 return, that is to say, for every dollar Uber puts in, it gets four dollars back.

The managers call an emergency meeting to explore their options. If they pursue a **Profit Maximization** strategy, they can lay off half the employees to free up $500,000. They can then transfer the research and development money to the operating budget to the tune of $1,000,000. Using the extra $1.5 million as an incentive, they can double driver bonuses, lure roughly 33% of Lyft's drivers to come over, and entice additional drivers from nearby cities to work in Los Angeles during the entire Olympic Games. The final bottom-line projection is a 35% increase in net profits and an extra $.20 per share dividend to the stockholders.

Hallelujah!!! For the profit maximization band, this is a hit single headed to the top of the charts. Get your fancy Montblanc pen ready to sign autographs at the next stockholders' meeting. Think about creative ways to spend those big performance bonuses rushing through the door.

For the shareholder value maximization party-poopers, however, this opportunistic strategy presents a problem. Traditionally, layoffs lower company morale, reduce employee loyalty, and create short-term inefficiencies in productivity. Valuable front-line producers, who know their worth in the industry, start to send out resumes. Trust within the company, as well as perceived viability for future opportunities within the organizational hierarchy, slowly erodes.

In addition, Uber Eats and Uber freight divisions, respectively, were already in a dogfight with competitors to gain a foothold in the marketplace. Now, the budget is gone. What are the odds they can catch up or regain their competitiveness, assuming the research and development money is eventually restored? An even gloomier prospect is the loss of investment dollars in driverless electric cars. All experts agree. Driverless electric cars are the wave of the future. Now that management has laid off the company's valuable brain trust of designers and engineers, Uber's much-touted strategic advantage over other competitors, what chance does the company have to compete for future market share?

Finally, the precedent of higher bonuses, although positioned by management as a temporary incentive tied to the Olympic Games, will not simply fade away. It's the same as a Christmas bonus, issued for years, and then suddenly discontinued. There's a psychological resentment among recipients that follows the discontinuation. Team members won't appreciate "less" next year.

No matter the company or industry, management has to decide which operational approach to pursue. Amazon lost money for years. It took over 14 years - 58 quarters after its May 1997 initial public offering - to produce the colossal amounts of profit demonstrated in recent quarters. Founder Jeff Bezos told investors if they were looking for a quick return in dividends, Amazon was the wrong company in which to invest. His commitment was to build a (Shareholder Value Maximization) customer-oriented growth company with a deep vertical infrastructure, a plan to dominate the industry for years to come.

In choosing an industry niche for your new business, why is the numerical context of these two profit objectives so important to you?

The FRIEND-OR-FOE research process **(the one we have designated to take the place of costly statistical sampling)** will involve an examination of companies within profitable industries. The objective will be to identify potential opportunities for your new business and the products or services you ultimately offer to the marketplace. So that your decision-making is not flawed, you need a clear understanding of what these bottom-line numbers actually mean. **Remember, profit is not the full story.**

Finally, if you decide to open a new Burger King franchise and the franchise team pitches you on a location projected to generate $200,000 in net profit (in your pocket), you should fully understand right then and there that net profit is not the full story.

♦ **McDonald's reported 2.3% same-store sales**

♦ **Burger King reported 0.8% same-store sales**

♦ **Jack in the Box reported [negative] 0.1% same-store sales**

During the same period, Taco Bell's same-store sales rose 6% and Chick-fil-A boasted a whopping 13.4%. Burger King's revenue is heavily dependent on $1, $2, $3 Dollar Menu a la carte value-oriented offerings. Chick-fil-A is selling higher ticket items based on customer service, speed, and simplicity.

With this chapter under your belt, you won't be swayed by profit promises. You have the knowledge to make an informed entrepreneurial decision. For this period, the Burger King franchise is in obvious decline. The $1, $2, $3 Dollar Menu promotions won't bring long-term growth. The projected $200,000 in your pocket doesn't look so good after all.

If the Burger King option was the first selection coming out of your *Golden Circle*, you just got slammed to the mat. The first round is over. Celebrate!!! **You just saved yourself a $400,000 loan for a Burger King Franchise.** Your money is still in the bank. It's time to send a fresh, new, promising selection into the ring.

 **ECONOMIC**

Don't worry. At some point, you will stomp your old economic opponent into the ground. In the end, you will find a fit that's right for you

70

DEMOGRAPHIC

Environmental Forces

Prepare to go toe-to-toe with the Demographic Bruiser in Chapter 14 ...

*I*nsight #4 explains the crucial role demographic forces play in choosing a business niche. As with economic forces, this burly opponent is also sweating numbers from his pores. But they are different kinds of numbers, numbers unlikely to make an accountant drool at the mouth. Neither will they attach themselves to a deposit slip on the way to the bank. These numbers belong more to a fortune-teller than an accountant. These numbers tell us what the future will bring.

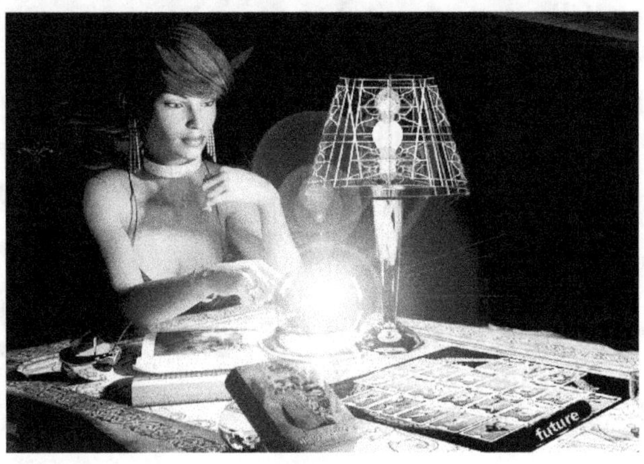

Back in 1994, MONEY magazine published a story about the sharp increase in shopping from home. That year, some 98 million consumers made $60 billion in non-brick and mortar purchases, mostly by calling a toll-free number listed in a mail catalog and on TV shopping channels. The internet was in its infancy then, and many publications referred to it as a mere fad, plagued by privacy, fraud, and free porn issues. When Amazon launched a year later, only 3% of Americans used the internet, let alone considered shopping online a viable option.

Yet, a few visionaries of commerce told us the great internet explosion was coming. In his 1990 book, *The Age of Intelligent Machines,* futurist **Raymond Kurzweil** predicted the rapid growth of eCommerce and the enormous potential impact of Artificial Intelligence on our lives.

In 2019, Consumers worldwide spent nearly $3.46 trillion online. Even for the non-tech Baby Boomer generation, consumer shopping habits have exploded. Big-box stores such as **Sears, Radio Shack, K-B Toys, Circuit City, Borders Books, Kmart, and JCPenney,** which depended on

mid-to-upper income demographic shoppers, were doomed. A few of these retailers such as **Radio Shack and Pier 1 Imports** have been bought up for pennies on the dollar. Wealthy social media influencers such as Tai Lopez see value in the long-standing brand names. None of these age-old leviathans can say they weren't warned

about the brick-and-mortar collapse. It's been coming for many years.

What Do We Mean by Demographics?

Demographics (or demographic research) is the study of people and population trends within specific categories. Traditional categories may include:

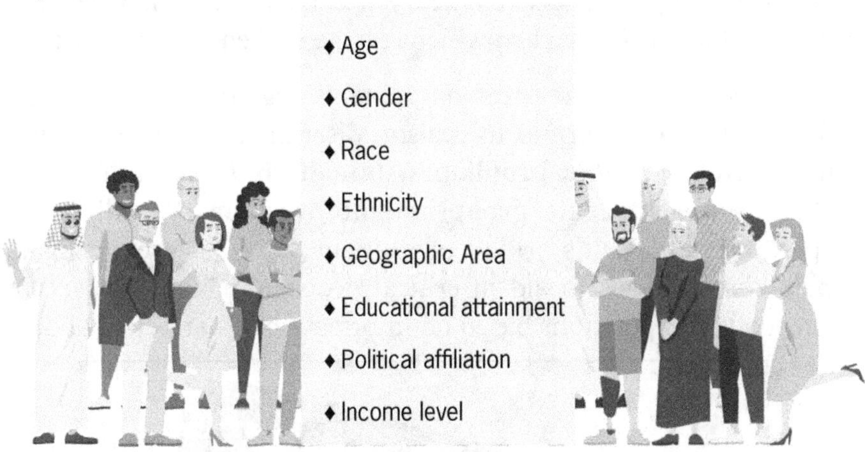

However, in recent years, with the massive amounts of data collected, the spread of Artificial Intelligence, and the perfection of scientific techniques using big data analysis, these categories have been expanded to include new, dynamic, meta-data categories such as shopper types, hours online, smartphone browsing, Google satellite tracking, and others, with a shift toward documented actions by certain profiles and the probability these profiles will take similar actions in the future.

Demographic numbers attempt to quantify the probability a certain type of person will do a certain type of thing. What is the probability a male over 60 years old who has been smoking all of his life will make more trips to the doctor than a 30-year-old male who has never smoked? You don't have to speculate about the reason the smoking question is on every medical insurance form you fill out. Number crunchers in high places are using demographics to reduce their payout risks. They have enough data to assign an "action index" probability number to each individual within a particular profile.

What is the probability an African-American teenager living in a high crime area like Viavant-Venetian Isles in New Orleans will have an arrest record, compared to a white teenager living in an upper-income Seattle suburb? If an HR manager has to choose a summer intern to pick up customer payments and take them to the bank, which teenager will she most often choose, and which resume will end up in the trash?

Let's lay all of the cards on the table regarding demographic profiling and its relationship to racism, discrimination, and cultural exclusion. **Demographic profiling within itself is not inherently racist, as some advocate groups might proclaim.** We all do it, multiple times a day. It's a kind of shortcut the brain uses to make complex computations to aid in critical decision-making. These are instantaneous computations based on information in our personal data

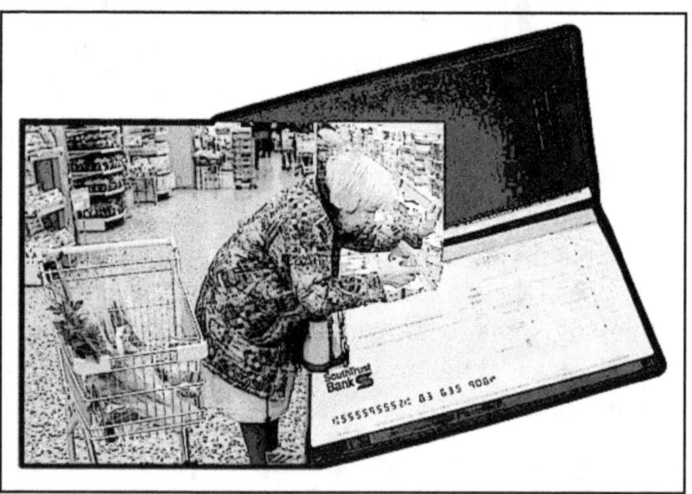

banks. The brain queries a jumbled mix of personal experiences and acquired knowledge to prompt an appropriate action.

Let's say you're in the grocery store, ready to check out. Three cashier lines are open. However, in line #2, an older lady with gray hair is fumbling with her checkbook and asking the cashier about the price she's being charged for ground meat. Your brain immediately queries your past experiences with elderly people on fixed incomes, who, in this day and time, are still writing checks. Somewhere deep inside your cerebral cortex, alarm bells go off. Without hesitation, you slide over to line #3.

In this simple profiling exercise, you have nothing against gray-haired old ladies. In fact, she looks a bit like your sweet Aunt Sadie. But your brain has instantaneously assigned a probability number to the potential slowdown. It compares that number to the number already assigned to your value of time (a time index that fluctuates from day to day). On that day, at that moment, your family is waiting. The time number overrides all other numbers and prompts you to move to another line.

The speed of this profiling apparatus is incredible. Most often, you are unaware of the process. There is no discriminatory or exclusionary intent against elderly people. And yet, your brain used this age factor (along with the checkbook) to make its recommendation.

Upside / Downside to Demographic Profiling

To explore the full upside/downside potential of this process, let's employ one more example. Let's say you are a security guard stationed at a console in a large shopping mall with multiple cameras scanning the interior and exterior of the building. You notice a brand-new luxury Mercedes pull up in the parking lot. Three young girls, maybe college-age, with heavy makeup, multiple tattoos, and multicolored rock band bleached hair, climb out. They're horsing around, shoving their iPhones in each other's faces, laughing out loud at the apparent images on the screen. Inside the mail, they enter a high fashion boutique and begin to browse.

A few minutes later, another new Mercedes pulls up. Three young African-American men in their early 20s get out. They also have multiple tattoos. Two have dreadlock hairstyles. The third man's baggy pants are sagging in the back, exposing his designer underwear.

Inside the mall, they enter a high-end jewelry store and start to browse.

Is the car stolen? Do they plan to shoplift in the jewelry store?

Alarm bells go off in the back of your mind. You call a fellow security guard on the radio to ask him to go over to the jewelry store and keep an eye on them.

Your profiling apparatus has assigned a number to their potential actions, the probable criminal actions these three black shoppers will take. But where did this number come from? You've had no personal experience with black men wearing dreadlocks. There have been no recent reports of shoplifting in the mall by young black men. You didn't bother to call the central security office to have them run the plates on the Mercedes to determine if it was stolen. But you immediately concluded the driver did not match the car.

This is the dark side of profiling, the predisposition toward an individual or group of individuals without probable cause. This is the reason so many police departments have been hauled into court and ordered to pay huge fines and settlements. They have assigned a probability number purely based on race.

Unfamiliarity breeds suspicion. Fear emerges from the deep wells of our subconscious mind. We don't always know why we have an aversion to certain people or certain cultures, or the source from which the pre-programming emanates. Grandpa said keep an eye on [all] Hispanics. They steal. So Roberto Goizueta, the first Hispanic CEO of Coca-Cola back in 1981, was no doubt

stealing from Coke … RIGHT?!!! My Grandpa wouldn't lead me astray.

What we must come to realize is if we allow our demographic profiling to be contaminated by personal biases, the results are untrustworthy at best, in most cases, totally flawed … and clinically dishonorable.

Let there be no doubt. **In this FRIEND-OR-FOE process to choose your business niche, you're going to use demographic profiling.** In making a commitment to apply systematic analysis rather than feel-good emotions based on lifelong pre-programming, there is really no way around it.

Demographic Insights That Drive Decision-making

♦ Nike targets individuals according to their age, life-cycle stage, gender, occupation, and generation. Although the fluctuating market is broad and dependent on other drivers, Nike primarily targets consumers between the ages of 15 and 40.

♦ According to a new study on frozen sweets, Americans over age 55 eat more ice cream per capita than any other age group. The average American eats ice cream at home 41 times per year. But the over-55 age group eats it an average of 56 times. Younger consumers between the ages of 18 and 24 prefer to buy ice cream from a premium shop, while female customers, 45 and older, put a high priority on branded ice cream. Brands like Blue Bell that focus on big rich flavors have an extremely high affinity index among African-Americans, more than 162, compared to Asians at just 59.

♦ Among current cigarette smokers, 40.8% are occasional smokers, fewer than 5 cigarettes per day, while over one-third (36.5%) reported smoking between 6 and 19 cigarettes per day. The majority (73.7%) began smoking prior to age 19. Among African-American high school students, cigars are the most commonly used tobacco product (8.8 percent); among Hispanic high school students, electronic cigarettes are most popular (15.3 percent). American Indians and Alaska Natives have the highest smoking rate of any racial or ethnic group.

Examples of demographics that drive decision-making might be reflected in the changing preferences of a generation of older Baby Boomers, switching from breakable glass containers to plastic containers, or the white flight of large segments of the population to the suburbs, or the "don't-want-to-get-married" trend depressing the purchase of expensive wedding rings by couples thirty-and-under.

Think about the elderly lady in the grocery store checkout line and the slow, inevitable death of the once commonplace paper check. In 2009, consumers and businesses wrote 28 billion checks. That number has been dropping about 1.8 billion a year. At that pace, according to a Philadelphia Fed study, by 2026, paper checks will go away entirely. Except for a few Kansas farmers, shopping at Big Al's Country Feed Store, consumers in all demographic categories prefer plastic, Smartphones, and Internet-enabled payment options like Square, Giropay, SwipeSimple , Apple Pay, Wallet apps, LevelUp ... AND cryptocurrency. We'll talk about this new crypto phenomenon in Chapter 11.

Demographics are more than curious facts that spice up dinner party conversations. Demographics are numerical insights that guide our strategic thinking and plot the most rational course forward for our journey ahead. Because of human evolution, 90% of the population is right-handed. If you start a company manufacturing baseball catcher's mitts, you wouldn't set up the assembly line for 50% right-handed and 50% left-handed mitts. The average age of a Miss Universe winner is 20.5 years old. If you're in Las Vegas, betting on the potential winner, you wouldn't put your money on

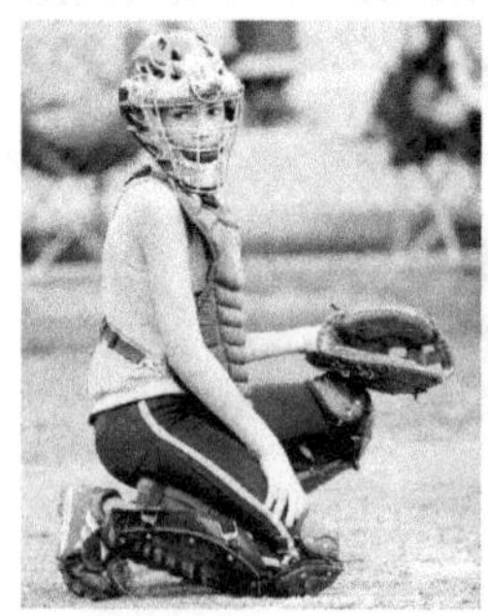

a 28-year-old contestant that barely slipped through the early rounds. Roughly 89% of all purchasing decisions are made by emotional drivers (a sense of freedom, a sense of fear, a sense of belonging, a sense of entitlement, a sense of standing out from everyone else) within the subconscious mind. If you're writing sales copy for a product, you wouldn't spend the majority of your words describing from which warehouse the product is shipped or how many screws are holding it together.

What if you owned a store that sold expensive bottles of wine. Let's say you recently received a new *Cabernet* that tasted extraordinary, with a reasonable markup, extensive distribution channel, and skyrocketing sales in other parts of the country.

Let's say you noticed a trend. Everyone that came in to buy that particular bottle of wine wore a red cap. You don't know from where these red cap customers are coming. What you do know is, based on this demographic observation, if you intend to spend your advertising dollars wisely, you need to target people with red caps.

How do you reach these red cap people without wasting money on people wearing green caps, blue caps, and yellow caps? The old shotgun approach of using television spots during the six o'clock news would be an obvious waste. Shrewd marketers in the advertising industry would tell you Google, Facebook, Instagram, 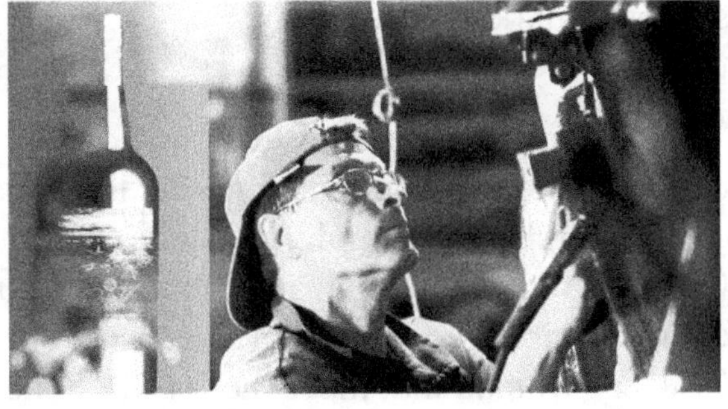 and LinkedIn offer the best opportunities for targeting.

Over the last decade, online marketers have accumulated mind-boggling data sets on billions of users. They know where the red cap people live, work, eat, and how they buy. In the same big data collection context as Apple, Amazon, and Google, Facebook maintains deep silos of information on all of its users.

These platforms are free to you. The information about you is priceless to them. Advertisers pay a pretty penny to get their products and services in front of billions of targeted prospects. In many disturbing ways (trends, addictions, inclinations, etc.), Facebook knows more about its users than the users know about themselves.

When it comes to digital (online) demographics, the metadata that accompanies the identity of a particular customer profile is equally as important as the profile itself. Metadata measures actions taken by potential customers while making the purchase.

Perhaps, the potential customer is a young, single woman under 30, logging on from a California zip code, browsing for dresses. Examples of metadata might be: how long she stayed on the page, how many clicks she made on sleeveless dresses, which colors and sizes she examined, and how many matching purses or shoes she bookmarked or added to cart.

This is powerful information for future targeting. The demographics, in combination with the metadata, drive the "future" offers merchants extend to specific profiles. If the woman from California kept clicking on stiletto heel pumps, this represents an expressed preference, an unmet need, not only by her, but (potentially) by every woman that meets her profile. The server drops a harmless cookie on her computer. **Stiletto heels ads start to chase her all around the internet.**

Let's take a final look at the red cap wine drinkers. Chances are they are online somewhere, if not Facebook or Instagram, then Google Search or YouTube or LinkedIn. Your next step is to gather as much information beyond the red cap demographic as possible. What type of car did they drive into your parking lot? What type of credit card did they use? What additional products did they buy to create some sense of association? Is your cashier capable of remembering to ask these wine customers how they heard about the product? Can you build in a reliable form of data collection at the register?

To increase the accuracy of your targeting online, you will need as much information about your red cap profile as possible. **Whataburger, the fastest growing regional hamburger chain in the south, uses receipt surveys to gather dynamic information about their customers.** The back of the receipt offers a toll-free number and website option.

If you call in or go online to fill out the short survey about your preferences and level of satisfaction, you receive a code for a free premium burger. The information is invaluable, not only to managers monitoring dissatisfaction in levels of service, but product planners on the lookout for new opportunities in (cheesy, spicy, crunchy) taste preferences.

The more you find out about your customer, the better your (ad spend, conversion rates, customer retention) results will be.

Putting It All Together

Now that you better understand how profiling works, let's see how your *Golden Circle* choice-of-the-heart lines up against the old demographic body slammer waiting for you inside the ring.

Let's say you like marketing, but not selling face-to-face. At fifty, you're surprisingly adept at e-commerce, customer trends, product selection, pricing, and distribution. You like fashion, specifically, fancy hand and shoulder bags. You hire an online agency to build your website and find a reasonably priced Chinese manufacturer to dropship these bags directly to your customers. Exploiting the benefits of dropshipping, you don't have to carry inventory or touch the product at all.

You know you have a quality product line and the style is unique. But sales for the first six months are quite pitiful, and you don't know why.

After some digging, you discover a pattern in your customer emails. Roughly 50% of the few customers you do have are asking for an update on delivery. What's taking so long? Your product line is good, but not that different from similar bags on Amazon. **However, Amazon is shipping out products in two days; delivery is five days max.** Your delivery from China takes three weeks ... with the worldwide pandemic, four to five weeks.

The product is fine. The metadata (the dissatisfaction expressed in the emails), however, signals disaster ahead. The current model, unable to compete on delivery, cannot sustain itself. Your business is eventually going under.

BUT WAIT! (Don't you just love when they say that in television infomercials?)

You have some options. You can carry inventory and take on the responsibility of shipping out the products from your garage ... just like Steve Wozniak and Steve Jobs did in the early Apple days.

You can also assign an extremely high priority to product differentiation; make it a critical building block within the company's corporate culture. **You will not sell bags that are not totally and remarkably distinctive from bags on Amazon.** You vow to beat everyone in your niche on quality and style, with same-as-Amazon delivery. Now, you have a fighting chance.

You haven't won just yet. But you haven't been slammed to the mat either. We will call this one a draw.

Keep your *Golden Circle* selection in the ring for now. We will visit it at a later time.

DEMOGRAPHIC

The whole matter of demographic profiling is critical. You want the numbers to spell out the probability for success in your chosen niche. You're more than able to accomplish this without a research company snapping up a huge chunk of your precious investment capital. The cumulative analysis of customer profile indexes, affinities, inclinations, preferences, metadata, and past actions rarely deceive you. The hard numbers about a right-handed universe will keep your decision-making both realistic and numerically based.

You've learned something here that's going to save you time, money, and other valuable resources. Stay true to the science. Avoid the creep of emotional bias. Apply these demographic profiling principles whenever you can.

TECHNICAL

Environmental Forces

Prepare to go toe-to-toe with the Technical Bruiser in Chapter 14 ... 

*I*nsight #5 explains the crucial role technological forces play in choosing a business niche. These forces might be something as simple as a slow internet connection, or an extended electrical power outage caused by a winter storm, or something as ominous as a ransomware attack by cybercriminals who lock up your computer files and threaten to shut down your entire operation if you don't pay.

Technological environmental forces refer to the rapid change in technology that leads to a strategic advantage in the marketplace, or an obsolete product or service that is no longer useful to the original customer base.

Five Popular Products That Technology Made Extinct.

♦ Manual Typewriters

♦ Encyclopedia Britannica

♦ Phone Booths

♦ 8-Track Players

♦ Floppy Storage Disks

Think about the beeper/pager and how useful it was in the 1990s. Having to wait at the office for an important call on their landline phones constantly hampered the productivity of people on the go. The beeper captured the market as an innovative enabling tool that mobilized communications and drastically reduced the missed-the-call / missed-the-deal syndrome.

Smartphones came along and eliminated the need for the bridge technology beepers provided. Consequently, beepers and all other associated products and services such as phone booths, token booth coins, transmission towers, repair shops, services issuing beeper numbers, and so on, went down the drain too.

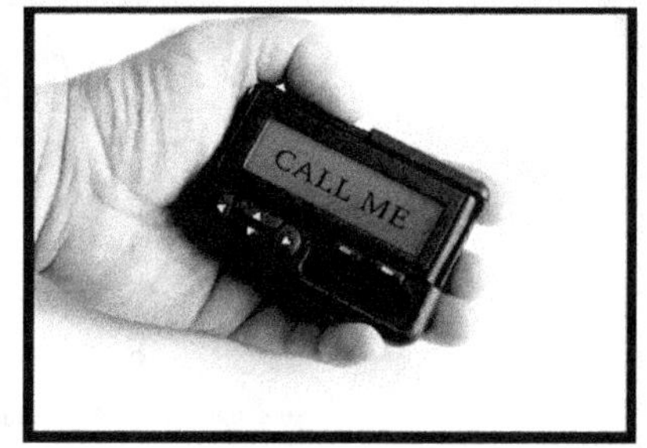

STOP AT THE NEXT PHONE BOOTH
AND CALL ME RIGHT AWAY!

Changing technology can usher in the sweet taste of increased sales and new market share to one player, and the pain and misery of uselessness to another. Apple and Samsung's faster chips and multiple features put early market leader Nokia out of the smartphone business. GPS replaced old Key Map Books. The cable companies, often characterized as greedy and overpriced, lost over 250,000 subscribers in a single year because of the staggering growth in on-demand web content sent directly to television sets and cell phones by multichannel streaming companies like SlingTV, Fubo, and Disney's Hulu. With the emergence of this new technology, the writing for cable and satellite monopolies is on the wall.

New Technology Comes With A Price

There is always a cost involved in delivering new technology. Pfizer spent almost $2 billion on Viagra R&D before the FDA approved the drug in 1998. No worries. The little blue pill has returned an estimated $40 billion in revenue over its 20-year span. Apple spent over $18 billion on research and development during its 2020 fiscal year, topped by Amazon with $22 billion in R&D. In a wildly competitive market, investment in new technology commands a huge chunk of the annual budget. Technology is changing at an unprecedented rate, and no one wants to be left behind.

Moore's Law states that every 18 months or more, computer processing speed doubles. The number of transistors that fit into a microprocessor reached over 10 billion in 2017. Remarkably, it was under 10,000 in 1971. In addition, a collision in related exponential technology advancements is taking place at an alarming rate. Every critical area of technology (hardware, software, infrastructure, artificial intelligence, cloud, etc.) is on fire and blazing out of control.

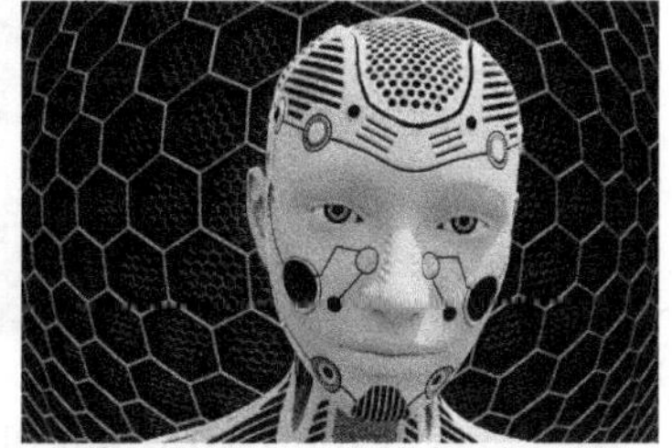

In 2021, technology spending will reach approximately $4 trillion. An expected 50 billion (AI) smart devices will collect and share data using black box codes humans can't read. By 2025, the web hosting services market will reach $77.8 billion. That same year, the speed of wireless communications will have quadrupled, and artificial intelligence (AI) machine learning will run most of our systems.

There is a flip side to the tech celebration. The cost of technology is not always expressed in dollars and cents. Sometimes, the impact is more accurately reflected in the human toll it takes on people who create, distribute, and use the technology directly.

A recent ten-year study by scientists at the National Toxicology Program, a division of the National Institutes of Health, demonstrated that exposing rats to high doses of cell phone radiation caused a brain cancer called **glioma** and a type of nerve tissue cancer called a **malignant schwannoma**.

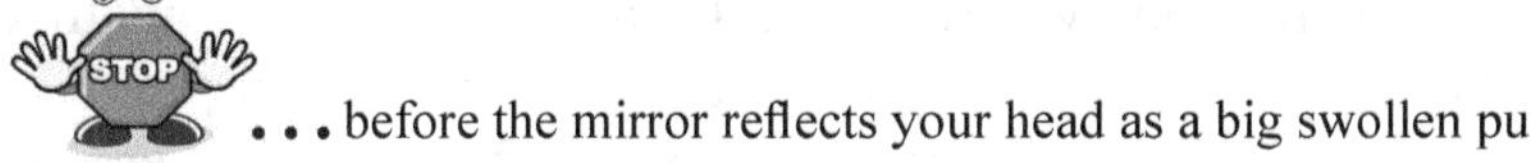

. . . before the mirror reflects your head as a big swollen pumpkin.

Because of the sample size, nature of the control group, and delicate extrapolations made from rodents to humans, the study has been deemed inconclusive, certainly not definitive evidence that heavy cell phone usage causes cancer in humans.

Over the years, scientists have conducted many studies on cell phone radiation related to cancer. But none have reached a tipping point of indisputable results. To accept this study as the **gospel truth** would be the same as accepting a single YouTube influencer's opinion about a product or service ... the exact (global warming) blunder that earlier chapters warned against. REMEMBER?

You cannot afford to limit your sphere of influence to a single source. You'll still follow the wisdom of the crowd. But your final decision should be based on many crowds, a diverse flow of multiple streams of information about the same subject matter from a variety of sources.

HOWEVER, don't be surprised if a decade from now, multiple studies definitively link cell phone radiation to cancer. It took almost that long for the United States government to determine that the technology used in **3M's defective Combat Arms earplugs,** caused thousands of military personnel to develop hearing loss.

Everyone is talking about 5G. But there was a time when 3G was the global technology wonder. AT&T was in a fierce race against time to roll out its new 3G cell phone network ahead of competitors. Subcontractors didn't have time to recruit sufficient numbers of qualified personnel or train them properly. They ended up hiring former pizza cooks, janitors, and delivery men to fill in the gap.

Between 2003 and 2011, at least 51 tower climbers fell to their deaths while working on cell sites. This is ten times the accident rate of the traditional construction industry. In instances such as this, not unlike the high death rate encountered during the construction of the Hoover Dam, real people took the hit. To compound the issue, each time a technician fell to his death, the pool of (pizza) tech workers in the cell tower industry diminished that much more.

Technology is not free. Sometimes, it's not even safe. Nevertheless, it is necessary ... indispensable to the evolution of humankind. From the Roman Empire's gruesome Greek Fire weapon that burned enemies to a crisp, to America's megaton atom bomb which took the same technological destruction to an infinitesimal level, over the centuries, technology has been the most consistent decipherer of victory and defeat. When the founder of Netflix, Reed Hastings, flew into Dallas to present his online video streaming idea to Blockbuster Video, they laughed him out of the room. In return, he used his laughable technology to put them out of business. Technology is the wildcard that everyone plays to gain a strategic advantage. To Baby Boomer who hate it ... **It's not going away.**

Meet The Church Media Guy from Church Training Academy.

He's a popular technology guru on YouTube, a welcome anomaly to a tech space dominated by the fast-talking, rule-breaking, under-30 marketing guru crowd.

He represents a breed unto itself, a handful of survivors who bucked the system and beat the odds and steamrolled their way into a wonderland of X's and 0's, a new Bill Gates frontier that didn't exist during their prime academic learning years. They are resilient,

shape-shifters who deployed precious time and grueling hours of trial and error to compensate for a lack of formal training. With one side of their brain teeming with millennial technology, and the other side, stacked with hard-nosed Baby Boomer business savvy, they are masters of both worlds.

It's important to understand the dynamics of this shape-shifters group's origin. Its existence is tied to an unrecoverable moment in time when technology was less complicated, less specialized, and growing at a much slower pace. Today, the same transition would be almost impossible. There's too much to learn at the start-from-scratch ground floor. And, considering today's blistering pace of innovation, without a concerted, ongoing, re-training effort, a shape-shifter's base knowledge would quickly evaporate into obsolesce.

The Bottom Line

All of the technological insight found in this chapter is geared toward our overarching goal of finding a compatible business niche. For the over-50 entrepreneur, the potential to open a successful technology business comes down to one question: **Are you a shape-shifter?**

For individuals in the over-50 bracket that are still struggling with their smartphones and remote controls, the answer is ... **No.** In corporate America, when it comes to technology, Baby Boomers are perceived as un-coachable, set in their ways, and expecting a high salary to reflect their traditional perception of seniority and self-worth. Even if a well-financed Baby Boomer bought an existing technology company, the decision-makers she ultimately pitched as potential clients would be in their early 30s, silently harboring the negative profile of another gray-haired, left-behind old-timer, out of her element.

Unless you're a battle-ready member of the shape-shifter's group, possessing a basic understanding of multiple technologies (content creation, file manipulation, platform distribution and sharing, cloud connectivity, storage, etc.), you wouldn't know who to hire and how to evaluate their performance. Most aspects of your core services would be very difficult to understand. Even if you were battle-ready, the FULL learning curve to reach the "expert" consultant level of any new technology would be very demanding and time-consuming.

It's not impossible, especially if you limit your involvement to low-tech (fidget, DIY, solar installation type) projects. There are excellent classes online (such as Codecademy, Udemy, The Great Courses Plus, and LinkedIn) as well as personal coaches available for a fee. But remember, your runway is shorter than a young roll-the-dice Millennial. Time is not on your side.

No matter the business you choose, you're going to use some form of high-tech or low-tech technology. Furthermore, "technology" should NOT be narrowly defined as some

kind of hardware or software program connected to a computer

screen. For instance, with the implementation of glow plugs and the single-tank SVO kit technology from Germany, you can run your fleet of diesel fuel trucks on French fry grease. That's unbelievable, game-changing "wow technology" in your face, and without a computer screen in sight.

But choosing technology products and services as your core offering in the marketplace is a completely different proposition, a low percentage bet for late-comers to the tech party. Thus, we will use our Baby Boomer business savvy and the rationale of our old crystal ball to close this chapter without putting our *Golden Circle* choice-of-the-heart selection into the ring ... at all.

POLITICAL

Environmental Forces

Prepare to go toe-to-toe with the Political Bruiser in Chapter 14 ... 

*I*nsight #6 explains the crucial role political forces play in choosing a business niche. These forces might include a new law banning the use of your best-selling pesticide, or a new tariff on Chinese imports, or the rise to power of a hostile dictator, or revolutionary extremists, taking over the oil fields in Libya.

Think about counties in Latin America such as Nicaragua, Ecuador, Bolivia, and Venezuela. Within these nations, there is no division of power. Absolutist strongmen rule with an iron fist. On any given day, a new law might triple your taxes; organized gang members might kill your best warehouse supervisor. The increasing wave of violence, corruption, and oppression has dispersed entire populations, sending millions in search of a better life in another country. Tragically, these desperate groups of migrants have given up on their own country, only to seek a new beginning in other countries in which elements of the host population consider them a threat.

Over the years, (legal and illegal) immigration has become a highly divisive social issue, leading in part to the Brexit vote in the UK and the election of Donald Trump in the United States. Should these new waves of immigrants be allowed to enter the country without deterrences or restrictions, large segments of the host population fear job losses, higher crime rates, and a disruption of the status quo. Some residents do not want them to enter at all.

As the debate rages on, two things are certain. **First, this will not be the first nor last high profile confrontation on immigration.** In the late 1880s, poor Irish immigrants were deported or blocked from entry based on the "public charge" clause. In 1882, the **Chinese**

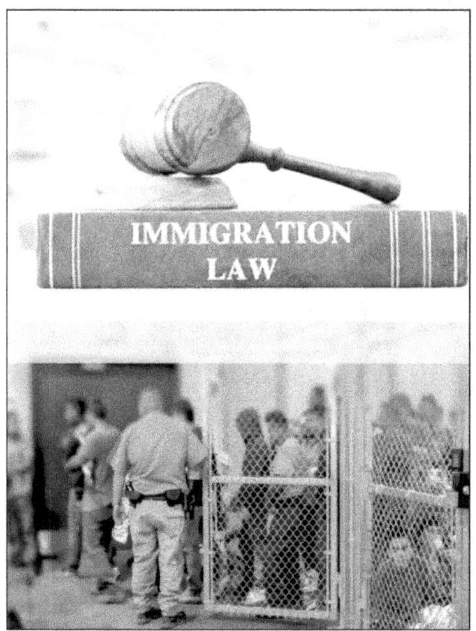

Exclusion Act prohibited Chinese naturalization and restricted immigration of Chinese laborers for 10 years. In 1952, the **McCarran-Walter Act** increased the power of the federal government to deport illegal immigrants suspected of Communist sympathies. In 2005, **REAL ID Act** created more restrictions on political asylum, curtailed habeas corpus relief for immigrants, and cleared the way for building extensive border barriers.

Secondly, and this is most impactive to your future business, **a capitalistic system cannot prosper and expand without a shadow economy created by illegal workers who are willing to accept a lower wage in exchange for opportunities that no longer exist in their own country.**

Most economists estimate the U.S. underground shadow economy at 11% to 12% of GDP. In 2018, that would be **$2.25 trillion to $2.46 trillion.**

This is huge. Furthermore, (since this is our political chapter) it exposes a great irony in the thought process of many Americans. The average conservative American business owner (using our profiling apparatus) will vote for a politician who advocates stricter immigration laws. That same business owner will search high and low to find the cheapest housekeeper/nanny, restaurant dishwasher, lawn cutter, rooftop tar worker, trash hauler, window washer … any reliable worker, no questions asked, to reduce expenses and save on the bottom line. The business owner is actively searching for the pool of workers he is voting to keep out.

As a new business owner, it is important to understand that social, political, and economic issues are not easily separated into tidy bundles and filed away. Whether camouflaged in bold macro terminology or complicated micro nuances, these issues will either help or harm your business. There is no neutral ground.

If you own a business on the Texas/Mexico border that imports hand-made products from Mexico, a sudden escalation of the import tax would devastate your profit margin. Cheap labor on the other side of the border matters. A politically inspired law to raise the rate would not create new jobs on your side of the border. It would, however, force you to sell at a higher price, which in the long run, would make you less competitive.

The big problem here is not a lack of upside-downside logic or reliable economic models to predict the future. The problem is the nature of the decision itself. It's 99.9% political, driven by a new sense of US nationalism. It doesn't have to make sense in an economic world.

Environmental laws, minimum-wage laws, and zoning laws are potent political decisions in disguise. They seduce the general population with glorious headlines and fix-all promises. For businesses operating in related sectors, however, they are critical disruptors that swell or diminish bottom line profits.

The Obama Administration's environmental policies were unpopular among automakers like Ford and General Motors. The mandate to increase fuel economy standards required auto manufacturers to produce smaller, more fuel-efficient cars, which were less profitable per unit. Having to report methane emissions required measurements and engineering studies that added costs.

Improving exhaust and waste standards required the installation of specialized technology.

These forced government mandates were similar to lawmakers requiring the auto industry to add passenger seat belts in 1964, not unlike the airline industry's mandate to add wind shear detection systems in 1988, and not unlike the construction industry's mandate to stop using cancer-causing asbestos in 1978.

These political decisions did save lives and help to preserve the environment, but at what cost to businesses operating in those highly scrutinized public arenas?

In a capitalistic system driven by profit, market pressures persist. The private

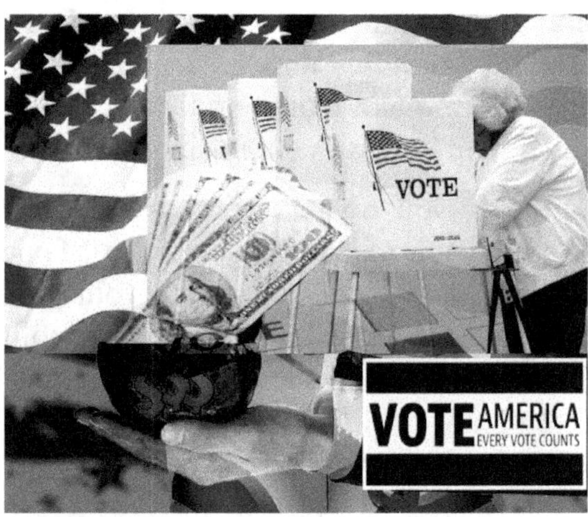

boardroom debate over **saved lives** and **lost profit** could not be more evident than in the implementation of a full shutdown of America's economy due to COVID-19. Even in the aftermath of dire warnings from the medical community and a spiking death toll, the Trump Administration received pressure from its (financially devastated) business constituents, and in turn, pressured states to reopen. Because of the rising death toll, states had to shut down all over again.

You might call it a political roll of the dice with an economic twist. Lives vs votes vs profit vs future prosperity all mix, precariously, with unpredictable results. The entire system, **the most powerful economic machine in the world,** runs on an awkward relationship between political decision-makers and influential capitalists who (with their wallets) decide who the decision-makers should be ... or who will receive enough campaign financing to have a fighting chance.

On average, a U.S. Senate race costs $10,400,000 to win. That can quickly surge to $30,000,000 or more in larger states. At one point, Governor Cuomo was spending half a million dollars a day on television and social media to win his gubernatorial race in New York. He spent tons of money, won the race, and almost immediately found himself caught up in a "political" sex scandal that tons of money couldn't overcome.

The impact of political decisions, made by political decision-makers, vetted by influential capitalists, trickle all the way down to the common workers on the street. Minimum-wage laws, for example, are extremely political in both conception and execution. Local and state laws dictate how far a union can go to organize a group of workers, and how much leverage a business has in discouraging union activity. With no "group" leverage, employees have to accept the wage scale offered by the company, or find somewhere else to work. Companies have the Constitutional right to pay what they feel is in the best interest of the company.

In theory, the lower the wage, the more capital the company retains with which to sustain itself and grow ... which, in the long run, should lead to more available jobs, accompanied by higher wages. Needless to say, that is in theory. In reality, the delicate balance between retained earnings and wages paid out to employees is far more complex. In Silicon Valley, growth might be contingent upon paying out huge salaries and bonuses to steal star technology players from the competition. In a slumping sales department, growth might depend on reducing base salaries and tying a hefty performance incentive to overall compensation.

The push-and-pull dynamics between companies and employees is a critical component in any company's success. As an entrepreneur, the moment you grow past one founder is the moment your push-and-pull session begins. Too much **bank capital** and not enough **human capital** will leave you with a pile of Blockbuster Video (temporary) cash, with no problem-solvers or visionaries around the conference table. Too much human capital and not enough bank capital will leave you with a GM-type union that dominates operations and drives you into bankruptcy.

TEAMSTERS' STRIKE

The National Labor Relations Act attempts to lay the groundwork for interaction between companies and unions. However, with union numbers dwindling, organizers often cut corners to recruit members. Likewise, employers often coerce, threaten, and retaliate against workers who are openly supportive of unions. In general, unionization leads to higher wages which may or may not lead to higher productivity and increased profits. But in a state like Alabama, where jobs are hard to find, Amazon's $15-an-hour minimum and first-day health care, sent union organizers running for the hills.

Top 5 Minimum Wage States

♦ Washington D.C. -- $15.00 per hour

♦ California -- $13.00 per hour

♦ Arizona -- $12.00 per hour

♦ New York State -- $11.80 per hour

♦ Connecticut -- $11.00 per hour

♦ Georgia and Wyoming bring up the rear at $5.15 per hour.

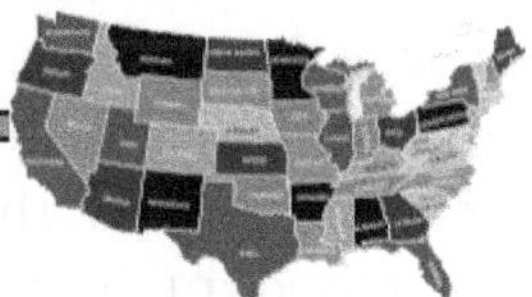

Top 5 Union States

♦ Hawaii

♦ New York

♦ Washington

♦ Alaska

♦ Rhode Island

In a high-tech, post-industrial economy, enduring the devastation of COVID-19, a business cannot operate without capital. **Although capital and labor have traditionally been indispensable compliments to each other, with the rise in automation, artificial intelligence (AI), and deep learning machines, gradually, labor has taken a backseat to capital. The process of efficiency has become more robotic in nature.** The pendulum has swung away from the necessity for a Bernie Sanders minimum wage to the proposition of value-added compensation. This is just a fancy way of saying you get paid what you're worth, and your worth is based on the (goal-related) value you bring to the operation.

In the short run, profits, flowing to the top of the food chain, increase. However, in the long run, as in the 1929 stock market crash, the foundation that undergirds the entire system deteriorates. A vast disparity in wealth distribution causes the bottom half of the population to gradually fall into cycles of income-starved, discretionary spending, unable to purchase the products and services the top half is trying to sell. **You might call it a form of cannibalism** in which the mouth is eating the feet so the feet cannot transport the mouth and the rest of the body to the food store to replenish the system.

In some instances, the culprit is pure greed. In the 1890s, **George Pullman**, one of the richest men in the world, had to be buried in secret, late at night, in a steel vault coffin. Because he had treated his workers so poorly, paying them starvation wages, the family was afraid bands of disgruntled workers would unearth his casket and drag his dismembered corpse through the streets.

In most instances, however, the primary flaw in the system is inconsistent "human" intervention. Someone has to determine a worker's true value to the operation. Large companies like Google and Microsoft employ sophisticated algorithms to reduce human biases, subjective assessment rewards, and external pressures such as quarterly profit goals. These recurring goals force managers to fudge on salaries to keep the budget in check. Most companies don't have these (Google) methods of evaluation in place. Thus, the system of value-added compensation is more **human** and **arbitrary** and **susceptible to external pressures** that have little to do with the worker's value.

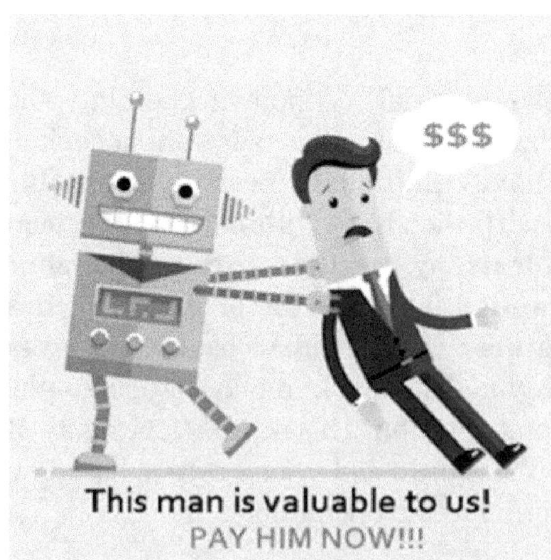

This man is valuable to us!
PAY HIM NOW!!!

In bad times, the pendulum swings hard toward salary caps and layoffs. In good times, the pendulum does not swing with equal voracity toward raises, benefits, and perks. "Human" managers/owners are more cautious (fearful of the future) than a performance-focused AI system would be. Based on the circumstances, the robots would give back as much as they had taken away. The system would indeed work. Humans, however, evaluating other humans, tend to error on the side of **future calamities.** Better hold something back. Invariably, *something* turns out to be the compensation-based value placed on workers.

For those startup entrepreneurs who still have a heart beating inside their chest, this is a tough moral proposition. The state of Georgia says, by law, owners are not obligated to pay more than $5.15 an hour. But who can feed their family on $5.15 an hour? With pressure from investors, fixed and variable expenses, price undercutting from competitors, and unpredictable dynamics of the marketplace, the new owner has to walk a precarious tightrope between profitability and the monetary value placed on human capital within a moral context. The owner has to make a profit. But he or she must also be able to sleep at night.

Owners must also consider the question of **"operational ownership"**. This is not ownership of the company itself. Management theorists define operational ownership as the willingness to assume responsibility for the desired end result. Owners of a project, event, or social movement understand the full ramifications of the project's existence and readily embrace obstacles associated with its ultimate success. In the old days, you didn't own the paper route. The newspaper did. But getting up in the morning at 5:00 AM, braving the cold wind and icy puddles and angry dogs, who could tell where the newspaper's ownership started and yours stopped?

Think about a scenario in which the CEO arrives on Monday morning in his new BMW; Tuesday, he drives his big family Lincoln Navigator; Wednesday, he rides in on his MTT Turbine Superbike motorcycle. At the weekly meeting, while punching numbers into his brand new $1500 iPhone MAX, he explains why salaries will have to be cut and people will have to be laid off.

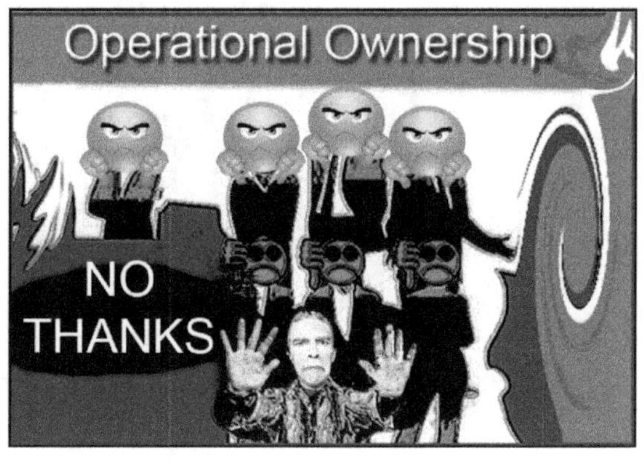

It's YOUR business. The political decision-makers in Georgia and Wyoming say you have the right to pay your employees **$5.15 per hour**. But who's going to take operational ownership of your projects at that hourly rate?

Team members, especially Generation X, know the score. They're not interested in making you rich with no indication you plan to take them along for the ride. Google, General Electric, FedEx, and other successful companies reward, heavily, for buy-in and operational ownership. You must do the same. Otherwise, don't complain when team members hear your grand vision of market dominance and spiraling profits, and say **"no thanks"**.

The tug-of-war between profitability and politically mandated pay scales, hammered out at the Statehouse, is not as cut-and-dry as you might think. The implication is that profitability and fair wages are mutually exclusive. In fact, studies show paying employees at a level that motivates them to be more productive actually increases profitability. But what level of compensation produces optimal productivity?

There are complex economic formulas (MPK/PK market equilibrium) that help to figure this out. But in the long run, each business is different. High turnover and employee disloyalty create their own intangible value. The politics are arbitrary, in that, each entrepreneur has to find his/her own way.

Starting A Business Based On Government Contracts

If you're competing for government contracts, you should understand that sweetheart deals are a bitter reality. In 2019, the United States federal government spent $4.45 trillion. Roughly 25% of awarded contracts were no-bid contracts. Political connections and contributions influenced the procurement terms specified in many government contracts as well as the ultimate recipient of the contract itself.

Let's say you own a construction company and want to bid on a new elementary school scheduled to be built in your district. When you read the terms of procurement, you find that any company desiring to bid must be headquartered locally and have a verifiable track record of successfully building five school/education buildings.

In all likelihood, any company that has already built two or three different schools without major cost overruns and lawsuits probably has the necessary expertise. A bit more digging reveals that only one company in town has built five schools. That company contributed heavily to most of the school board members' re-election campaigns. The contract was obviously written for the board's deep-pocket contributor.

The further you move away from the actual hammer and nail work, up the ladder, to the decision-makers that approve the project, the more politically astute you'll need to be. **To start a business aimed at winning government contracts requires a lot of weekend golf, dinner meetings, barbecues, birthday cards, and campaign contributions.** Your big machinery and expert plumbers and electricians won't mean a thing until you learn how the political game is played. This is not just in America, but all over the world.

In Chapter 14, the Over-50 Entrepreneurial Assessment-Q9 identifies a particular profile that does well at this. **It's called the PERFORMER///PROMOTER.** This Ronald Reagan/Magic Johnson type is fun-loving and outgoing. He or she seeks an audience to listen to their stories and adventures. He loves being the center of attention. She is people-oriented and dislikes being alone. If you feel an affinity  for constant high-level hobnobbing and fraternizing, and gradually building your connections with the powerbrokers in your niche, then throw your choice-of-the-heart selection into the ring.

Finally, political factors can affect your business indirectly. If the City Council allows oil frackers to come in and contaminate the local waterways with drilling concoctions of chloride, barium, strontium, and radium, the probability of a large fish kill is very high. **If you're a commercial fisherman, that means your business dies with the fish.**

Political decisions by oblivious stakeholders can have a disastrous impact upon your business. As an entrepreneur, you cannot ignore the arbitrary deal-making that may not have had your explicit demise in mind. Political (toxic subprime derivative type) suicide takes out bystanders too. The smallest, ill-conceived governmental exemptions, reclassifications, and grandfathering in of your deep-pocket competitors can send your business tumbling to the ground.

Treat political environmental forces as a moving target that can change with unexpected disfavor. Be ready to move in quickly and move out quickly. A single election can put you in business or out of business, depending on how you placed your government sector bet. Don't get angry because wind turbine subsidies have dwindled to a drop in the federal bucket. Big oil and gas fossil fuel advocates have regained their powerful voice with lawmakers. The once-promising renewable energy horse is back in the barn, if only for a season. With the election of a new President, the "renewable" barn doors may again fly open.

If not, it doesn't mean you have to leave the energy sector entirely. There are countless emerging technologies that offer the smart entrepreneur an opportunity to pivot out of a dying market and into the latest big thing government policymakers feel an obligation to fund ... electrocatalysts that convert carbon dioxide and water into ethanol; exotic ways of manipulating fusion reactions into stable energy sources; high energy (IFPC) military laser weaponry for shooting down enemy drones, disabling boats, and flying helicopters.

With the right combination of researchers, scientists, and proposal writers, the government will pay. **They don't care if you're over fifty; might even prefer that you are.** The principal component is not the science. Rather, it's your ability to cultivate political relationships and make the precarious forces of government work for you.

SOCIAL

Environmental Forces

Prepare to go toe-to-toe with the Social Bruiser in Chapter 14 ...

*I*nsight #7 explains the crucial role social forces play in choosing a business niche. Social forces might be an animal cruelty boycott against the use of mink and fox fur, or bloody social unrest in South Sudan that blocks the critical export of gum Arabic for paint production in the United States, or the Occupy Wall Street Movement of 2011, a massive protest against corporate greed and the growing inequality between rich and poor. The chaotic marches and sit-ins threw financial trading for a tailspin and disrupted normal business activities for merchants throughout the New York City financial district.

When Breast Cancer prevention activists accused Revlon of using chemicals linked to cancer in its cosmetics, the company, after years of denial, bowed to growing social pressure and removed certain  long-chain parabens and DMDM Hydantoin from its product line.

Nevertheless, many cosmetics manufacturers are still under fire. An in-depth list compiled by watchdog site Styles and Resilience shows the continued widespread use of Carcinogenic in cosmetics.

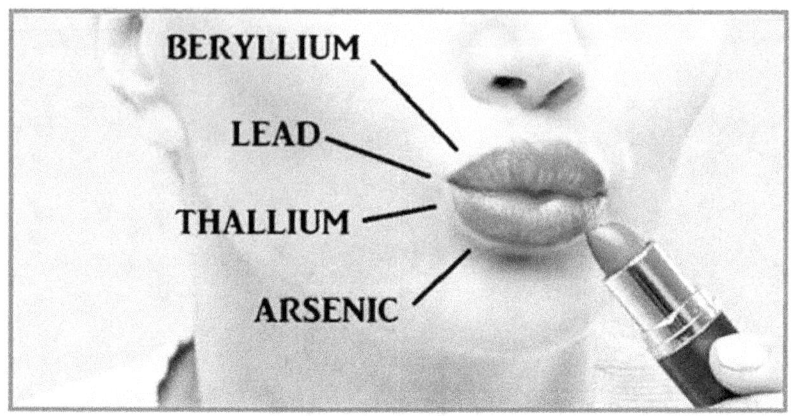

List of Top Ten Carcinogenic Lipsticks - 2018:

♦ (#103c), Stargazer Lipstick

♦ (#1005 Red Lizard), NARS Semi-Matte

♦ (#410 Volcanic), L'Oreal Colour Riche

♦ (#125 Pink Petal), Maybelline Color Sensational

♦ (#165 Tickled Pink), L'Oreal Colour Riche

♦ (#580 Ruby Remix), CoverGirl Queen Collection Vibrant Hues

♦ (#27 Mauvey), Sonia Kashuk Luxury Lip Color

♦ (#748 Heroic), L'Oreal Intensely Moisturizing Lipcolor

♦ (#025 Warm Brick), CoverGirl Continuous Color

♦ (#475 Mauve Me), Maybelline Color Sensation

During the mid-90s, labor organizations targeted Nike for allowing suppliers in third world countries to exploit poor, under-aged workers. Life Magazine published a story that used the headline "Six Cents an Hour", displaying a Pakistani boy sewing Nike soccer balls.

The company's name became synonymous with slave wages, forced overtime, and arbitrary workforce abuses. The noisy social protests slowly morphed into an economic disruption, spilling over into sales and profits.

Initially, Nike denied responsibility for conditions in factories the company didn't own. But as public protests and media reports increased, Nike agreed to create an extensive system for monitoring and remedying factory conditions in its footwear and apparel supply chains throughout the world.

In recent years, industry giants (Tyson Foods and Cargill) have come under pressure from public safety advocates to ban the use of antibiotics to treat sick chickens. Studies show the practice makes germ-fighting medicines less effective in humans and contributes to the spread of dangerous drug-resistant bacteria including E. coli, salmonella, and S. aureus.

Similarly, the overuse of antibiotics in the meat industry has contributed to the rise of an antibiotic-resistant population in the United States. Food experts project, by 2050, this widespread industry practice of juicing animals with drugs will have caused the deaths of an estimated ten million people a year. U.S. antibiotic-resistant infections have already caused over two million illnesses and 23,000 deaths prior to 2019. This translates into a $70 billion burden on society each year.

The U.S. Food and Drug Administration has introduced voluntary recommendations to phase out the use of antibiotics as growth promoters, and require veterinary approval of antibiotics in feed and water. Walmart has introduced voluntary guidelines limiting suppliers to only use antibiotics to treat and prevent diseases, and not for growth promotion.

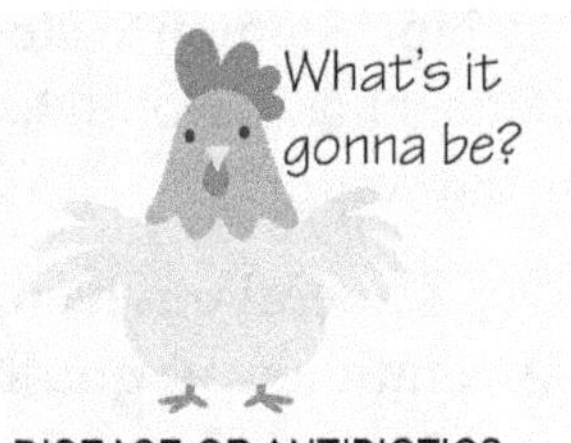

DISEASE OR ANTIBIOTICS

Reaching back to our previous chapter, the voluntary recommendations policy is an excellent example of political forces at work. Despite the apparent health hazards caused by the practice, the government decision-makers are under pressure by industry lobbyists NOT to take formal action against the industry... 

"Hey, managers responsible for company profits. Please do the right thing, okay?"

This complicity by the FDA won't last forever. As more people die and social pressures increase, the obvious next step will be a total ban on the use of antibiotics in agriculture. Keep in mind, if you enter this meat and poultry distribution niche, more stringent government policies will affect you as well.

Recognizing and adjusting to changing social norms is a critical aspect of choosing your business niche. If you open a restaurant and, because of COVID-19, find social norms moving toward less dining in and more home delivery, does your menu lend itself to "live healthier" social trends, that is to say, a greater demand for organic, gluten-free, self-contained lunch bundles, delivered by Uber Eats? Let's put it another way. Does your health-conscious offering of soups, salads, broccoli, stuffed 

zucchini, salmon cakes, and hot bread taste the same in a plastic container as it would having been brought out to the customer's table by the waiter?

Social environmental forces don't readily give a pass on expectations of quality. Today's customers are short on loyalty and long on demands. The grocery store manager cannot expect customers to accept soggy grapes and rotten tomatoes because the COVID-19 pandemic has disrupted the food supply chain. Monsanto can't remove the cancer-causing ingredient glyphosate from Roundup weed killer and still expect customers to buy the product if it doesn't kill weeds.

There is always pressure to deliver. Fresh seafood flown in from Alaska BETTER be fresh. If you stop using the cancer-causing preservative formalin to keep it fresh, you have to find another way to deliver the **"fresh"** you promised.

In the late 90s, when SBA loans for underserved communities and inner-city economic zones were plentiful, this **"customer expectation lesson"** was the hard lesson that many minority business owners learned. Because these businesses were minority-owned in minority communities, based on a sense of pride and future economic independence, shop owners expect the "community" to support them. These psychographic drivers were sufficient to bring in traffic for a short period of time. In the long run, however, customers expected these entrepreneurial beacons of hope and empowerment to compete on all the traditional points of differentiation ... **quality, price, selection, return policy, and so on.**

This was an impossible dream. There were bubbly customer service reps and clean restrooms at McDonald's across the street. Budgets were too tight, however, to order customer service training at Crenshaw's Catfish Kitchen. If Walmart and Walgreens were buying wholesale railroad boxcars of toothpaste on a single order, forcing manufacturers to issue huge volume discounts, how could these small minority shops, (ordering a box of twelve), expect to sell at the same price? Customers from the surrounding community might pay a little more, but not a lot more. In the end, market forces overrode socioeconomic forces. No one gets a pass.

If you open a beauty supply shop, will you STOP carrying your best-selling shampoo because it contains parabens, still legal, but linked to breast cancer all over the world? There are no protesters marching outside your door. Your customers don't have a clue. If your moral code doesn't stop you, one bad day of viral exposure on social media certainly will.

Each day, billions of internet users trust social media to inform them of the unraveling status of their universe. It would take only one research-savvy customer to discover your contaminated hair shampoo, your alleged blatant disregard for safety. How long would it take for that customer to drop your business in the grease?

Earning his honored place in the annals of American heroism, one man, **Jeffrey Wigand**, almost single-handedly brought down the cigarette industry. He announced to worldwide media sources that cigarettes were giving smokers at least five different types of cancer.

Even more horrifying, cigarette companies possessed irrefutable clinical proof of the carcinogenic effect on humans. Yet, for decades, and fear of lost profits, they had chosen to hide the truth.

There is a twofold lesson here that new entrepreneurs must memorize with both sides of their brain. **First, customers expect you to deliver. As empathetic as they may appear to be, no one gets a pass. Ultimately, they will find other sources to satisfy their needs.**

Secondly, you must never underestimate the power of social environmental forces in your *Golden Circle* selection. Don't choose a business niche that forces you to cut corners in order to survive. Don't find yourself bribing Nigerian officials or sleazy inspectors on the New Orleans waterfront. You might endure for the moment. But eventually, a tidal wave of condemnation and public backlash will catch up with you. You're over fifty and your runway is short. Why take a chance?

Food Lyon's Social Demise

Years ago, the Food Lyon chain had to shut down all of its grocery stores and move out of Texas. Someone filmed a store manager rubbing down old meat with Clorox bleach to bring back its tantalizing, fresh, red color. The butcher plastered on a new expiration date to give their revitalized product a brand new week of selling time. Old meat turned into new profits, and for a brief moment, quarterly sales figures made everyone smile.

The company's home office in North Carolina inevitably paid the fines. But the social impact was too much. Customers never forgot, never forgave, were not even willing to consider a below-cost, bargain price on cereals and can goods. Day-after-day, the media milked the story. With all stores empty, they had to shut down.

When you put your choice-of-the-heart selection in the social ring, remember your opponent is going to use a million posts and tweets and Likes and Shout-outs to slam you to the mat. Don't choose a business niche like a smoke shop or abortion clinic or disposal unit for nuclear waste if you're not ready to go toe-to-toe with the negative spin doctors in an unending battle to control public opinion.

You say your sex doll brothel business brings true value to the marketplace. They say you need to be run out of town. Ultimately, you spend more time fighting than building your brand.

Your operating capital is limited. Your runway is short. Avoid niches with these built-in confrontations, or you'll never get your business off the ground.

If you're ready to walk the tightrope between increased profits and social consciousness, then let's move on ... to the next chapter ... **NOW!!!**

PHYSICAL

Environmental Forces

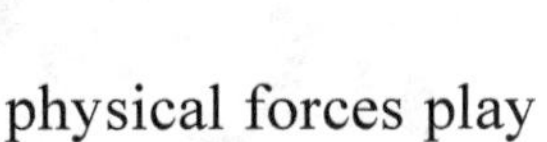

Prepare to go toe-to-toe with the Physical Bruiser in Chapter 14 ...

*I*nsight #8 explains the crucial role physical forces play in choosing a business niche.

Think about the disruptive forces of global warming. The cause-and-effect is physical. Temperatures increase, polar ice caps melt, sea levels rise, coastal cities are engulfed, weather patterns become more severe, and entire populations retreat to higher ground. But if we put on our analytical specs and dig below the surface, we discover a more compelling story, the extent to which social, economic, and political factors contribute to our demise. Irresponsible coexistence with the planet (factory pollution, poor waste disposal, and forest depletion by urban populations throughout the world) has multiplied the greenhouse effect, trapping carbon dioxide, methane, and other harmful gases in the atmosphere. These gases block heat from escaping and damage the protective ozone layer.

Though some spiritual gurus might disagree, our molecular existence starts with the "physical". Physical environmental factors undergird the other environmental factors. You might have an excellent business plan, a well-differentiated product line, superior channels of distribution, and dedicated, well-trained employees. But if you operate out of Venice Beach, California, Back Bay, Boston, Ocean Drive, Miami, San Juan, Puerto Rico, the Mekong Delta region of Cambodia, the Solomon Islands in the South Pacific, Maputo, Mozambique, The Netherlands, or Fortaleza, Brazil, it doesn't really matter. By 2200, when the oceans rise by 20 feet, you're going to be underwater.

There is an exaggerated misconception about the power of the internet and its global connections. Time and time again, proponents of internet commerce remind us we're all connected, all floating around in one big happy soup. With the click of a mouse, we can become millionaires, never having to leave the comfort of our home. This empowering sense of global equality, however, is quite misleading.

Certain professions require certain physical locations, that is to say, you can't be a ski instructor in Arizona or a big-time Hollywood talent agent in Biloxi, Mississippi.

Farmers need land and shipbuilders need water. In these instances, you can't disparage the importance of physical factors by deploying an internet connection or relying on the click of a mouse.

There are other reasons your physical location matters.

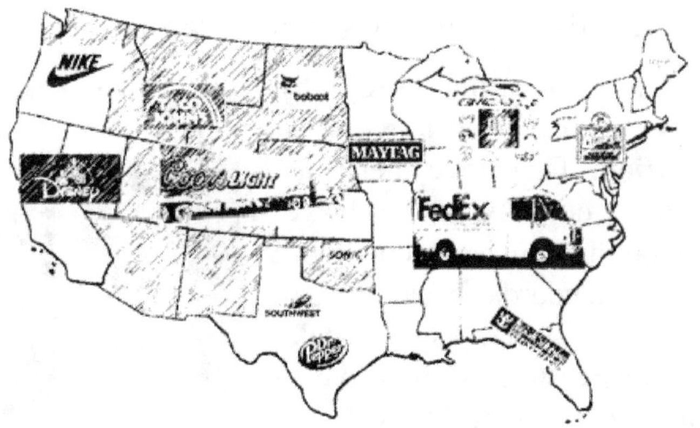

Talent Pool

Once your company reaches a certain point in its growth cycle, you will need to hire team members. Successfully attracting critical skill sets may very well depend on the makeup of the local job market and the premium salaries you'll have to pay to recruit top talent to the boondocks of Sleepy Valley. If, however, you're already in Silicon Valley, some hotshot software engineer might be willing to give your startup a try.

Roughly 72% of all job applicants want to find work in their current metropolitan area. However, people are willing to move if the opportunity is overwhelming. Highly-paid computer technicians, software developers, and engineering candidates are most susceptible to a relocation offers. More money is the attention-getter. But money means less if the company has a reputation for creating a "cool" employee-oriented culture.

Most Baby Boomers have heard about the new "cool" work cultures ... video games, pool tables, exercise rooms, free Friday lunch, flexible hours, and work areas with no partitions or walls. In the back of their minds, the old-timers are wondering when the real work gets done. They are astounded to find that these surface perks are just the tip of the iceberg. Companies like **Google, Apple, and Facebook** give employees time to work on pet projects that have nothing to do with their assigned workload, and offer free company-sponsored career classes, industry certifications, and hours of dedicated mentoring by senior managers.

It's easy to understand why Google has to force employees to take a vacation. They love their jobs so much, they don't want to leave. Their daily production is much higher than industry standards because they are fully engaged, overly eager to take **operational ownership**. They strive to eliminate any doubts about the value of their contribution. They don't want some outsider to come in to take their place.

What does this new "cool" work standard mean to the over-50 entrepreneur?

It means the prospect of selecting a physical location moves to the front of the pack. You're just getting started so you don't have a reputation for "cool". You don't have the capital to outbid the competition for top-rated talent. Rather than expect people to relocate to your home office, you have to take your home office to where your prospective talent exists in abundance.

If your new company is driven by AI technology, you might consider moving to one of the top seven cities that technology gurus prefer ... **San Francisco, San Jose, New York, Los Angeles, Seattle, Boston, and Austin.** If you're in the medical field, you need to operate in close proximity to multiple hospitals and trauma centers, as found in **Houston, Baltimore, and Boston**, cities in which qualified medical personnel dominate the workforce.

Building a remote team using sub-contracted internet programmers and virtual assistants from the Philippines is an early alternative, but certainly not a permanent solution. You want people there with you, growing as the company grows, espousing the company's vision, and replicating decision-making that reflects your core values. Completing a remote function such as web development or writing sales copy is one thing. Building a team of key core contributors for future growth is another.

Relocation is an exquisite way of saying moving. Moving is the abbreviation for the harsh reality of moving away. We'll talk much more about relocation in Chapter 14.

Your business is going to grow in phases. As a smart visionary, you must think past the **"just you"** phase. To grow, you're going to need other team members. From which great incubator of human capital do these team members emerge?

Give yourself a shot at the best talent. Go where they are. Build a "cool" organization, and at some point, no matter where you are, they will come to you.

Let's move on.

Investment Network

If your business continues to grow, you'll reach a point in which outside investment is a practical option, most likely, a necessity. Even if you continue to self-finance or bootstrap with family members and friends, the very act of meeting with experienced investors broadens your knowledge base and exposes you to innovative financing opportunities you might otherwise overlook.

Think of it this way. If you're a college kid, hanging around your uncle's NBA practices, chances are, through observation and redundancy, your skill level will improve. If you decide to go Pro, someone in that elite sports circle will introduce you to an agent and tell you which teams to avoid. **Your "physical proximity" will afford you benefits your internet connection can't provide.**

Regulations and Incentives

In Arkansas, 39 of the 76 counties are "dry", meaning the sale of any kind of alcoholic beverage is absolutely prohibited. In Georgia, you can't get drunk until after church. State law does not allow the sale of alcohol on Sunday before 12:30 PM. Illinois prohibits horse racing on Sunday. Iowa requires all car dealerships to be closed on Sunday. Bergen County, New Jersey bans all types of work on Sundays except in grocery stores, gas stations, pharmacies, hotels, restaurants, and other entertainment venues.

Depending on your business niche, physical location can play a major role in boosting or depressing your profit potential. State and local laws may restrict your access to customers on specific days and prevent the movement of goods and services in preparation for the following work week. In California, landlords must abide by a new law limiting rent increases to 5 percent each year plus inflation, but never above a cumulative total of 10 percent. Also, designating someone as an independent contractor rather than an employee has become a lot more restrictive. If you, the representative of the company, direct their daily course of work, or if the worker's job is part of your company's core business, you can no longer arbitrarily label them as a contractor.

If you remember the nationwide scramble by Newark, Miami, Chicago, New York and other municipalities to woo Amazon HQ2 headquarters to their fair city, then you probably remember the unprecedented incentive packages these cities offered.

Amazon vowed to bring 25,000 to 40,000 jobs to Long Island City in Queens in exchange for $3 billion in state and local tax subsidies.

The deal fell through. The problem was, in a union state like New York, Amazon was perceived as anti-union and brought a reputation of dehumanizing workers with pressure-packed shipping quotas that sometimes required workers to "urinate in bottles" to meet deadlines.

Amazon resented the public, humiliating trial-by-fire of its employment practices, and withdrew from the deal. No one knew that months later, Amazon would be caught up in a scandal, accused by the Federal Trade Commission (FTC) of stealing roughly $61 million in customer tips from workers to subsidize delivery drivers' hourly wages.

Physical location matters. In almost any other state (states in which the union did not play a major role in local elections), the manner in which Amazon treated its employees would NOT have come into question. The potential payoff in job creation and long-term taxation would've been too attractive, especially to states already operating at a deficit.

Amazon learned a lesson about the nuances of choosing a location. New York learned a lesson about the consequences of refusing to look the other way.

When choosing a physical location for your new business, consider these nine factors:

1.   Built-in legal restrictions that keep you from competing in your niche (avoid).

2.   Access to favorable product distribution channels.

3.   Vertical integration advantages such as primary suppliers just across town.

4.   Access to talent and investment funding.

5.   Long-standing competition footholds that keep you on the outside, looking in (avoid).

6.   Easy access to transportation such as airports and trains.

7.   Safety for your employees and contractors.

8.   Availability of decent housing and good schools.

9.   Traditional weather and climate threats (avoid).

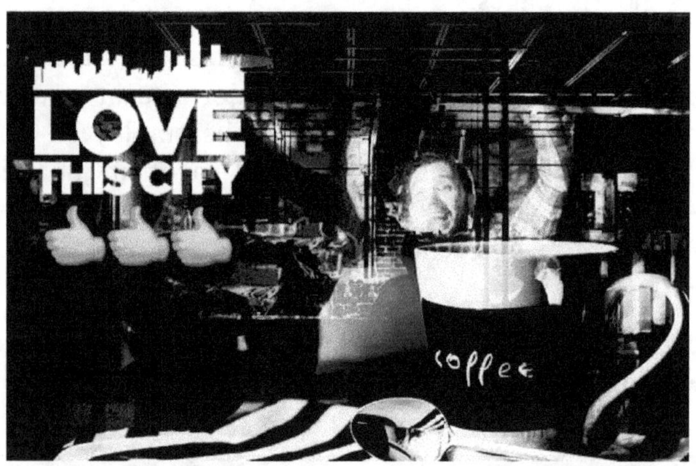

Give yourself the best possible chance for success. Don't let physical environmental forces pin you to the mat. Find a location that works for you, not against you. Build a "cool" work environment, and soon, the best industry talent will come knocking at your door.

 **PHYSICAL**

THINKING TIME

*I*nsight #9 explains the critical types of thinking your brain must employ to choose a compatible business niche. What is "thinking" in the first place? Is it the same as "learning"? And how can we use these processes to pick a winning product or service as our perfect offering to the marketplace?

Thinking Like You've Never Done Before

Let's begin by getting our terminology succinctly squared away. It's important to understand what's going on inside that thick skull of yours and why you think the way you do.

The brain is a masterful creation. No one completely understands its processes and functionality. We know it receives information from the outside world through our five senses: sight, smell, touch, taste, and hearing (Studies of the savant syndrome strongly suggest there are more.). These instantaneous transmissions often flow in at the same time with varying degrees of urgency. It is the brain's responsibility to give priority to these bits of information and direct the other parts of the mind and body to respond accordingly.

The brain controls our thoughts, speech, memory, movement of our limbs, regulation of our organs, and other critical functionality within our body. Although these tasks are delegated to certain regions of the brain, the entire system is interconnected. One part of the brain calls upon another part of the brain to complete its assigned task, no different from the marketing department calling upon the shipping and receiving department to deliver grand opening signs to a new location.

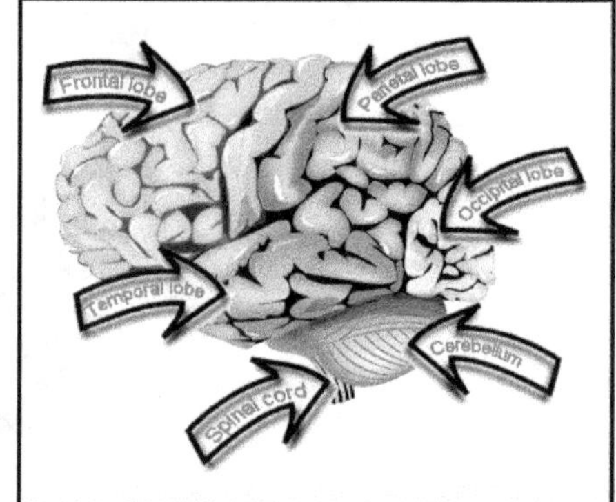

The cerebrum is the largest, most dominant part of the brain. It is composed of right and left hemispheres, joined together by the corpus callosum that transmits messages from one side to the other. Each hemisphere controls the opposite side of the body. If a stroke occurs on the right side of the brain, your left arm or leg may become weak or paralyzed.

In general, the left hemisphere controls speech, comprehension, arithmetic, and writing. The right hemisphere controls creativity, spatial ability, artistic and musical skills. In the majority of the population, the left hemisphere is the side that controls hand usage and language. All of this amazing horsepower under the hood is necessary for us to engage in the cognitive process we call thinking.

The Essence of Thinking

It takes this entire complex apparatus of regions and networks and neurotransmitters for thinking to take place. Thinking is more than the conscious activities of processing information, solving problems, and making decisions. It is the sum total of all we have learned (long-term memory) patterned against new information (short-term memory) in order to create a meaning association and assign a value and category in which the new information can be stored.

Let's say you were walking in the forest. You see the grass move and hear a rattling sound coming from a pile of dead branches near your foot. Your fight-or-flight instincts suddenly kick into gear. Immediately, almost instantaneously, you backpedal from the branches and look for a snake.

The new information (sound, movement, and location) triggers a reaction from your long-term memory of movies, books, and folklore about rattlesnakes. In other words, your instinctive retreat from potential danger does not come from the thinking/ rational part of your brain.

Rather, the command to move comes from the warning produced by your long-term memory. The thinking part comes in afterward the act as a means of justifying or giving credence to your decision to retreat.

All systems are still connected. Your brainstem relayed a command to increase your breathing and heart rate. The primary motor cortex (M1) generated an instantaneous neural impulse to make your legs move. But it was the clump or volume of long-term memory containing the "rattlesnake file" that prompted your initial, panic-stricken reaction.

... Take a deep breath. Wrap your thinking around the essence of thinking.

This clinical mapping of brain behavior may feel counterintuitive. In reality, it reveals a commonly misunderstood fact about the way we humans make decisions. Sometimes, we think we're thinking, when, in essence, we're reacting to a clump of past memories embedded deep inside our subconscious mind. **This is the same complex mental process we talked about in Chapter 1 (Baby Steps).** Our brains run on automatic most of the time.

This innate tendency to think you're thinking is counterproductive to your selection of a business niche. You do the research, gather the information, and start to analyze its impact upon your Golden Circle selection. Instead of looking at the full potential of your choices, you allow the familiar, trusted clumps of long-term memory to restrict the opportunities staring you in the face.

Have you ever had a mentor or close friend say, *"You're looking at this the wrong way"?*

This means you're viewing the information or current circumstances using the restricted, linear (avoid risky unfamiliarity) capacity of your long-term memory. **You're not thinking.** You're reacting.

Let's say you purchased a big, shiny, luxurious, gas-guzzling SUV. A few months later, someone ran through a stop sign, totaled out the vehicle, and put you in the hospital for several weeks. You're angry at the careless driver, angry about your spoiled plans to go on vacation, angry at the length of time it took the hospital to figure out the right pain medication, angry you'll have to

wear a cast on your broken arm for the next two months.

Then, one day, your friend comes to visit you at the hospital and says, *"You're looking at this the wrong way."*

He reminds you that you really didn't want the SUV in the first place. Your wife got caught up in the deep-cushioned seats, airplane instrument dash, and shiny wood grain paneling. With a newborn at home, her point about needing more room was valid. But a minivan or large crossover would've done the trick. Your auto/ home insurance has doubled. Your gasoline expenses have doubled. A simple oil change is now $200. The paint warranty prohibits your driving through a regular car wash. A weekly hand wash is almost 50 bucks. Don't add wax, or you'll have to shell out a $100 plus tip.

Your friend reveals the true benefits of your current circumstances. The vehicle can't be repaired; it's going to be totaled. The other driver's insurance company has already made an initial offer to pay off your balance and put another $15,000 in your pocket for personal injuries. The follow-up offer will probably be $20-$30,000 to keep from going to court. You'll be out of the hospital in a few days; out of the arm cast in two months; enough money in the settlement to undo an unwise, emotionally driven dealership fiasco; enough to purchase something more practical, something more in lines with your current financial goals ... *Hallelujah!*

The same information was right there in front of you. But it took your friend to point it out.

Your friend used a well-known methodology called holistic thinking. This type of thinking takes into account the full ramifications of all of the information as an interconnected whole. You might say it's a wide-net thought pattern encompassing various paradigms and theoretical outcomes. The word *holism* comes from the Indo-European word *kailo*, which means whole, intact, or uninjured. It represents a "deliberate mentality" through which a person recognizes the inter-connectedness of elements that form larger patterns.

If you invade North Korea and knock out their nuclear missiles before they can launch, they still have 1.3 million ground troops. China will enter the war with 100 times more missiles and nuclear firepower and 2.1 million ground troops. With formal agreements of Communist solidarity already in place, the Russians will enter the war with thousands more nuclear missiles, some with biochemical payloads (deadly man-made viruses that make the Coronavirus seem laughable), and with another 1.1 million ground troops. **The United States' 1.3 million ground troops are not enough, not even close.** If you DON'T use your nuclear arsenal, you will lose. If you DO use your nuclear arsenal, and usher in worldwide mutual destruction, the whole planet earth will lose.

This is holistic thinking at its highest levels. This theoretical model suggests you will win the war against North Korea, but lose the earth in the process. Where will you hold your victory celebration? Who will drive the carloads of scorched, skinless, radioactive skeletons in the ticker-tape parade?

Thinking is "deliberate". You make a conscious, rebellious, objective-driven effort to pull yourself away from familiar norms of the subconscious mind to examine the validity of other possibilities.

In 1633, astronomer **Galileo Galilei** was convicted of the high crime of heresy for rebelling against the Catholic Church's long-standing doctrine which stated the earth (not the sun, as Galileo claimed) was the center of the universe. If you can envision the powerful Catholic Church as your subconscious mind and Galileo's rebellious pursuit of an unfamiliar possibility as the risky process of thinking, you will understand why thinking is so difficult. By deliberately uncoupling your thought process from the familiarity and bias of long-term memory, you have nothing to go on but the empirical evidence in front of you.

In choosing your business niche, you will do the research, that is to say, you will gather the empirical evidence before you. This is the easy part. The answers are there. You just need to find them. **The hard part is unlinking yourself from the bias of long-term memory and actually "thinking", rebelliously and independently, to reach an objective conclusion.**

To complicate matters, there are many types of thinking processes. As we explore these types, understand that, once you choose your business niche, these processes don't simply go away. **You will call on them again and again throughout your entrepreneurial journey.** The more you understand the application and usefulness of each, the more proficient you will become in making good decisions and navigating the marketplace.

Holistic thinking

Since we've already discussed this in detail, we need not spend time re-explaining the concept. This type of thinking takes into account the full ramifications of all of the information as an interconnected whole. Always remember your friend at the hospital and his presentation of the big picture, free of the biases of long-term memory. If you apply this approach in all of your decision-making, you will avoid many unforeseen consequences farther down the road.

Synthetic thinking

Synthetic thinking examines the combination of components in a complex whole, explaining the behavior of an interconnected system from the inside, out. Analytical thinking teaches us "how", while synthetic thinking teaches us "why" with an emphasis on the impact of all parts working together.

Every system is contained inside a larger system … the heart in a body, the engine in a vehicle, a solar panel on a home's energy grid.

The objective of synthetic thinking is to de-aggregate the function of a system with all its working parts from the larger

system in which it exists, to understand each part's contribution as it relates to the whole. Sometimes, when considering the task of dismantling a system, synthetic thinking and holistic thinking are used interchangeably.

Organizational thinking

No matter how large or small, formal or informal, each business has an organizational culture. Organizational thinking focuses on evaluating and enhancing systems driven by people, structures, and processes that operate together to make an organization run. Problems that show up in the finance department may very well originate in marketing or shipping.

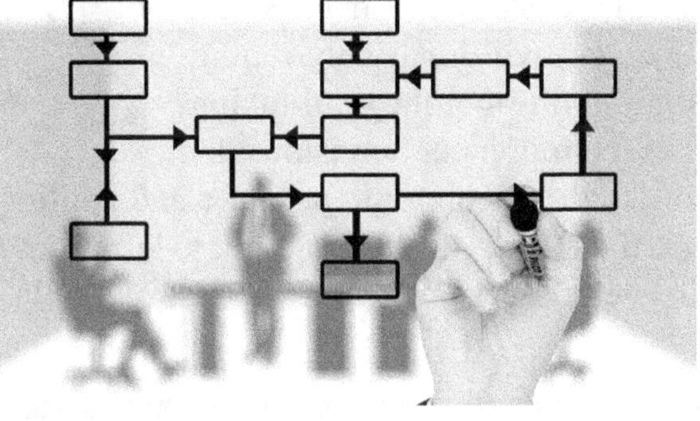

Purging people and processes in finance is not going to resolve the issue. Organizational thinking promotes an adaptive, broad-based approach to problem-solving that considers the interaction of all parts that make up the total organization. This approach strives to identify inefficiencies and root out hypocrisy and bias in organizational practices and decision-making.

Strategic thinking

Strategic thinking involves the effort of owners and other company stakeholders to apply unique business insights, experiences, competencies, and expertise to create competitive advantages for the organization. Strategic thinking analyzes tactical opportunities within the environment, pushing against familiar boundaries and challenging conventional wisdom to develop game-changing results. In many ways, this process is counterintuitive. You are working right to left, step by step, from future to present, from the end objective, back to the beginning enablers of the end objective. Because of an inherently fuzzy future, bold new strategies often fail. But those that succeed, such as **UBER, Netflix, and the iPhone**, tend to reshape the entire industry.

What is your strategy for moving a product from inside your brain, to the warehouse, to the customer's front door? The plan will invariably require some form of strategic thinking. The entrepreneur envisions the  customer, opening the package and smiling with satisfaction. He or she then works backward, right to left, from that customer satisfaction freeze frame to make the vision a reality.

Rational Choice thinking

Rational choice thinking, also known as rational action theory, is a model for understanding individual decision-making based on the social, political, and economic options available to all individuals. The basic premise of rational choice thinking is that aggregate social behavior results from the behavior of individual actors, each of whom is making individual decisions that affect the whole. As mentioned in Chapter 2, this process can easily be seen in the **Wisdom of the Crowd** syndrome. The drivers in  front of you flip on their signal light and move into the left lane. Not able to visually observe the reason for their collective effort to change lanes, but believing your lane is impeded, you instinctively move to the left lane too. The wisdom of the crowd influences your personal preferences. Rational choice thinking examines the association and interconnectivity of these individual choices.

Paradoxical thinking

Paradoxical thinking is the flip side, counter-intuitive process of assigning value to the negative traits of an individual, thereby empowering the full range of that individual's skills and attributes to achieve desired results.

Paradoxical thinking goes against the flow of generally accepted truths and assumptions in viewing life's problems. It perceives an individual's positive attributes and negative attributes as being inseparable, making up their relational whole. A father might be a workaholic. But the wife and children benefit from the resulting financial security. A football player might have an overly aggressive personality, but is the leading tackler in the entire NFL. **These dualities go together in a complex, inseparable framework.** Those who see life as a rigid, linear process have

difficulty accepting this type of thinking. We might send Steve Jobs to therapy for yelling and screaming at coworkers. The question then becomes, within the connectivity of his brain, would he become more creative or less creative once he's cured.

Safe Island thinking

Safe Island thinking is a highly complex approach to peaceful coexistence between potential rivals through the use of compromise, sharing, empowerment, facilitation, and/or alliances. In many ways, this approach is the exact opposite of Reductionist thinking, as it seeks to pacify rather than conquer, and share rather than hoard. *What?!!! Share?!!!*

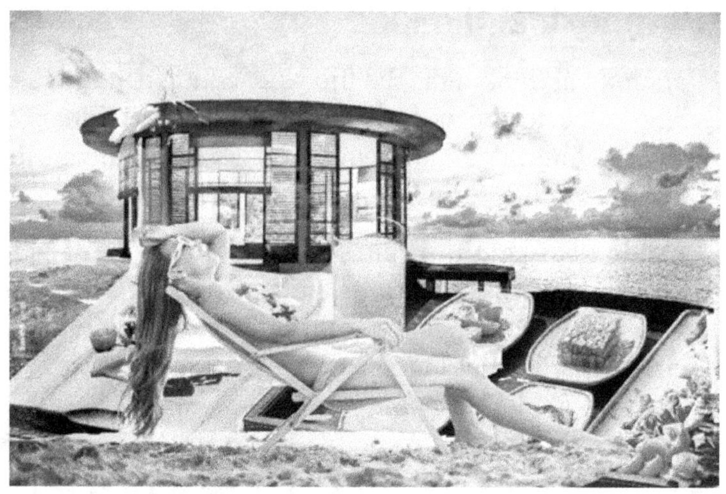

Imagine being on a tropical island with everything you wanted ... ten wives (Solomon had 700 wives, but we won't be greedy), exotic gardens and fruit trees, crystal spring water, herds of cattle and horses, rooms stocked with electronic gadgets, and ancient silver and gold mines with limitless, untapped veins of ore.

Still, you have one problem. There are three other islands in the area, all with substantially fewer resources than yours. Some populations are barely subsisting with intermittent periods of famine and starvation. Increasingly, the other islanders have begun to raid your island by night, stealing food, livestock, and precious minerals, even kidnapping a couple of your wives (luckily, the two nagging wives with perpetual honey-do lists). The more the word spreads about your prosperity, the more invasions you experience, the more property losses you suffer. (Spanish conquistador Hernán Cortés kept hearing about the gold and riches of the Aztec Empire and eventually overthrew them. Word gets around.)

Your initial reaction might be to build up your defenses; hire mercenary soldiers to guard the coastline, and perhaps, build a wall. But, within the context of Safe Island thinking, these solutions are both shortsighted and hypocritical in addressing the *real* problem.

The real problem is the clash between wealth and poverty, the haves versus the have-nots. In the distance, starving islanders see you eating steak and lobster. They become desperate, resentful, and demand a piece of the action ... by any means necessary.

Thousands of years of history, hundreds of books on theocracy, modern clinical research, and personal profiles of successful individuals express the same sentiment. Predominantly, almost without exception, people living prosperously feel no innate obligation to share. Whether earned through inheritance, unscrupulous dealings, or years of sacrifice and hard work, **it's THEIR property. They resent the idea of someone coming along, expecting a free ride.**

Safe Island thinking seeks to bridge the gap through compromise and pacification. Rather than building a wall to keep out invaders (at least, temporarily, as they will eventually find a way over it or under it or around it), Safe Island thinking tries to resolve the problem by eliminating the reason invaders want to come in the first place. The objective is to take away the incentive.

... Brace yourself. Your subconscious mind is about to scream in agony.

To the dismay of many Americans, the United States has been employing Safe Island thinking for many years, sending billions in foreign aid to places like Mexico, Haiti, Central America, Africa, and Russia (yes, Russia), and signing trade agreements such as NAFTA to give regional poor countries a boost.

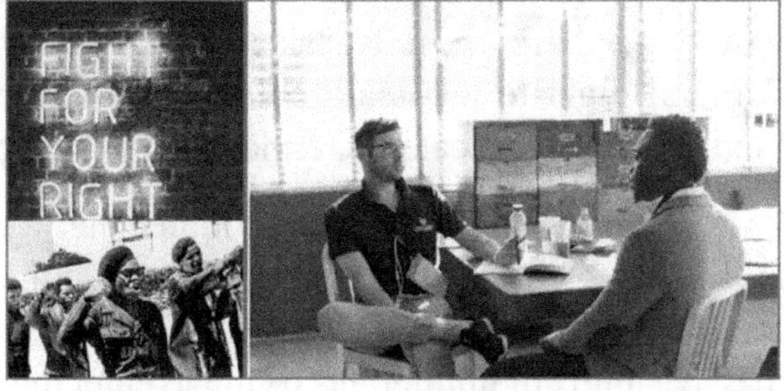

Back in the 60s and 70s, when the United States was on the verge of a race war, the U.S. government used policies grounded in Safe Island thinking (Affirmative Action, Job Corps, and free college grants and tuition) to get angry black protesters off the streets and into the workforce. For potential protesters involved in the fight for equality, the stakes (historic, unprecedented employment offers) became too high to get involved in daily marches or join the Black Panther Party on the front lines. You had to choose between social activism and your new role as the first black face in Exxon's accounting department, making $80,000 a year, and planning a family trip to Disneyland. It was personal risk/reward assessment at its most basic tier.

Historians agree these sophisticated Safe Island strategies were not only instrumental in averting another civil war, but, as an unexpected payoff, brought an invaluable source of diversity to corporate America, allowing U.S. companies to compete more vigorously in the global market.

As far back as the end of World War II, **Roosevelt, Churchill, and Stalin** used Safe Island thinking to carve up the world into

three domains, with each leader agreeing NOT to interfere in the affairs of the other leader's territory. Churchill could colonize countries rich in minerals like Palestine, South Africa, India, and Cameroon. Russia could crush independence movements and annex eastern countries like Albania, Bulgaria, Poland, Czechoslovakia, and Hungary. Roosevelt would get help from Russia to fight the Japanese whose ancient Samurai, fight-to-the-death culture did not embrace surrender of any kind, and have (defeated) Germany split into zones favorable to the U.S.

During the early years immediately after the War, the United States spent billions (trillions in today's dollars) frantically rebuilding England, Germany, and Japan, even Russia, to a smaller degree. With the massive influx of immigrants trying to enter the U.S., Safe Island thinking was an easy sell to American taxpayers. **"Let's get these war-torn countries rebuilt and in order so their people won't come here, flood the workforce, and drive our own economy into the ground."**

No need to come here.

Your country is going to
be just fine.

In this instance, the overriding objective of compromise and pacification was summed up in one word ... **treaty**. In corporate America, however, managers refer to the same type of arrangement as an ... **alliance contract**. As a new business owner, unless you understand the value of these contracts, you will forever find yourself building walls and fighting unnecessary wars.

In 2004, sworn competitors Samsung Electronics and Sony signed an agreement to split the cost of research and development to build flat-screen LED televisions. In 2013, Ford and Toyota formed an alliance to jointly design a new futuristic hybrid vehicle. Apple and Microsoft formulated an alliance to design a mobile operating system. Amazon (Kindle) and Apple (iPad) forged an agreement to allow the distribution of Amazon e-books through an iPad/Kindle app.

Safe Island thinking requires a conscious and deliberate detachment from ego-driven outcomes. Force (to contend with bad actors) is still on the table, but viewed as a last resort. The whole idea is to have potential adversaries so intrigued with the benefits of their own island, they have neither the time nor desire to invade yours.

Admittedly, Safe Island thinking has become a much harder sell. In 1961, **President John F. Kennedy** used it to find his way out of a nuclear standoff with the Russians. This approach totally inflamed his Joint Chiefs and military advisors who saw no other viable solution except to go to war. Safe Island thinking is similar to a chess move that voluntarily relinquishes short-term power for a long-term gain. However, within our human evolution, is an overriding instinct to conquer rather than compromise. **Passively working out a deal that benefits both parties just doesn't FEEL the same**, nothing to facilitate a round of cold beers for the heroes and

a victorious slap across the back. Our subconscious will remind us that to the victor go the spoils ... all of them, including the right to dictate the terms, and punish the opponents who had the audacity to challenge us.

We've spent a great deal of time on Safe Island thinking. It's just that important. **So many new business owners go under, choosing the hard road instead of the smart road**. (This is especially difficult for entrepreneurs with a **STRUCTURED///OVERSEER'S** profile in the Over-50 Entrepreneurial Assessment-Q9.)

Don't allow your "them vs us" ego to drive you out of business. Keep up your guard. But remember. Sometimes building a bridge can be far more profitable than building a wall.

Reductionist thinking

Reductionist thinking, sometimes referred to as Machiavellian thinking, is a self-focused, self-rewarding approach to behavior that suppresses emotions and places no value on shared payoffs or personal attributes such as empathy, modesty, and restraint. **Rather, reductionist thinking tends to promote winning, hoarding, and control of others.**

Astoundingly, there are modern psychological studies that show an alarming 12% of the population would **give up a portion of what they have to prevent a peer from having anything.** This is a protective measure to reinforce a sense of entitlement. Clinical studies define extreme levels of entitlement as a toxic narcissistic trait, tied to people who feel frustrated, unhappy, and inherently more "deserving" than others around them. For these individuals, deliberately pushing others down to elevate their own personal status is a preferable, go-to solution. Any means to achieve self-reward, including lying, cheating, bullying, sabotaging, picking winnable fights with inferior adversaries, and even withdrawing from the process, is justified as long as it leads the reductionist thinker to a personal win.

Lateral thinking

Lateral thinking, coined by **UK psychologist Dr. Edward de Bono**, involves solving problems by an indirect, nonlinear approach, typically through viewing the problem in a new and unusual light.

This technique uses distortion and exaggeration to create lists of "outlandish" possibilities to move the discussion forward. Many lateral thinkers were involved in the construction of the Panama Canal and NASA's program to go to the moon. If all of the soldiers won't fit on the plane, a lateral thinker might suggest equipping each soldier with a flying suit. If a beverage is not selling well in  an aluminum can, a lateral thinker might suggest using a pouch with a straw. Lateral thinking erases the restrictive boundaries of normalcy and opens up new possibilities that would not have been considered using a linear approach.

Innovative thinking

Innovative thinking, sometimes referred to as creative thinking, reflects the ability to look at challenges from a fresh, uncommon perspective and find unusual solutions to apply. People who demonstrate this ability usually possess a rich imagination that allows them to envision things out of the ordinary. New ideas may stem from looking at old ideas from a fresh perspective, improving each iteration until a totally new product emerges. The evolutionary method of creativity reminds us every problem that has already been solved can be solved again in a better way. Successful architects, designers, and screenwriters tend to use innovative thinking throughout their daily routine. It's right brain thinking with a left brain twist.

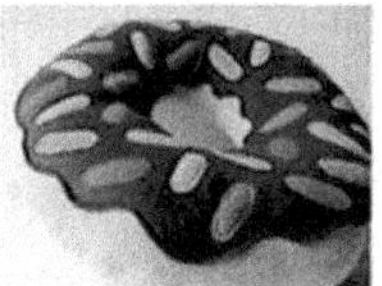

DOUGHNUT PILLOWS

There are other less-mentioned forms of thinking. But this proprietary list will be more than enough to protect you from the latent tendency to *pretend* you're thinking inside the restrictive cradle of your subconscious mind. Real thinking is not easy. It requires a deliberate effort to unlink from the bias of long-term memory and allow all of the amazing horsepower under your hood to fire unrestricted, free of pre-programming, on all cylinders.

In the next chapter, you'll get a sweet taste of your incredible new thinking processes unbridled. This is your powerful entrepreneurial future. Celebrate! The journey has just begun.

THINKING UNBRIDLED
Open The Gate

*I*nsight #10 offers a simple example of thinking power unbridled. You've learned enough about the physiological and theoretical sides of thinking to put on your boots and spurs, climb aboard the bucking bronco, and give the FRIEND-OR-FOE gatekeeper the nod. Now, let's open the gate.

Theory is good. But practical application is even better. For the purposes of this book, we have embarked upon a specific journey to expand our knowledge of the thinking process so that we might:

(1) Effectively choose a business niche

(2) Once the business is operational, maximize our decision-making in choosing products and services for the marketplace.

Though not identical, both tasks are very similar ... and ongoing. **There is no reason to believe your initial choice of a business niche will be your last choice.** The marketplace is dynamic, ever-evolving, eternally demanding tweaks and pivots to match customer demand and environmental forces of which you have no control.

Thinking Application - From Theory To Practice

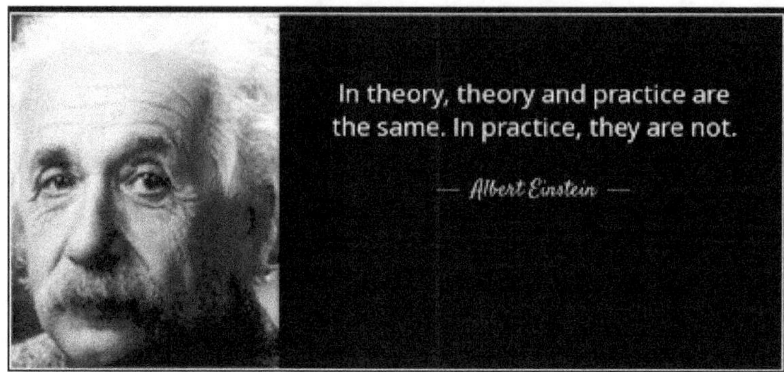

You might start out running an employment recruitment agency with candidates coming to your office to fill out paper job applications that are faxed to potential employers. Then, the new World Wide Web comes along and companies are suddenly able to host their own job boards and database-driven, instantly accessible online applications. To help companies reduce the cost of so many full-time employees on payroll, you pivot to outsourcing and managing contract workers. But new Congressional labor laws redefine the meaning of contract workers, making them equivalent to employees who do the same work inside the company and warrant the same pay and benefits. Your services as the "middle" contractor/ employer are no longer relevant. You pivot and pivot again until you end up as a high-paid Human Resources consultant, showing companies how to incorporate Artificial Intelligence (AI) into their hiring and evaluation schemes.

In this scenario, you never left the industry for which you had a passion. You simply pivoted to the next big thing.

In all honesty, "simply pivoted" is an understatement. There is nothing simple about these critical, do-or-die, life-resuscitating moves.

You will use every ounce of thinking power to make these bold and unpredictable decisions. There is no guarantee that any of your options will be the right one.

This chapter presents a "best practices" example of how to apply your deep well of thinking resources. This process is not easy. You learn, improve, and evolve as you go.

The good thing is, at some point, you won't have to do it alone. As your business grows, you will bring along team members who possess an inclination toward certain *ways of thinking*. Specific to the challenge of pivoting, your creative visionary types will come up with solutions that never crossed your mind.

The previous paragraph might lead you to believe the process of incorporating a top-notch, quick-thinking, diversified group of team members into your organization is automatic. It is NOT. In fact, without the proper hiring priorities, it's almost impossible. Studies (an excellent one by the Kellogg School of Management) have shown **that inexperienced startup CEOs have a tendency to hire people who look, act, and think like them**. Similarities in experience, attitude, political views, and physical appearance all increase the likelihood that the CEO/owner, acting as the hiring manager, will connect to a younger rendition of herself.

This should not come as a surprise, given the protective, risk-avoiding nature of the subconscious mind. The new owner observes a parade of unfamiliar faces, marching into her office, armed with their flimsy pieces of doctored history, confirming their readiness for the job. No wonder her subconscious mind is turning flips, searching for any beacon of familiarity that might engender trust and confirm a shared belief system compatible with her long-term vision.

The problem is, in this critical stage of team-building, the well-intended subconscious mind will lead most new entrepreneurs

astray. If you hire people just like "you", you limit the brainpower of the organization to your modes and methods of problem-solving. When major crises come, and they will come, there will be no Steve Jobs or Mark Cuban or Robert L. Johnson upstarts sitting around the conference table. There will be only you and your less experienced carbon copies.

Hiring carbon copies of "you" leads to what psychiatrists call "Groupthink"

Consider a twelve-member jury panel, deliberating a life-or-death verdict. If eleven members vote "yes", that newly formed "yes group" quickly transforms into a unified force of expert criminologists, determined to convince the holdout to vote with the majority. As time passes, persuasion tactics escalate into personal attacks and skewed reasoning. In most cases, for the sake of being accepted as part of the group, the dissenting juror gives in.

This phenomenon is no different from the self-authenticating lure of membership in an exclusive country club. Except, in a business environment, the stakes are much higher. **Groupthink offers a cohesion of purpose (a perceived higher purpose) as well as mutual validation among like-kinds.** Navigating each precarious step of decision-making, you know your comrades have your back and you have theirs. As with Enron and Bernard L. Madoff Securities LLC, not even the law can stand in your way. After all, the law is beneath your higher purpose. The lawmakers wouldn't understand.

One day, you will reach that critical hiring stage in which you glance over your shoulder to make sure Groupthink is not slithering up from the rear, extinguishing the few, precious, innovative sparks still left in your brain.

But for now, it's just you. You are the team. Let's open the gate and see what happens.

Portable Lighting Business

Let's say your *Golden Circle* exercise points to a passion for camping, hunting, and other outdoor activities. You also like to work in your outdoor garage, tinkering with electronics, tools, and gadgets that, with a bit of Radio Shack modifications, operate more efficiently than the version they sent from the factory. This is a great TECHNICAL /// CRAFTSMAN profile which you will learn about in Chapter 14.

Like Netflix founder, Reed Hastings, you must solve a usability problem. Frustration with the market's current selection of inferior outdoor flashlights leads you to explore the portable lighting industry as a business opportunity. You decide to take your entrepreneurial swing.

You purchase a few out-of-date, bargain basement consumer surveys from Nielsen and Wood MacKenzie. (Old studies are all over the internet.) You discover that, because of the skewed multiplier effect of retiring Baby Boomers, camping and hunting activities are growing by 30% annually. You also discover that both campers and hunters have expressed strong dissatisfaction with the current selection of flashlights available for critical nighttime activities.

You have reached into your deep well of analytical thinking.

How do you know? Because you are spending your days combing through the research numbers, comparing the results of historical data and information analysis.

Information analysis is one of the primary components of analytical thinking. **Analytical thinking (sometimes called critical thinking) is the process of gathering relevant information and identifying key issues related to this information.** It involves a step-by-step approach that allows you to break down complex problems into single, manageable components. This type of thinking also requires the comparison of data from multiple sources. You identify possible cause-and-effect patterns and draw conclusions from these patterns to explore workable solutions.

You do NOT have to be a statistical expert. It's really not as complicated as it might seem.

Let's say you're a transportation official in Boston, trying to reduce the number of suicides off the Tobin Bridge. To gain a broad-based perspective, you'll need to compile multiple datasets. You call officials throughout the nation. In California, 20 people jumped off the Golden Gate Bridge; in Michigan, 15 off the Mackinac Bridge; in New York, 18 off the George Washington Bridge; in Philadelphia, 10 off the

Walt Whitman Bridge, and so on.

After 100 datasets, you see a pattern. Roughly 80% of the victims are intoxicated, jumping from the east entrance, between the months of September and December, close to a full moon. The stats have spoken. If you're the Boston official, you'd better get your crews out to put up nets and barriers before the first full moon in September and beef up holiday patrols.

Back to the critical steps of launching your new flashlight enterprise.

In this research and analysis phase, you continue to use analytical thinking to dissect the attributes of the top-selling flashlights. You discover most models are unacceptably fragile, the equivalent of cheap metal cylinders that cannot be dropped or banged or subjected to any kind of heavy impact without damaging the circuitry and rendering the light inoperable.

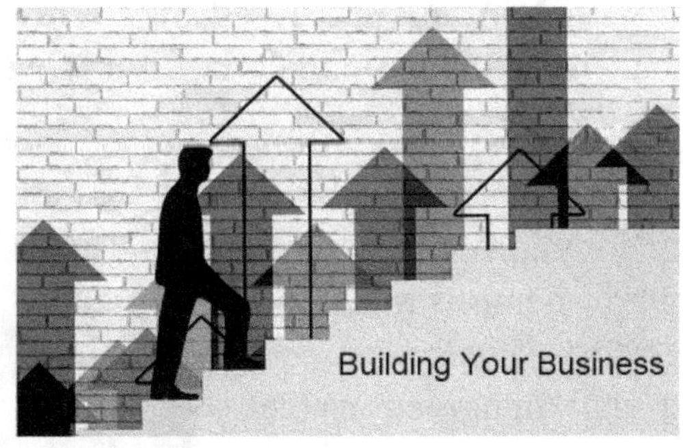

It's not just the cheap metal housing around the circuitry that's creating a problem, but the cheap circuitry, itself. The housing is imported from China; the circuitry from Vietnam. Existing competitors appear to be using a low-cost strategy, competing almost exclusively on price. You suspect there might be a product differentiation opportunity (similar to what Chick-fil-A is using against Burger King) to introduce a high-end, durable, and long-lasting flashlight.

Perhaps, your product can become the Lexus in that underserved outdoor category. For now, you assign a working name to your envisioned line of superior flashlights. You called it **"Big Bright"**.

You sit down with Hank, a retired engineer, who's bored and is looking for something challenging to do. Together, you come up with a new design that improves the circuitry components and places them in the center of the cylinder, protected by a hard rubber enclosure. Your new design also replaces the cheap metal housing with a sturdy, lightweight, non-corrosive titanium outer shell.

. . .

You have moved to innovative thinking. How do we know?

You have started to create. Using the research you've gathered about the marketplace, you have begun to make something new.

Innovative thinking (sometimes referred to as creative thinking) reflects the ability to look at challenges from a fresh, uncommon perspective and find unusual solutions to apply. People who demonstrate this ability usually possess a rich imagination that allows them to envision things out of the ordinary. New ideas may stem from looking at old ideas from a different perspective, improving each iteration until a totally new product emerges.

Technically, creative thinking began when you assigned your new product line a name. Where did the name come from? You created it based on all of your life experiences, patterned against the new information you gathered. You pulled it out of the darkness, into the marvelous light.

Brain waves are oscillating electrical voltages in the brain, which generally measure no more than just a few millionths of a volt. When we engage in creative thinking, our brainwaves shift from gamma mode (problem-solving) to a more reflective and restful alpha mode. We are still problem-solving, but indirectly. We are not in the cloud, but floating above it. During this thinking mode, we have the ability to see the problem in its totality, along with emerging solutions we were unable to see in the cloud.

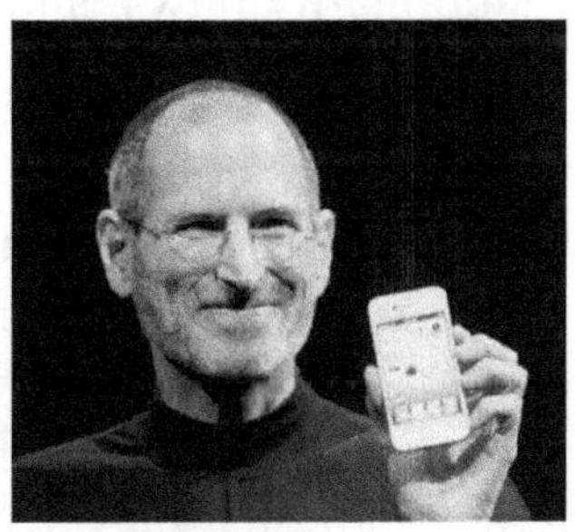

"Creativity is just connecting things. When you ask creative people how they did something, they feel a little guilty because they didn't really do it, they just saw something. It seemed obvious to them after a while. That's because they were able to connect experiences they've had and synthesize new things."
... **Steve Jobs**

After paying a local lab to develop several fully functional prototypes at $3,500 each, you begin testing your new high-end flashlight. Don't stress. Prototyping is an expensive wildcard. This initial investment is quite reasonable, considering the first Xbox One controller prototype, released in 2015, cost roughly $100 million. The iPhone 1 prototype was $150 million.

You make a few calls; enlist the help of a few campers and hunters you've known over the years. You set up one-on-one meetings and begin to extract their "unbiased" opinions about your new flashlight.

This is something new. You have moved to the "think-aloud" method of thinking, employed in product usability testing.

One of the many narrowly focused, technical forms of thinking, we did not talk about this in our original list of protocols.

Originally introduced by **Clayton Lewis at IBM,** the think-aloud method of thinking is used in the product design and development phase to gather data about the true usability of a product. The extracted information may include the potential for total rejection of the product by users, as well as the impact of physical size constraints, structural engineering hazards, mechanism functionality flaws, and so on.

The term true usability is connected to a common phenomenon called the endowment effect or **divestiture aversion effect**. It refers to an emotional bias by the owner of the product who, after spending so much time and effort, places an irrationally higher value on the product, much more than what the marketplace thinks it's worth.

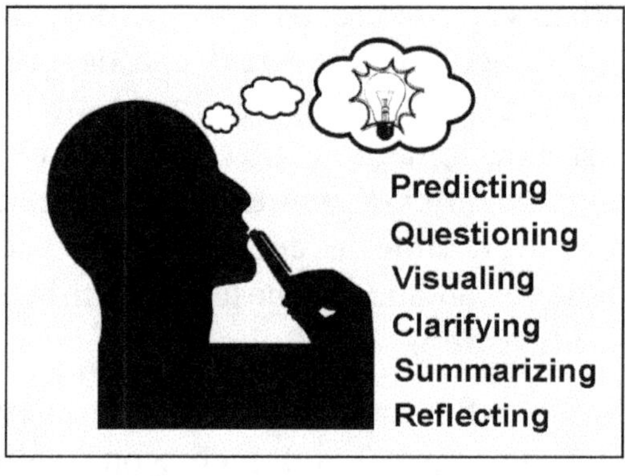

The whole idea of incorporating the think-aloud protocol into usability testing is to capture the explicit and unbiased reactions to your product by knowledgeable but disassociated parties, that is to say, observing in real time what potential users are looking at, thinking, doing, and feeling while interacting with your product. The cumulative responses of all test subjects alert you of potential problem areas further down the road.

There is one important thing to keep in mind. If you conduct these usability tests employing the help of people you know, you must "vehemently" convey your objective, and that is to capture their brutally honest opinion. If they sugarcoat their responses for the sake of your feelings, **they are costing you money and deceitfully leading you down a path of destruction, the very thing you are trying to avoid.** Be polite but heavy-handed in this matter, or you will end up with a friendly that-a-boy pat on the back and an empty wallet.

Let's move on.

You have just completed the final phase of testing and optimization. With a few minor tweaks, you are now ready to introduce your **Big Bright** flashlight to the marketplace. In upcoming months, several hunting, fishing, camping, and general outdoor conventions and trade shows are scheduled for the region. With a bit of strategic thinking, you draw up a plan to rent a booth at each event and present your prize flashlight directly to outdoor enthusiasts, the target market with the greatest potential to appreciate your upgraded standard of quality and durability.

Your anticipation soars through the roof. You can't wait. You can't sleep. Hopefully, your pounding (over-50) heart will hold out until the first trade show comes to town.

A week before the first show, you get a call from Hank, the retired engineer who helped you develop the original prototype. He has just read a featured article in his monthly science magazine on titanium. **The article states that titanium dioxide**

has recently been classified by the International Agency for Research on Cancer (IARC) as an IARC Group 2B carcinogen possibly carcinogenic to humans. The test results show that high concentrations of pigment-grade (powdered) and ultrafine titanium dioxide dust caused respiratory tract cancer in rats exposed by inhalation and intratracheal instillation.

You can already see competitors running ads, flooding the social media channels, and sending out tons of emails saying, "Don't use **Big Bright** flashlights. THEY'LL GIVE YOU CANCER."

Of course, titanium dioxide dust is completely different from your titanium flashlight casings. But who's going to take the time to read the fine print? Processing in the human brain takes mental shortcuts. These shortcuts, known in psychology as heuristics, act as a way for the brain to conserve energy and work more efficiently.

Broad associations, profiles, and big-picture takeaways are the decision-making tools upon which we rely to get us through the complexities of the day. The details are there. But seldom do we take time to scrutinize them.

You have moved to holistic thinking. How do we know?

Because the primary focus of your thinking is on linkage and big-picture analysis. You have linked all external environmental factors (economic, demographic, social, technological, political, and physical) to your existing market equation as an interconnected whole, a visionary web of cause-and-effect events that potentially support or sabotage **Big Bright's** ultimate success. You have taken it upon yourself to predict the future.

Linkage is not some esoteric business theory thrown around the classrooms at Harvard or Yale. Linkage is a real, quantifiable phenomenon that touches every conjoining part of the total profit-and-loss equation.

When it comes to holistic thinking, linkage facilitates the "thinker's" ability to deal in probabilities, that is to say, the chance that a future event will occur as part of a chain reaction, instigated by past and/or present events. Holistic thinking translates into a sophisticated bet that something is going to happen before it happens.

In a previous chapter, we talked about the slow, inevitable death of the once commonplace paper check. In 2009, consumers and businesses wrote 28 billion checks. That number has been dropping about 1.8 billion a year. **According to a Philadelphia Fed study, paper checks will go away entirely by 2026.**

If you own a commercial printing press operation with a substantial amount of paper check business, the writing is on the wall. Pivot to a new niche, or go out of business.

The legendary hedge fund manager, Dr. Michael Burry (the same guy who made millions on the GameStop fiasco), who saw the 2008 subprime derivatives meltdown  coming five years prior, made $725 million for his clients and a cool $100 million in clear profit for himself. He linked the artificial housing bubble to the reckless lending practices by mortgage bankers to the unregulated, free-for-all exchange of worthless subprime derivatives based on millions of homeowners (often approved using a one-page, no income verification loan application) who couldn't pay their mortgages.

In your potential face-off with titanium linkage, negative social fallout can sabotage your entire product roll-out. **Holistic thinking points to a high probability that human brain patterns and mental processing shortcuts will lead potential customers to link your flashlights to cancer.**

Whether you choose a business niche, introduce a new product or service to the marketplace, or reposition an older line that has gone soft, **the same step-by-step methodology** applies. These thinking processes help to tune out personal biases and tune in rational decision-making.

Fortunately, the **Big Bright** roll-out is not over. With all of the "thinking" horsepower under your hood, you easily rev up your engine and move smoothly and confidently into the familiar problem-solving lane. One little misunderstood misfit from the vast selection of metals in the periodic table is not enough to extinguish your dream. The main thing to remember is you're walking away from an option (component), not your dream roll-out as an entrepreneur.

Back to the research drawing board. Research means gathering new data and analyzing the hidden solutions it potentially contains. You need an "alternative" metal that's as strong and durable as titanium, but with no *perceived* medical downside. Lower costs and ecological factors lead you to two workable options ... lightweight Martensite steel or Zirconium.

Go, Big Bright!!!!!!!!!

In your new advertising sales copy, you change a social media disaster into a strategic benefit. Zirconium is lighter than titanium, more hypoallergenic, less likely to corrode when exposed to water, and yet, just as durable. You'll spend a few thousand more for a new zirconium prototype. But it will be well worth it.

Are you beginning to see how successful entrepreneurs pivot, improvise, and reset? In the next chapter, we will explore our top ten recommended options for a business niche. Remember, you ARE who you ARE. Some opportunities belong to you. Others don't. You will learn a great deal more about who you are in Chapter 14.

Meanwhile, let the unbiased methodology of research and analysis lead you through this upcoming chapter on potential business niches. Your *Golden Circle* selection process becomes more powerful and explicit as we go. Let its empirical findings (not your emotions) have the last word.

TOP TEN STARTUP OPTIONS

*I*nsight #11 examines the most promising business niches for startup entrepreneurs at this unprecedented moment in time. Depending on your preferences, life experiences, and base skillsets, the practicality of each opportunity will appear as a traffic signal light, alternating between red, yellow, and green. Thorough research has the potential to change the light to a different color. But don't speed. This is an exercise in sound strategy and analytical calculation. **You're much smarter now.** Allow your deep well of thinking resources to make sure you get through the intersection, safely, and with the greatest chance for success.

CRITERIA

The selection criteria for these recommended business niches is based on three factors:

Growth ... industry is expanding, NOT contracting as with desktop computers, house phones, and retail bookstores.

Saturation ... market share is still splintered among smaller startups, NOT consolidated under a few big players such as Comcast and AT&T, well-established chieftains of commerce that easily rely on size, discounting, and brand familiarity to dictate market protocols.

Barriers to Entry ... you have a reasonable opportunity to enter the market without a Doctorate Degree from Yale, or nuclear plant certification from Congress, or Lockheed Martin security clearance.

Top Ten Recommendations:

◆ Write A Content Specific Blog

Blogging (an early abbreviation for weblog) is just internet jargon for an online journal or information-based website offering insight and tips about a specific category of topics. Perhaps, you are an expert Lexus mechanic, or organic gardener, or antique gun dealer. You share trends, tips, and proprietary insight about these subjects and get paid, either through selling advertising or consultant fees. Posts and articles in print lead to audiobooks, which lead to YouTube videos, which lead to speaking engagements and class modules online.

Most successful super bloggers such as **Wellness Mama** and **Gary Vaynerchuk**, concentrate on one narrow subject area. As the audience builds, advertisers come knocking. Sponsorship and influencer opportunities follow with larger payoffs. Google Adsense and YouTube provide strict analytics about the quantity and quality of the audience viewing your content. The more you grow your audience, the more you get paid. Google sends out a 1099 tax statement at the end of the year.

♦ Dropshipping

In the past decade, this business model has created hundreds of rags-to-riches millionaires, mostly young entrepreneurs under 35. **And no, dropshipping is not dead.**

The business model is based on a simple strategy. An individual finds an inexpensive product in another country, usually China, Vietnam, or India. The individual advertises the product online at a substantial markup. A product that costs $20 might be advertised on Facebook for $99. When a customer buys the product, the individual sends an order to the vendor in the foreign country to mail the product directly to the customer, without the individual having to touch the product at all.

Although this niche is very profitable, there are many pitfalls to this process.

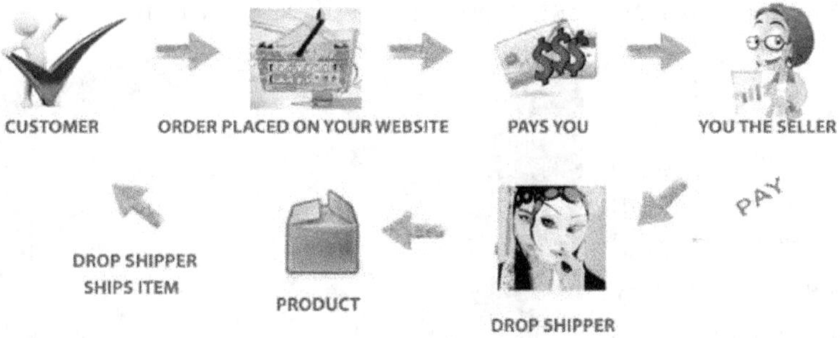

Customer returns and products, lost in shipping, are a nightmare. Tracking numbers may not reflect the true origin or status of a product at a given time. Customers may not get all of the products they ordered. With no explanation for days, Facebook's advertising platform might reject and freeze your ongoing advertising campaign. Still, if the purchase and delivery processes go well, the hefty profits lay the groundwork for other warehousing models that offer more control.

There is a steep learning curve here, nothing you can't master with an investment of time, patience, and determination. Most successful millionaire dropshippers paid expert mentors to get them on the right track. When compared to the costly mistakes you avoid in the long run, the mentoring classes are a reasonable investment. Just go to YouTube and do a search on dropshipping mentors. Stay away from scam artists who have no experience, track record, or references. Their business model is selling expensive classes.

♦ AIRBNB Booking Agent

Airbnb, Inc. (shortened from the original name AirBedandBreakfast. com.) is an online marketplace for securing or offering lodging for travelers and tourists who seek an alternative to the traditional hotel experience. Property owners in over 65,000 cities list their apartments, homes, boathouses, family cottage, etc. on the Airbnb website at a transparent, predetermined rate, along with dates and times these properties will be available.

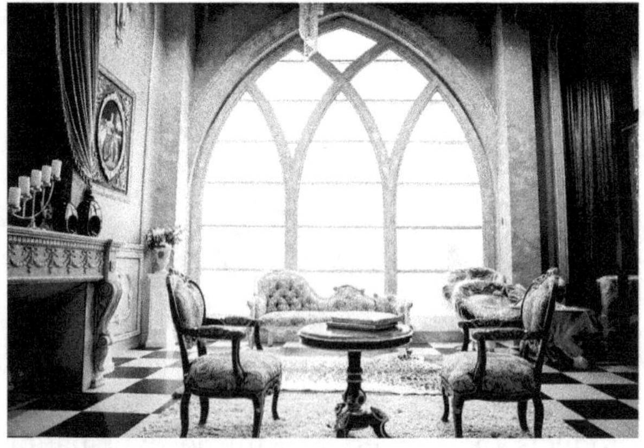

Travelers pay Airbnb in advance. Once the guests check in and claim their stay, PayPal releases the money to you. Airbnb does not own any of the listed properties, nor does it host events. Rather, it acts as a broker, receiving a 3% commission on each booking from the property owner, and between 6% and 12% from guest travelers. Airbnb covers each booking with $1,000,000 in property damage protection.

The upside of this business niche is that the Airbnb model is very scalable. You could lease multiple properties, then add upgrades and amenities such as big screens, workout rooms, massages, on-site "homemade" specialty meals, and local limo drivers for big Super Bowl caliber events. It's possible, once you understand the needs of your target customers, to put together custom entertainment packages, generating a 100% markup or more. Affluent target groups are willing to pay for convenience, security, and a slice of life that offers something new.

The downside of this model is the wasted time interacting with potential customers who never close the deal. The market is very dynamic. People are fickle and change their minds. Vendors get sick or decide something else is more important. You cannot manage the human factor (chaos) alone. Like any hotel or resort, team-building is critical. Early in the game, you'll need a reliable partner.

Another way to generate income on Airbnb is to rent a property you don't own. If you are able to find owners in your city that are tired of upkeep and rent collection responsibilities, you can take over those properties for a percentage of the income generated on Airbnb. To maintain complete control over the property, you might contract the property as the official renter at a steeply discounted price (guaranteed income to the owner) with permission to remodel the property without owner restrictions, allowing you to accommodate Airbnb travelers looking for something exotically different.

If you have an inclination toward real estate and you like hosting gatherings, meeting interesting people, and adding spice to the old tourist traps in your area, this is definitely a potential business opportunity for you. For more details, visit the Airbnb website.

♦ Orthotics / Prosthetics Supply Rep

The entrepreneurial opportunity here is huge. Let's get the technical definitions under our belt.

According to The World Health Organization, a Prosthetist / Orthotist is a healthcare professional who provides specialized treatment for patients who need added support for body parts that have been weakened by injury, or disease, or by disorders of the nerves, muscles, or bones. An orthotist works under a doctor's orders to design, fabricate, and fit custom-designed bracing to help each patient's mobility and independence. The major difference between orthotics and prosthetics is that, while an orthotic device is used to enhance a person's limb, a prosthetic device is used to replace a limb entirely. Both specializations must be certified by the American Board for Certification in Orthotics, Prosthetics and Pedorthics or the Board for Orthotist/Prosthetist Certification.

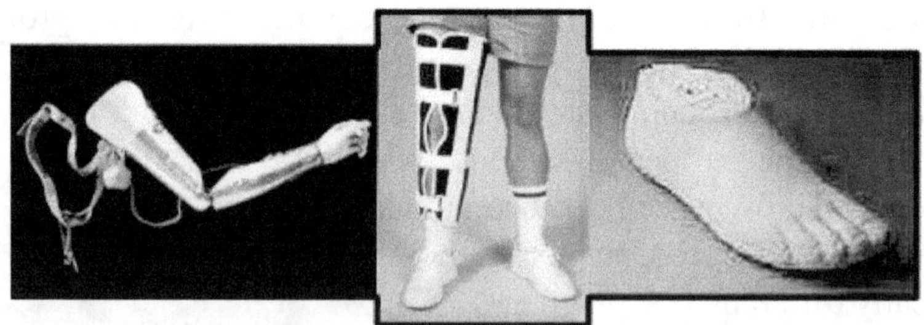

It is important to understand that these healthcare professionals use "raw materials" to make devices to meet the specific needs of each patient. The range of required materials is extensive and may include fiberglass, Kevlar®, carbon, hybrid skin sheets, wiring, foam molding, and other fabrications.

Some pre-assembled parts such as immobilizers, sleeves, straps, hinges, and limb attachments form the basis for custom design bracing or replacement apparatuses that healthcare professionals fashion into one-of-a-kind, single patient devices.

These devices are expensive. A myoelectric prosthetic hand might cost upward of $20,000; a shoulder, $61,655. The lifetime cost for prosthetics and medical care for loss of a single arm for a veteran of the Iraq or Afghanistan wars is roughly $823,000. In one instance, a man who lost both arms due to electrical shock received experimental thought-controlled arms at a cost of $6 million.

The market is growing exponentially. With the introduction of new artificial intelligence (AI) enhancements, suppliers are

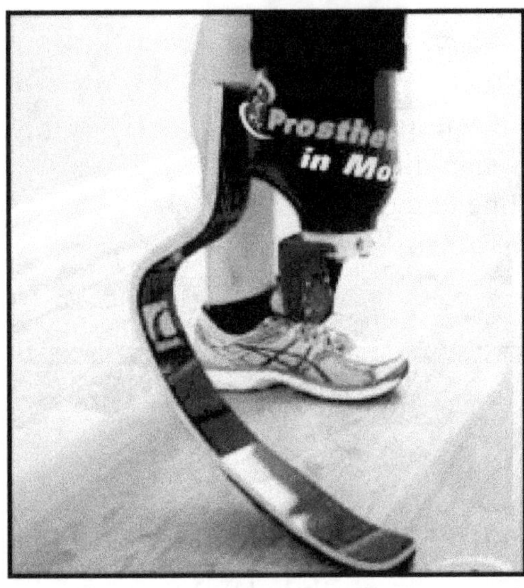

scrambling to keep up with the latest technologically advanced products that push into the market and make their most promising inventory obsolete. They need expert help to reposition their product line. And they need marketing representation on the ground in cities with large medical facilities where healthcare professionals are demanding better products and faster turnaround.

There are many opportunities to develop relationships with manufacturers and suppliers to help them increase market share and grow their customer base. These are the top ten by revenue.

1.   Stryker Corp. - $9.9 billion

2.   DePuy Synthes   - $9.3 billion

3.   Zimmer Biomet   - $6.0 billion

4.   Smith & Nephew   - $4.7 billion

5.   Medtronic Spinal   - $2.9 billion

6.   DJO Global   - $1.1 billion

7.   Integra Lifesciences - $883 million

8.   NuVasive Inc.   - $811 million

9.   Globus Medical   - $545 million

10.   Wright Medical   - $415 million

These manufacturers have deep pockets and new products entering the market each month. They would gladly pay a strategic rainmaker with contacts in the medical industry to move their product line to the next level. People who are good at relationship selling will do well in this niche.

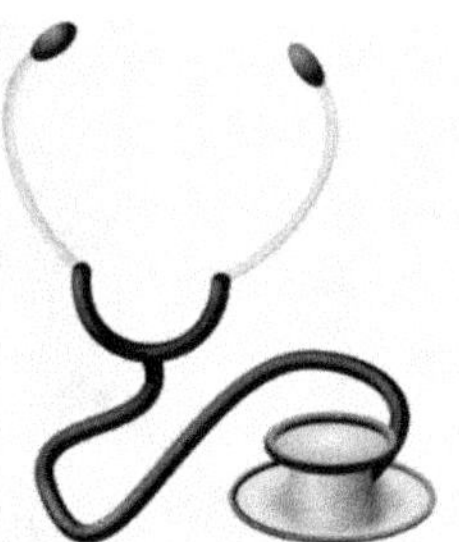

♦ Pack-it /Move-it Specialist

If your initial thought is a crummy little UPS Store on the corner, waiting for customers to stumble in with an arm full of poorly wrapped boxes, asking you to tape them up and send them away, then think again. On the other hand, if the nightmare you envision is your 50+-year-old body straining to pick up a box of pots and pans, hoping one of your young muscle-bound employees will give you a hand getting it on the truck, you're still wrong.

Roughly 40 million people move each year. The pack-it/move-it business is very lucrative; the execution angles are almost unlimited, none of which have to involve YOU, personally, strong-arming boxes from a smoldering attic, or driving a big truck to Kalamazoo.

Like all successful businesses, this business is a problem-solving model. Packing is a problem. Moving is a problem. Tracking goods in transit is a problem. Temporary storage is a problem.

Which problems you decide to tackle and how you solve them for your clients is left up to you. **Executed properly, your customer service, logistical savvy, use of state-of-the-art AI inventory, and tracking platforms can gradually drive your local competition in the ground.**

Think of market leader Blockbuster Video and newcomer Netflix. At one point in their head-up struggle, both offered customers the same movie-viewing service. Their approach, however, was totally different. Ultimately, Blockbuster got left behind.

In the pack-it/move-it business, many ole-school services are still struggling to keep up with a new consumer market of tech-savvy Generation X, Xennials, and Millennials who want to know where their belongings are at all times, why the packing options are so limited, and why the manual labor-based prices are so high. Large companies that pick up the cost for their executives to move from region to region are looking for more value-added services. There is a demand gap in the marketplace that is not being met.

In this business, you don't have to get into residential packing at all. There are countless suppliers and manufacturers who struggle with shipping out their orders each day. You have the option to concentrate on product fulfillment and nothing else. Think of how many companies would value your expertise in developing a customized packing and shipping system specifically for their product line. Think of how many mid-range suppliers would like to turn their inventory management over to a local partner, similar to the arrangement Walmart created with its vendor-managed program (VMI). This system frees managers to focus on the core competencies that generate their actual profits.

You will have to overcome several barriers to entry. In the long run, however, these same barriers work to your advantage to reduce competition. You will have to hire trustworthy employees who know how to pack breakables, perishables, heavy equipment, and other valuable materials. You will need to purchase or lease equipment such as trucks, pulleys, wrappers, and other supplies (e.g. bubble wrap, boxes, plastic wraps, and markers). You will need the proper licenses, certifications, and extensive insurance coverage.

Finally, you will need computer software that gives you a competitive edge in all aspects of moving, tracking, and storing inventory. Companies in India offer this programming dirt cheap. These software packages come with free training and will be your secret weapon for time and cost efficiency, all securely located in the Cloud.

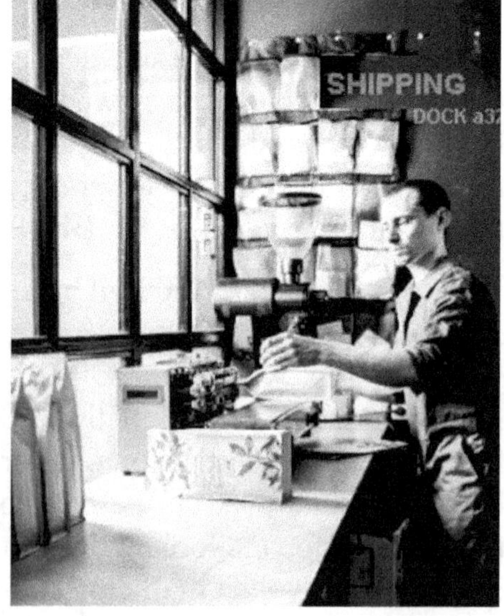

Gathering, sorting, weighing, packing, insuring, and shipping items through a secure, efficient, Cloud-based system is a headache that companies will gladly pay your team to manage.

♦ Pet Sitter Services

We have already talked about this niche in earlier chapters. Let's view a short refresher and move on.

Pet sitters provide daily care for pets while their owners are on vacation or out on the town. The sitter may go to the owner's home or have the owner drop off the pet at the sitter's facility. In addition to caring for pets, sitters general provide an assortment of services including:

♦ Provide food and water

♦ Walk dogs

♦ Clean litter boxes

♦ Brush fur and teeth, and carry out other types of grooming

♦ Give medications, if applicable

Sitters may specialize in the type of pets they prefer such as cats, dogs, birds, fish, small mammals, reptiles, and amphibians. Regardless of the specialization, the key to a successful sitting business is added value services such as training, exercising, and

grooming, under a standard monthly contractual agreement. Otherwise, demand for sitter services may be sporadic and unpredictable. A few once-a-year vacation customers is just not enough.

One added value approach is to partner with veterinarians who can pre-sell your nail clipping or party-dressing add-on services. A simple contract to split the proceeds will give the vet an incentive to pitch your service to established clients who trust him or her, thereby saving you an excessive amount of time and money trying to hustle business.

Also, planning a pet party and providing a free photographer (part of the package) is a great way to solidify your relationship with clients and extend your income stream.

You won't get rich in this niche. Serving upscale customers can average between $60-$70,000 per year. But if you have a good rapport with people and enjoy this type of work, there are plenty of opportunities. Consult **The National Association of Professional Pet Sitters** for additional information.

♦ Tutorial Coordination

Education has evolved, and with it, the method by which tutors make their expertise available to students needing help. In the old days, someone came to your house or met you at the library, or outside the classroom. Sometimes the process involved a long, monotonous call on the old landline phone.

Today, the tutorial function has been supercharged with cutting-edge technology, interactive engagement, and a repurposed emphasis on convenience and pre-structured learning.

With COVID-19's disruption of traditional learning protocols, computer-based learning has become the most popular tutorial platform. Three categories dominate this preferred method of tutorial support:

Video tutorials

Providers offer this form of learning through a series of short, sequential videos they either own or lease. The user (learner) pays a subscription fee to access the videos on a secure website that restricts unauthorized freeloaders by tracking cookies and IP addresses. The tutorials are available for a certain period, perhaps, 12 months. After that, unless renewed by the user, access to the website expires.

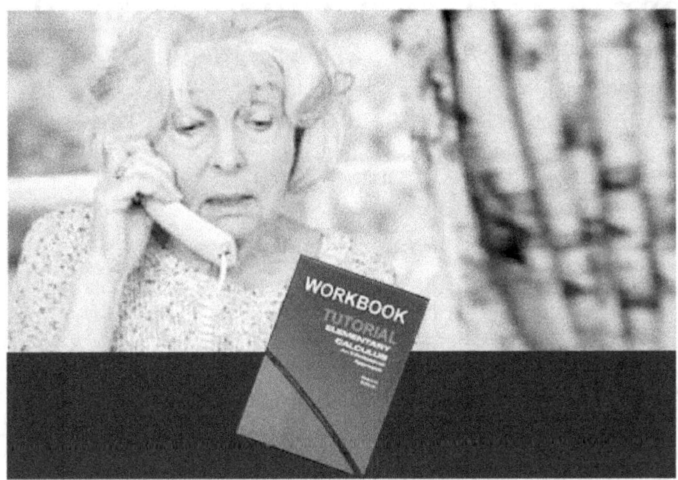

Come on, Henry. Are you looking at your workbook or the Encyclopedia?

Interactive tutorials

This is video learning, but more sophisticated in context.

In this scenario, viewers follow on-screen instructions attached to a physical workbook or online pop-up questionnaires that viewers have to complete before moving to the next module. An outstanding example of this is the online defensive driving course that teaches driving protocols and tests comprehension in sequence. You can't get away from the AI logic. You may choose to skip any section. But if you can't pass the attached survey questions for that section, you can't move forward. Too many wrong answers and you get kicked out of the course.

Webinars

With this method, viewers participate in real-time lectures, online tutorials, and/or remote workshops using web conferencing software such as **GoToMeeting, Microsoft Team, and Zoom**. A live, skilled, well-polished facilitator is the key to this type of tutorial model. This is one-on-one tutoring on steroids, with each target group requiring different learning materials and objectives.

The market is diverse with an array of opportunities for:

♦ Schools, Preschools, and daycare institutions

♦ College prep programs

♦ Tutoring

♦ Test prep services

♦ Testing centers

As a business niche, the possibilities are unlimited. You might create a series of relevant information-packed videos that bring in subscription revenue for years. You might decide to dominate a niche such as astronomy, pay Carl Sagan-type influencer professors to be guest lecturers, and partner with NASA on exclusive streams that none of your competitors are able to obtain. Or, you might hire the experts who wrote the SAT to break down its critical components on your pay-to-access SAT / ACT preparation website.

Finally, if you have the necessary operating capital, purchasing a franchise such as **Kumon Math & Reading Centers** offers an alternative way to enter the market with hands-on business and training support for roughly $100,000 per franchise. Choose the entry strategy that's best for you.

♦ Blockchain & Cryptocurrency Master

This is the future, full of unlimited profit and growth potential for over-50 entrepreneurs who are willing to dig into a steep learning curve. Most (Steve Jobs / Warren Buffett) entrepreneurs who make substantial amounts of money in a particular industry get in early. By the time the masses catch up to universally accepted trends, the early adopters are already there, manning the collection gates.

Let's get the technical definitions under our belt.

A Blockchain is a type of digital notebook or spreadsheet containing information about ongoing transactions. Each transaction generates a hash. Each block refers to the previous block, and together, in combination, represents the technical term: Blockchain. As it spreads over more and more computers, a Blockchain gains value as a legitimate record source, with transparency, accessibility, and verifiability within the network, as each participant has a full copy of all Blockchain transactions.

Cryptocurrency is an internet-based digital or virtual medium of exchange that uses mathematical algorithms to map data of arbitrary size to a bit string of a fixed size and is a one-way function, that is, a function which is practically impossible to invert. A cryptocurrency is secured by cryptography, which makes it nearly impossible to counterfeit or double-spend. Many cryptocurrencies exist on decentralized networks that rely on Blockchain technology. The most successful and well-known cryptocurrency is Bitcoin. Music star 50 Cent accepted 700 bitcoins as an alternative form of payment for his 2014 album "Animal Ambition". Those coins are now worth over $30 million.

Though Bitcoin and Ethereum are probably the most popular coins in the market, there are many other coins that have grown in popularity and net worth. Here are the top ten coins thus far:

- ♦ **Bitcoin**
- ♦ **Ethereum**
- ♦ **Litecoin**
- ♦ **Cardano**
- ♦ **Polkadot**
- ♦ **Bitcoin Cash**
- ♦ **Stellar**
- ♦ **Chainlink**
- ♦ **Binance Coin**
- ♦ **Tether**

The term "crypto" refers to complicated cryptography which supports the creation and processing of digital currencies across decentralized platforms. Because these cryptocurrencies are generally free from government control, they are inherently risky investments, but limitless in upside profit potential. A small unknown Elon Musk-supported Dogecoin might swell 900% in twelve months, or go broke with no one to hold accountable. The market is the wild west of investing and open to anyone who feels they have the fastest draw.

There are many ways by which Blockchains and cryptocurrencies generate revenue.

Attracting Funding

Oddly, one way of generating revenue is by attracting funding from investors who see a promising future, but don't have the capabilities for research and development in-house. Companies such as Goldman Sachs and Overstock.com have invested in projects like Axoni, Ripple, Digital Assets, Blockchain, and Bitman. Some prominent banks such as JP Morgan, Wells Fargo, and Bank of America have also shown interest in this technology. Publicly traded companies such as MicroStrategy, Tesla, and Galaxy Digital Holdings have adopted Bitcoin as a reserve asset, and hold direct control over their Bitcoin funds. **Some investors believe that Bitcoin and a few other cryptocurrencies will one day be worth more than gold.**

Flat Fees And Transaction Fees

Companies make money by building and maintaining a network between a consortium of partners. They charge each user partner a subscription fee or transaction fee for the activities tied to each partner on the network.

One promising example is Paxo Crypto Brokerage that dominates the decentralized finance niche. They have the capability to make stock trading instantaneous which, in all likelihood, would have eliminated the GameStop/Reddit fiasco.

Another example of the huge potential of cryptocurrency is R3. R3 is an enterprise software firm that focuses on distributed database technology. It leads a consortium of over 200 members, such as financial institutions, banks, trade associations, and Fintech companies. The main aim of R3's consortium is to develop Corda – an open-source distributed ledger platform, designed to work within finance to operate complex transactions and restrict access to transaction data.

Well-known players in the airline industry such as KLM Royal Dutch Airlines are applying Blockchain technology to facilitate intercompany settlements process with its subsidiaries. Crypto technology is gaining more traction each day.

Cryptocurrency Wallet Storage

Cryptocurrency wallet companies are springing up everywhere. A wallet is a software program, online platform or a hardware device that holds the official keys used to send and receive various blockchain cryptocurrency tokens. Companies such as **Coinbase Wallet, StakedWallet.io, Jaxx, Exodus, and Electrum Wallet** are in fierce competition to earn lucrative fees for storing keys in a secure environment. Otherwise, international hackers would steal the keys, sell the coins, and vanish into thin air.

Cryptocurrency Speculation

Many Blockchain companies issue tokens, or an investment company that holds a large amount of a certain cryptocurrency works toward promoting their tokens and increasing their market value. Once the value increases, these companies (such as Factom and Lisk) sell the tokens to the speculators at a profit.

This wild west business niche is first come, first serve with a steep learning curve. Any entrepreneur who loves adventure, speculation, and the ground moving beneath their feet should consider the many business opportunities found in this niche. You might buy a coin or token and sell it for profit. When the price drops again, you might buy it back and wait for the roller coaster to start up, all over again. As the industry continues to grow, those who get in

early have the greatest chance to reap potential profits. **High risk ... high reward.** Who's willing to ride the roller coaster from hell?

♦ **Firearms and Ammunition Store**

If you're located in one of the Southern states (Texas, Louisiana, Arkansas, Oklahoma, etc.) where survivalist sentiments are high, this might be a business opportunity for you.

Survivalism is a movement of individuals, groups, and communities which actively prepare for emergencies, including possible disruptions in social and political order. These disruptions will create anarchy of such a devastating magnitude that traditional society will disintegrate into two groups: survivors (who are prepared) and victims (who will be lost because of a lack of preparation). With the same doomful expectation, the world's super-rich are building impenetrable fortresses and bunkers, a roughly 300% increase in demand each year.

These survivor groups purchase a wide range of survival equipment ... nonperishable foods, water purification systems, stand-alone generators, and repurposed home shelter components. But central to their preparation for inevitable anarchy is the ability to defend themselves and their families. **This means guns and lots of them.**

Americans bought 13.9 million firearms in 2019. NICS background checks conducted in December 2019 claimed second-place honors on the all-time- record list for the period.

In March 2020, responding to the Coronavirus outbreak, more than 3.7 million total firearm background checks were conducted through the FBI's background check system, the highest number on record in more than 20 years. An estimated 2.4 million of those background checks were conducted for gun sales. That's an

80% increase compared with the same month of the previous year.

Handgun sales are playing a critical role in the market's inflated activity. Since 2014, annual handgun unit sales have handily outpaced annual long-gun unit sales. Gun stores across the nation have experienced record sales of firearms and ammunition. These stores generated $11 billion in annual revenue and, between 2013 and 2018, experienced a 3.8 percent annual growth rate.

In the aftermath of horrific mass shootings in Boulder, Colorado and Atlanta, Georgia, lawmakers are pushing for stricter background checks and a total ban on assault weapons. This is not a new push. In recent years, after each school shooting, the same urgent calls for stricter gun control have filled the airways.

Despite these proposed anti-gun initiates, the laws stay virtually unchanged. The right to bear arms is an emotional, hot-button issue, too controversial for lawmakers (expecting to get re-elected) to appear soft on the constitutional right of all citizens to own a gun.

The issue is in no way related to hunting squirrels and deer. Gun control advocates want the big military assault weapons off the street. They hope to eliminate the mentally deranged shooter's ability to walk into a school and kill 20 children with the single pull of a trigger. Survivalists, who fully expect a civil war, don't want to be caught patrolling the streets with a BB gun. If the government starts to take away guns, at what point will they stop?

The stalemate is long-lived, deep, and in the near future, insurmountable. Gun sales are not going away anytime soon.

The greatest downside for potential store owners, however, is technology. At some point (very soon), new laser weapon technology with fingerprint security will make steel guns and lead bullets obsolete. With growing military investment and testing, it's already here. Some store owners are going to be stuck with millions of dollars in old, obsolete inventory that no one wants to buy.

♦ Franchise Broker

Franchise brokers are independent middle contractors that earn a commission from national franchisor companies such as Subway, McDonald's, Ace Hardware, Ben & Jerry's, and UPS Stores by facilitating the purchase of franchise packages to would-be entrepreneurs.

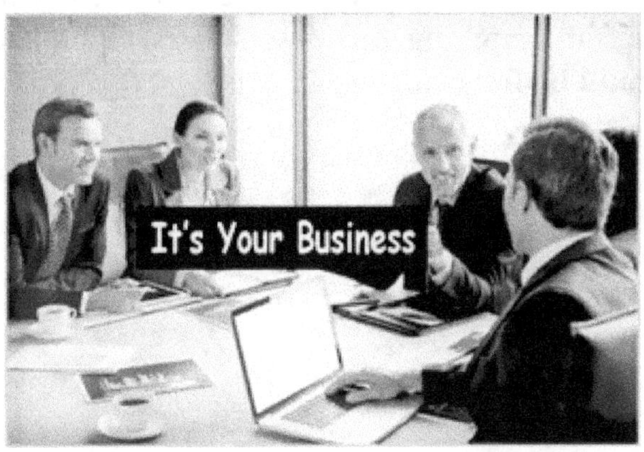

The broker's service may include:

♦ Advertising available franchise opportunities

♦ Vetting potential buyers

♦ Providing local market statistics and insights

♦ Brand assessment and feedback

♦ Securing tentative agreements with retail landlords

♦ Identifying investor banks and lending groups with an inclination toward franchisees

Over the last decade, the number of franchise brokers has exploded, increasing from a rag-tag group of a few hundred early adopters to over 1,500 in the United States alone. While the number is growing, only a relatively small percentage of franchisor companies use broker networks. The franchise business is very competitive. Every dollar paid out to a broker is a dollar off the net sales revenue to franchisor companies. If the brand is strong and people are beating down the door (as with Chick-fil-A), there is no need to pay a broker. However, new franchisor companies that are just entering the market need all the help they can get.

There are many opportunities to scale the business based on reputation for delivering high-quality customers, reduced length of closing cycle, and social networking expertise. **If you enjoy the bridge model of matching business sellers to business buyers, this niche could be for you.**

KEYS TO DECISION-MAKING

*I*nsight #12 examines the seven keys to decision-making. There is an old saying, **"garbage in ... garbage out"**, which simply means a flawed process renders a flawed end result. If you approach a decision about your business niche, asking the wrong questions, gathering irrelevant data, and allowing personal biases to pull you away from your primary objective, you will invariably choose the wrong niche.

At this point, we know too much about the painstaking research and deliberate scrutiny successful entrepreneurs invest in critical decisions to rely on sloppy due diligence. We've gotten smarter whether we like it or not. There's no way we're going to flip a coin or open a fortune cookie or wait for rich Uncle Floyd to come to us in a dream. We need something more concrete, a proven process that presents our options in an orderly manner with an emphasis on objectivity and cumulative (economic, demographic, technological, political, social, physical) facts.

Below is a reliable seven-step framework for making a decision, any decision that allows rational problem-solving to guide the end results. **You're not an AI robot.** Passions and emotions will come into play. These seven steps, however, keep emotions from hijacking the process and resist the built-in caution of your subconscious mind.

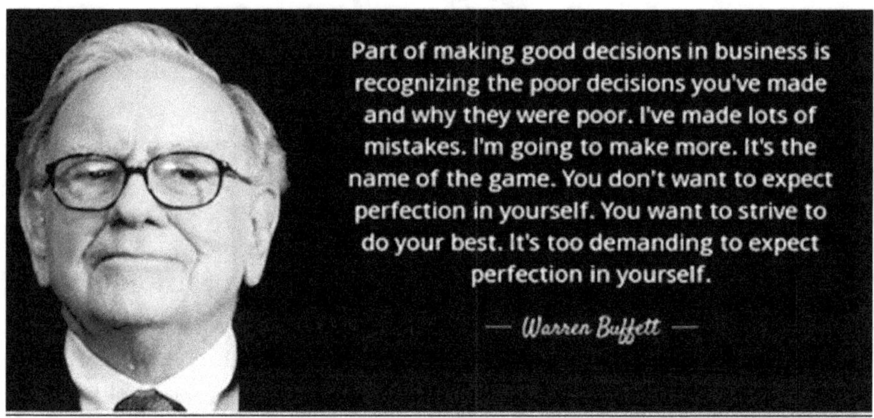

STEP 1 - IDENTIFY THE PROBLEM YOU NEED TO SOLVE

This first step is not as easy as it might appear. An old car might start to smoke and run hot. The problem, however, is not the smoke, nor the overheated engine. The problem is the clogged $9.99 thermostat that's about to ruin a $2500 motor.

The symptoms, or events connected to the symptoms, are just the tip of the iceberg ... easy to see, easy to mistake for the real problem that's manifesting in patterns and trends below the surface. In this book, we have identified the problem as the common inability to select the best business niche based on your experiences, skill set, and circumstances. But is that the real problem?

If we dig deeper, we might find the real problem is not having enough money on which to retire, or seeking happiness and fulfillment after living out the majority of your life inside an unfulfilling, corporate jail. It might be missing your familiar, time-consuming work routine after retirement, and finding inactivity more a form of torture than reward.

Take a few steps back. Widen your trajectory and frame your questions to make sure you're really addressing the problem at hand and not the logistics of an option downstream. Once you have identified the "real" problem, you can move on to the next step.

DO YOU SEE
THE REAL PROBLEM?

STEP 2 - GATHER RELEVANT DATA ABOUT THE PROBLEM

You will remember that gathering data is research, and research involves analytical thinking. You want to use as many reliable sources as possible to confirm or dismiss your hypothesis. One loud-mouth influencer on YouTube is not enough.

Relevant data is both quantitative and qualitative, that is to say, relevant data sheds light on the "what" (In the beginning, New York State had the highest number of reported cases of COVID-19) as well as the "why" (a combination of population density, early sense of invincibility among a younger population, and aggression of purpose that resisted idleness and sheltering). The data should shine a light on the underlying cause-and-effect relationships that created the problem and facilitate its continuation in the future.

In 1978, after many years of struggle, Wang Laboratories (Wang PCs) relocated to a large three-tower office complex in Lowell, Massachusetts. With over $2 billion in sales and 35,000 employees, the company had finally arrived.

During the mid-1980s, however, the entire computer industry experienced stagnant growth. **The Massachusetts Miracle**, an unprecedented period of prosperity in Boston's high-tech and financial services sectors, was winding down. The computer industry was moving away from minicomputers and mainframes, toward PCs and desktop workstations. For Wang

Laboratories, this was a bad omen of things to come.

To add to the company's internal woes, marketing guru and CEO John Cunningham stepped down to run a smaller company. Dr. Wang then insisted his son, Fred Wang, take over the day-to-day operations.

Under young Fred's tenure, many research and development products failed to gain traction, debt ballooned, and sales declined. At one point, Fred Wang announced fourteen major hardware and software products and ambitious delivery dates. Only a handful of these products were close to completion, and many of them had not even been started. The deliveries were notoriously late; some products were never delivered.

The credibility of Wang Laboratories hit an all-time low.

The father eventually fired Young Fred and replaced him with Rick Miller, a former executive from RCA. Though Miller guided Wang Laboratories through a massive restructuring and sold off many of its assets and subsidiaries, he could not save the company. In August, 1992, owing over $550 million, Wang Laboratories filed for bankruptcy.

This brief history of Wang Laboratories offers an ideal opportunity to misidentify the real problem. The data suggests the entire industry was in a severe state of transformation, and Young Fred, ill-equipped, with no visionary prowess, drove the company into the ground.

If we dig deeper and totally detach ourselves from the scapegoat mentality, we discover the real problem was the all-out, wholesale strategic bet Dr. Wang made on mid-size minicomputers and mainframes, with no thought of cross-compatibility to other popular desktop software in the industry. Yes, Young Fred's incompetence contributed to the demise of Wang Laboratories. But a shortsighted product strategy doomed the company to failure.

Regarding our personal quest to choose a business niche, we must remind ourselves the data is interconnected. By nature, data is illuminating, instructive, and impartial to the protective biases of the subconscious mind. It wants to shine a bright light on the raw patterns and implications beneath the surface, even if the revelations conflict with our wishes and desires.

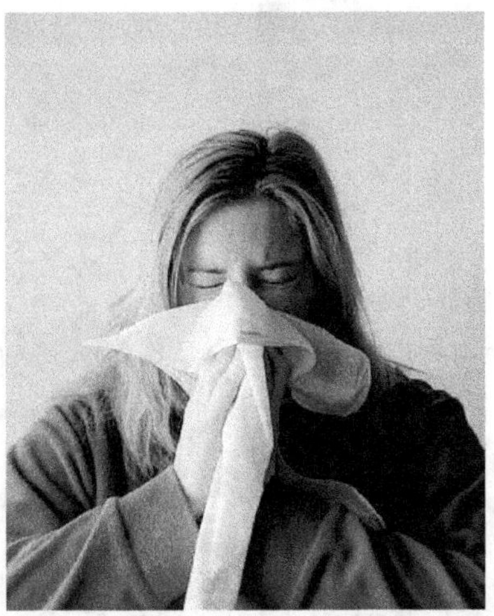

If you're interested in opening up a smoke shop, the data will warn you that your clothes are going to be drenched with the smell of smoke. No matter the income. When you come home night after night and set off your wife's allergies, you are moving toward a divorce.

Don't fight the data. Let it lead you. Revelations about your real problem are patiently waiting. Let's move on.

STEP 3 - IDENTIFY YOUR OPTIONS

What are your options? You might not like any of them. Nevertheless, you must identify them, if for no other reason than to filter them through the rational and deliberate process of elimination. **Sometimes, you eliminate 90% of option (A) and then keep the remaining 10% to be executed in conjunction with option (B).** But how can you cherry-pick the best parts of option (A) if you refuse to recognize its legitimacy in the first place?

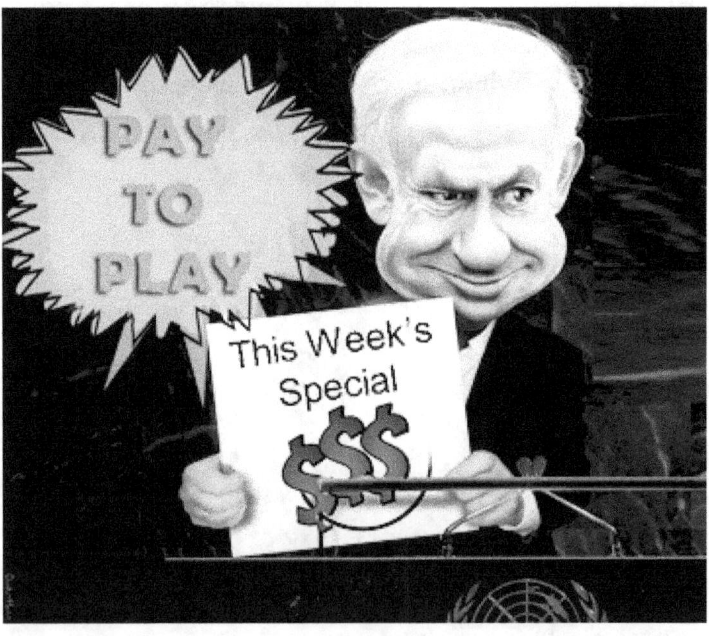

Let's say you have a prohibition on your international product. You need to get an import/export exemption through Congress, but don't like dealing with sleazy politicians.

An alternative option might be to hire a Washington lobbyist to negotiate the deal for you. On a decision matrix, both objectives, getting the exemption and avoiding sleazy politicians, are being met, but only because you kept ALL options (tasteful and distasteful) on the table.

There are three ways to create a viable list of options:

♦ **Research** ... through the normal channels of books, newspaper articles, internet websites, classes, forums, and paid survey results.

♦ **Personal interviews** ... facilitated by seeking advice from skilled experts and mentors willing to share their intimate experiences with you ... free or for a fee. Think about a retired teacher who has taught for 30 years, or a seasoned truck driver who has rambled the open roads for a lifetime. Their valuable insights and private silos of knowledge cannot be replicated by a news article or research report. These are soldiers of war, returning from the battlefield with one-of-a-kind nuances and perspectives. Their minds are cluttered with innovative options that have never made it to print.

♦ **Triangulation** ... which is just a big word for advising yourself outside of yourself. Ever wonder why it is so much easier to give advice to others, and yet, reject the same advice for yourself?

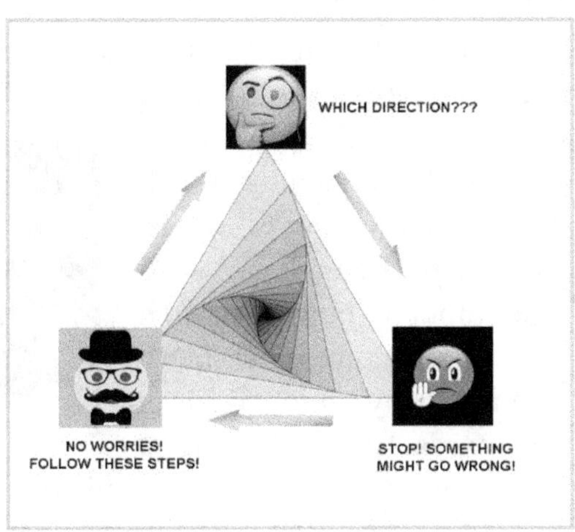

In advising others, we become an independent third party, a psychiatrist without a license, offering our professional, structured, unbiased advice for repair and reconciliation. That part of them needing guidance is not really hearing from us, rather, an independent triangulated extension of us.

This same state of triangulation exists when we allow our independent third-party advisor to present rational options to us, those unique and promising "potential solutions" not yet tainted by the emotional bias of our subconscious mind.

Some experts refer to this state as the option visualization chain. You evaluate an option based on the potential impact it will have on your past, present, and future. You visualize the benefits of being a part of the in-crowd ... cool, carefree, and rebellious. For 20 years, you smoke a suave, manly, you-ain't-the-boss-of-me pack of cigarettes a day. Then, at fifty, you find yourself in a hospice fighting three types of cancer. The options belong to you. So do the consequences.

You might be thinking: Yes, an option we choose today might affect our present and future. But how can it alter our past?

Think about Enron. The unscrupulous decisions made by top executives drove the company into the ground. The present, and all of its false glory, was abruptly ended. The future potential of the company would never be realized. But if we dig deeper, we see the past, literally rewritten before our eyes. Enron Stadium, the official home stadium for the Houston Astros, was almost instantly renamed. Charities immediately removed Enron 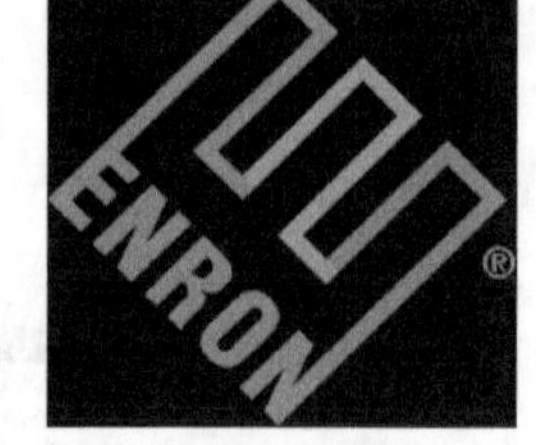 executives from their Boards. Enron, the company everyone revered, suddenly became the company everyone wanted to forget. Their glorious past legacy was erased. Everyone cleared their nostrils of the stench and moved on.

Option visualization places options on the list vetted by the full spectrum of time. You must ask the question: What benefits, pain points, and consequences await, YOU, the decision-maker just over the bend? Can you massage and repurpose the options to fit your specific needs? Are you setting yourself up for misery further down the line?

Options are complex and interconnected. Take your time. Unravel the inner workings below the surface. Carefully choose your plan of action. And then move forward.

STEP 4 - WEIGH THE EVIDENCE

Let's say this another way. Give weight to the evidence. In other words, **give a numeric value to each option**. We'll talk about this more in the final chapters. But for now, think of it as assigning a qualitative and quantitative value to each possibility.

Let's say you have two men in your life, and it's time to settle down. The two men represent two options on which you'll base your future happiness and prosperity. Both emotionally and rationally, you want to get this right. But, to assign a numeric value to each potential husband, you have to determine what's most important to you.

Would-be husband #1 is a romantic, spontaneous, music-loving motorcycle nut, a job-hopping corporate misfit that keeps you laughing all of the time. **Would-be husband #2** is a handsome, neatly dressed, well-mannered product of old insurance money with a huge corporate future and an expressed passion for family and children.

You have to decide which characteristics are most important to you. If your life has been a roller coaster, and stability and predictability are now your greatest priorities, **Would-be husband #1**, despite his happy-go-lucky romance and laughter, is going to receive a lower numeric ranking. If, on the other hand, you're a $200,000 a year nurse anesthetist with a small nest egg in the bank, and determined to find a compatible soul mate, **Would-be husband #2's** family insurance empire and earning potential won't mean a thing.

Your numeric assignment sheet might look something like this:

Add up his profile numbers...

1. Good with finance ... +10

2. Thoughtful and considerate ... +10

3. Heavy smoker ... -8

4. Good hygiene ... +6

5. Snores and snorts in his sleep ... -9

6. Hates pets ... -7

7. Strong sex drive ... +9

9. On the phone or visiting mother each day ... -10

10. Prefers truth (and consequences) over deceiving ... -8

Grand Total = Dump Him!!!

Weighing each option means assigning a numeric value that correlates with your particular circumstances. If you hate guns and any discussion of violence against other human beings, no matter the lucrative profits and continued market growth in gun store ownership, your scorecard of priorities is going to point you away from firearms and back to a Baskin-Robbins Franchise.

STEP 5 - CHOOSE YOUR OPTION; GO ALL-IN

Wedged deeply into the traditional fibers of decision-making, this is one of the hardest parts ... **taking action.** Because of fear, past failures, and a human aversion to uncertainty, we all have a tendency to cling to the interim steps before implementation. **There is really no such thing as a perfect option.** Yet, we spend an inordinate amount of time searching for one. When we peel back the layers, we realize our subconscious mind is working hard to shield us from disappointment. The longer we wait, the longer potential failure stays outside the gate.

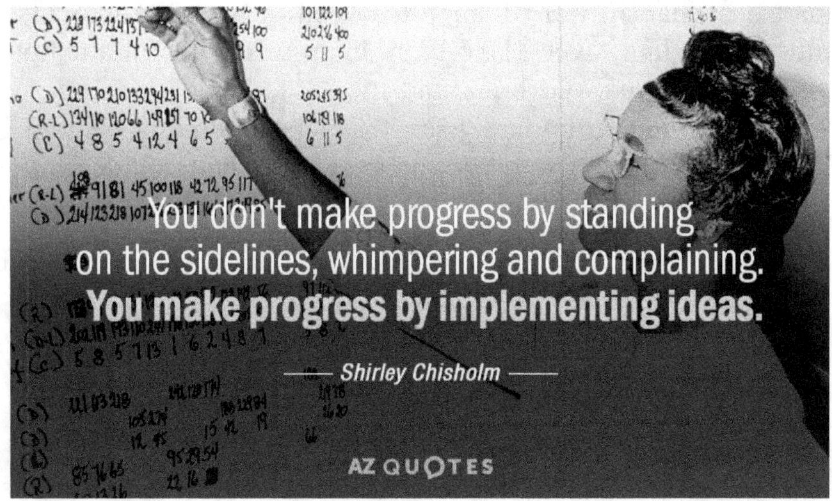

When you've researched your "known" options, choose one and move forward. Don't tip-toe around. Swing for the fences. If it's an unworkable option, you'll know soon enough. Backtrack. See if your option is redeemable in a different form or iteration. Step up to the plate and swing all over again.

STEP 6 - COMMIT MORE RESOURCES

What happens when your initial steps of implementation don't move the needle?

In 1994, Viacom acquired Blockbuster for $8.4 billion. Over the next 15 years, Viacom burned through roughly $300 million a year (negative red ink down the well) to try to recover Blockbuster's lost legacy ... lost to Netflix, a company they could have purchased for $50 million in 2001. By the time Blockbuster filed for bankruptcy in 2010, the company was drowning in $1 billion in debt and worth only $24 million. From 2010 to 2018, Kmart chairman Edward Lampert poured in massive amounts of jumpstart funding, over $11 billion, in an unsuccessful attempt to revive the 135-year-old brick and mortar retail icon, Sears. Year after year, trying to bounce back from the relentless beating by Walmart and Amazon, and with no answer to the toxic derivatives recession in 2008, Sears lost 96% of its value.

The chain has sold off most of its popular appliance brands and real estate assets. Indeed, it's a sad day for the ole school sentimentalists who grew up riding down the escalators and crunching on Sears buttered popcorn, and young beauty queens, trimming the big Sears label from the back of their high school prom dresses.

The once-mighty retail juggernaut is no more than a ghostly skeleton, left over from the glorious days Baby Boomers remembered and cherished years ago. A few stores (55 locations) are still open. But how long will that last?

Pumping more resources into a rescue operation does not always translate into shattered hopes and dreams. In 1997, when Apple was on its last leg, Microsoft swooped in with a $150 million investment and saved the company. In 2009, the US government saved bankrupt Chrysler with a $12.5 billion government assistance loan. In 1974, a few years into the delivery company's fledgling operation, FedEx founder Frederick Smith owed $24,000, but didn't have it. Armed with the company's last $5,000, he took a weekend trip to Vegas, won $27,000 and pumped it back into the company.

If you believe in your entrepreneurial startup, then go "All-In". You might have to restart the operation several times. There are no guarantees. Examine your financial obligations such as employee wages, rent or lease payments, unnecessary fees, and hefty finance penalties. Almost always, creditors are willing to work with you if you ask.

Both logistically and emotionally, you will recognize the point of no return. If you can't save the business, don't extend your depleted resources on irretrievable sunken costs. It's time to move on.

STEP 7 - SHUT IT DOWN

When is it time to close down the company?

This part is not easy. With so many precious hours of blood, sweat, and tears invested in your business, it's difficult to trust your own instincts in recognizing the dreaded point of no return. Here are seven clues offered by entrepreneurs who have gone before you:

♦ You Aren't Meeting Revenue Projections ... not even conservative breakeven numbers that might offer a ray of hope.

♦ More Than 50% Of Your Revenue Is Dependent On One Client ... which is a (predictable) time bomb tied to the standard rate of client turnover in your industry. Understand. This client attrition happens no matter how well you deliver goods and services.

♦ Your Product/Service Is Not Ranked Number One In Either Price Or Features ... you have no bragging rights. You can't compete. You are not able to establish a competitive edge.

♦ Your Personal Health Has Depreciated ... including noticeable phases of mental and physical exhaustion, changes in personal temperament, and lapses in cognition. People hate to see you come through the door.

♦ A Decided Lack Of Enthusiasm In Your Original Mission ... it's getting harder and harder to come to work.

♦ Your Key Employees Are Leaving ... people have begun to abandon ship.

♦ More Creditor Calls Than Client Calls ... you are dodging phone calls each day.

If you see the writing on the wall, you can't simply turn out the lights and go home. There are still due diligence steps you'll have to take to protect yourself from skeletons creeping out of the closet on your next venture .... that right, your NEXT venture. You are so far from giving up. **Most successful Silicon Valley gurus fail two to three times before they become the startup legends we read about.**

Here are eleven common steps you need to follow:

1. Write down an orderly and strategic shut-down procedure.

2. Get with employees or partners for a serious and honest breakdown of reasons and timetables.

3. Collect payable on outstanding accounts.

4. Meet face-to-face with key customers and inform them in a way that will preserve the relationship.

5. Cancel business licenses and permits, but leave a single bank account open for late receivables.

6. Consider bankruptcy options.

7. Sell off assets if possible. Competitors may offer to buy them.

8. Get a CPA to prepare a final set of financial statements.

9. Close the doors.

10. Take time to mourn. Celebrate all that you have learned.

11. Get right back out there on another project.

Decision-making is best executed with a plan of action, right down to closing the doors and saying goodbye to one venture, while transitioning into another. Be proud of your flops. They represent badges of courage and precious learning experiences that will propel you to future triumphs. If making business decisions were easy, everyone could do it. Everyone would have a fat bank account and a glorious success story to tell.

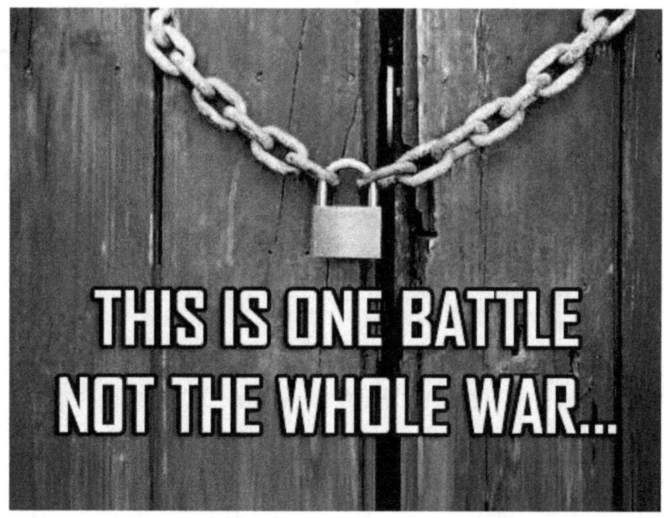

But we know better. We know that hard work, solid decision-making, and relentless persistence are the keys to entrepreneurial success. Stay out of the emotional, subconscious, feel-good zone of decision-making. **Some Christian entrepreneurs try to hide in a cloud of spiritual and philosophical gerrymandering.** "Maybe God doesn't want me to be a business owner."

This is an old lie of appeasement, contrary to their own faith. If God gave them a vision, why would he suddenly take it back? Failure along the way does not negate the mission. Be rational and data-driven. Walk through the process. This is just one battle. Make prudent decisions that will give you the best chance for future success.

DECISION-MAKING HELP TOOLS

*I*nsight #13 examines three premium software applications that mitigate human distortions and biases from contaminating the decision-making process. **No matter our inclination toward objectivity and rational thinking, we all fall victim to personal biases.** Over-50 candidates lead the way. These are common, often invisible influences that sway our judgment on both the conscious and subconscious levels.

Before we look at the help tools used to avoid these psychologically embedded blunders, let's thoroughly examine the blunders, themselves. Here are the top five biases that cloud our decision-making and keep us from choosing the best options at our disposal.

Top 5 Human Biases

♦ Anchoring Bias

Anchoring bias is a tone-setting bias that occurs when an individual is overly influenced by an initial range of values that limit future considerations. If someone offered you two tickets to the Super Bowl for $5,000, without doing any research, you might counteroffer $3,000 and consider the purchase a bargain.

If you're in the market for a new house, and the agent takes you to five homes in the same neighborhood, all with swimming pools, when you visit the sixth house that has no pool, even though you don't swim and don't want the additional maintenance costs, your inclination might be to assign the home a lesser value. **The initial five homes have set the tone or "anchored" the value.** Your subconscious mind eliminates the sixth home from the range of viable possibilities, based on the five anchoring homes.

In choosing a business niche, you might find yourself comparing franchise offers. A Burger King franchise might cost $3,000,000; a Taco Bell franchise might top out at $2,500,000. Conversely, to open a new Chick-fil-A might cost roughly $20,000 with no threshold for net worth. The expensive anchoring prices of the other popular franchises would lead you to believe there was something lacking with Chick-fil-A. In fact, in the first six months after a Chick-fil-A opens in a particular market, customer traffic falls an average of 5.4% at Wendy's and 4.4% at Burger King locations within 1.5 miles radius. Nearby McDonald's locations see short-term traffic declines of 1.5%.

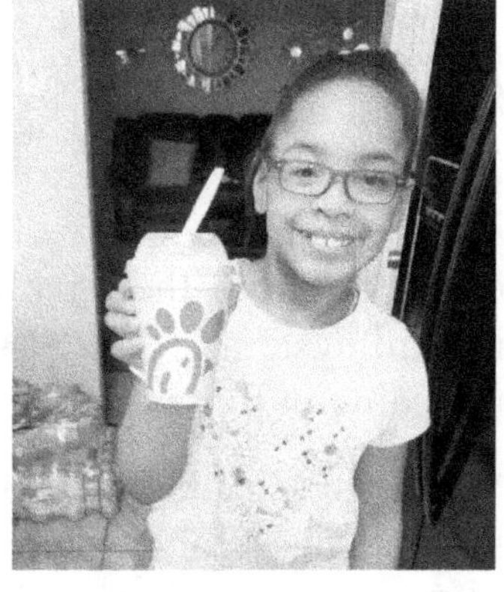

In addition, Chick-fil-A's average unit volumes are the best in the industry, with the average location making $4.6 million a year. By comparison, Burger King's average unit volume is $1.4 million and McDonald's is $2.8 million, much of which is based on value meal discounting. No matter the industry, no one really wants to bet their future on a "discounting" strategy. It's a volatile, unpredictable roller coaster ride geared toward short-term profit objectives rather than long-term market share.

Without an awareness of anchoring bias, you might make a decision based on the initial price ranges set by less valuable franchises simply because they spoke the loudest or put their offers on the table before anyone else. Value is more about the fundamentals of the operation and less about who speaks first.

♦ Self-Serving Bias

Self-serving bias is the attempt to enhance one's self-esteem by attributing positive events to one's self, but negative events to external factors including the actions of others. Self-serving bias involves the perceptual process of taking credit for perceived good and shifting the blame to others for perceived bad. (You might call it the Washington DC political square dance.)

Incompetent bosses use this technique a great deal. Studies show that over time, self-serving bias becomes less a deliberate

deception to avoid responsibility, and more a distorted internal belief system, concocting an alternative reality to undergird low self-esteem. These bosses speak a great deal about loyalty, do not tolerate any deviation from their reality, and develop subtle punishment-and-reward systems **(B.F. Skinner's operant conditioning behavior)** to deal with those who believe or disbelieve.

In selecting a business niche, you might be tempted to blame the franchise marketing team for deceiving you or not presenting all of the facts. This is how they tricked you into buying the franchise in the first place. This is the reason it failed.

In reality, the fine print contained all of the facts you claimed were hidden from you in a web of deceit. But you never took the time to read them, or get a lawyer or CPA to read them, or conduct due diligence research with other current owners to get a better perspective of the pitfalls of ownership. Instead of learning from your mistakes and applying the knowledge to future entrepreneurial opportunities, self-serving bias entangles your brainpower in a nonproductive witch hunt for someone else to blame.

◆ Confirmation Bias

Confirmation bias is the tendency to search for, recall, believe, and promote information that confirms or strengthens one's personal convictions or values. **When people desire a certain idea or concept to be true, they feel motivated to confirm that concept is valid and supported by expert opinions and irrefutable evidence.**

Their research is skewed toward positive reinforcement of their original belief. All other possibilities are cast aside as being fake news, unreliable, and a misrepresentation of the facts.

If you want global warming to be a myth, you cling to the few renegade (seekers of truth) scientists that declare melting polar ice caps and rising seas a natural phenomenon. If you work for an oil company that pays you $200,000 a year, you WANT to believe the seekers of truth. If you ride a motorcycle without wearing a helmet, you go on YouTube and watch all of the Harley experts who have been riding for twenty years, head-to-pavement, and are still in one piece.

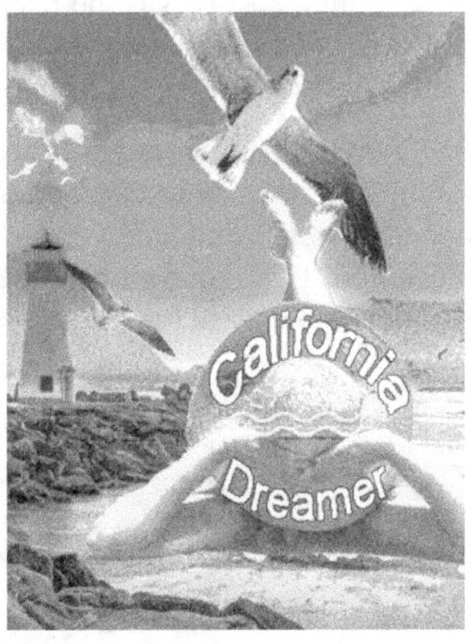

If you WANT to start your business in sunny California, you downplay the continuous earthquakes and expert predictions of the catastrophic "BIG ONE" that is overdue and expected any day.

Your confirmation bias will dig up old newspaper articles by foggy-brain tectonic plate alarmists from thirty years ago, spreading warnings of doom and gloom. No need to worry. Who can say what the future will bring?

♦ Sunk-Cost Bias

Sunk cost (retrospective cost) bias refers to the tendency to follow through on an underperforming activity or purchase that is not meeting one's expectations. In this scenario, a sum has been invested in the past that is no longer relevant to decisions about the future. Sometimes, we refer to sunk cost as the Concorde fallacy after the failed supersonic Concorde jet program in which governments insisted on completing despite the jet's dreary potential for a positive return on investment.

Sunk cost bias is the reason people finish movies they don't enjoy, or eat a full plate of food, even though they were completely stuffed halfway through the meal.

If, over a period of time, the business niche you choose is failing, and your only two options are (1) continue to invest in the operation or (2) shut it down, if you choose to shut it down, it doesn't mean you'll get your money back. It only means you avoid losing additional money in the future.

There is a psychological justification for sunk cost behavior. Studies reveal that people show an inclination to throw good money after bad rather than appear wasteful or imprudent. These individuals also place a higher probability for success on a particular outcome, once they have invested in it. Their self-validating reason is that any rational, like-minded visionary would have seen the same outstanding potential for reward. They did not make an assessment (mistake) that any "reasonable person" in the same position would not have made. Once again, the subconscious mind has stepped in to protect them.

The lesson here is simple. **If you continue to invest in a business niche that has failed to show reasonable promise, do so because you still believe in it, not because you hope to cover up your mistake.** After all, if your initial selection of a business niche rewards you with valuable experience and transferable knowledge to the next project, then it's not a mistake at all.

◆ Bandwagon Bias

Bandwagon bias, sometimes called "Group Think", refers to a psychological phenomenon in which people take a position or carry out an action primarily because other people are doing it. This is a decision to "join in", sometimes, despite their own beliefs, to the point of overriding their core values. The primary motivation is to align themselves with the group and gain acceptance as a member.

We have already talked about "Group Think" in Chapter 10. Consider a twelve-member jury panel, deliberating a life-or-death verdict. If eleven members vote **"yes"**, that newly formed group quickly transforms into a unified force to convince the holdout to vote with the majority. As time passes, persuasion tactics escalate into personal attacks and skewed reasoning. In most cases, for the sake of being accepted as part of the group, the dissenting juror eventually gives in.

If everyone in your family is involved in an Amway multi-level marketing distributorship, and each family gathering is focused on Amway activities, you might be inclined to get involved as well. **You join the family bandwagon for acceptance, and sacrifice your own passions for the sake of the group.** There is a high probability this decision will not work out well. Your *Golden Circle* compatibility may be in an entirely different niche.

On all levels of cognitive thinking, people want to be right, admired, and accepted. They want to be on the winning team. In order to wade through the massive communications clutter, they observe other people in their social group to decide what's "right". If it appears everyone else with whom they identify is doing something, the average person presumes that action is the correct thing to do ... right down to handling rattlesnakes in church, or taking off their mask and mingling with the people who have COVID-19.

Social proof has been around for a long time. In the old days, it was called "testimonials". People would proclaim the benefits of a new product and then imply that you were stupid and totally left out of the savvy in-crowd if you didn't get the product for yourself. This "in-crowd" strategy still works very well. People don't want to embrace the hard job of thinking. AND ... they don't want to be left out.

Reducing The Impact Of Biases

One way to mitigate the impact of biases upon your decision-making process is to employ decision-making software applications, sometimes referred to as Decision Support Software. TransparentChoice, Power BI, Powernoodle, TIBCO Spotfire, airfocus, Yonyx, Zingtree, and QlikView are just a few of the most popular options in the marketplace. These decision support tools don't really care about satisfying the wishes of your Amway family clan, unless you explicitly tell them to. **These tools seek to identify the most rational, cost-effective solutions, based on the priorities you established when declaring the existence of the problem.**

Let's say, after repeated warnings, your kids won't clean up their room. These decision support software applications force you to declare and prioritize your "true" objective. Is your objective to simply keep the room clean for purposes of organization and hygiene? Is your underlying motive a desire to teach your children life lessons about the responsibility of ownership? Or is the most troublesome aspect of the dirty room their disobedience and disrespect?

The support software will force you to assign priority to the outcome(s) your protective, subconscious mind might ordinarily brush aside or try to avoid altogether. Depending on the priorities you set, the software might recommend hiring a weekly maid or enrolling the kids in some kind of character-building, accountability camp ... or just shipping them off to a foster home and turning the space into an indoor grow room for marijuana.

Brilliant!$!

Decision Support Software prioritizes objectives, evaluates alternatives, and simulates results. With the advent of highly sophisticated artificial intelligence (AI) algorithms, there are many proficient, data-driven decision-making applications to help you choose a business niche that is right for you. Based on affordability, effectiveness, and ease of use, the cost of these tools ranges from a one-time licensing fee of $40, to a renewable subscription of $20,000 a year.

Each tool comes with a series of performance specialties. For instance, **1000minds Decision Making** is an excellent tool for data analysis, decision tree analysis, and sensitivity analysis, that is to say, comparing equal preferences using subtle, side-by-side categories of importance, and then vetted through a strict question-and-answer interview system. **Competency Management by CABEM Technologies** builds competency models, identifies hard and soft skills needed to reach prescribed competency levels, and tracks the progress of all team members seeking credentials or certifications to reach their competency goals. **Decision Lens'** strong suit is to deploy new routines of communication and collaboration within the decision-making and planning processes to capture the best combinations of value, cost, risk, and balance in your company portfolio. This optimization of resources is a critical step in attracting new investors and driving up stock prices.

Although these tools will be invaluable in future business operations, in this phase of your entrepreneurial journey, your whole objective is to select a compatible business niche. **That means deploying tools that identify, prioritize, and match your personal capabilities and inclinations to opportunities in certain industries or markets.**

This is important. Earlier, we mentioned the difficult task of matching your unfiltered, unbiased core personality as a uniquely fashioned individual with a particular market opportunity. But let's take a step back to understand the true meaning of our search for market niche compatibility.

This search has a name. It's called identifying core competencies that make you a **"niche fit"**. Core competencies represent an individual's fundamental knowledge, ability, and expertise in a specific skill set. **Core** implies the individual has an intrinsic inclination toward matters in a specific area, and is an ideal candidate for future learning in that area and related areas. The cumulative competency mix of all team members, both internally and externally, represents your organization's core competencies. But your organizational structure comes after you identify the business niche for which YOU have a passion, the one YOU plan to pursue.

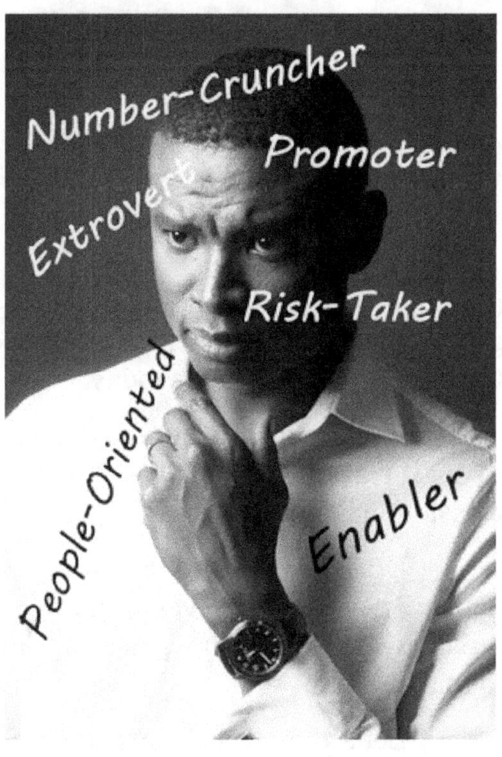

At this point, you should easily grasp the necessity for some kind of "save-me-from-myself" **decision software.** There are so many ways to stumble; so many ways to force a compatibility match that isn't there. When we look back at the many critical decisions we've made without these decision-making tools, we realize how often we've distorted priorities and inflated the value of fathom opportunities based on our hidden biases and strong desire to plow ahead.

Indeed, we can now recall the missteps and blunders. We may have invested thousands of dollars into Little Susie's piano lessons when, in fact, (we refused to acknowledge) Little Susie

hated the piano and spent her free time outside, among the trees and grass and flowers, on her way to becoming the highly successful California botanist she is today.

Are the people at Google, Apple, and Amazon that smart to get it right every time? No! They're just smart enough to use the decision-making tools that give them the edge.

Decision Support Software Applications are not a silver bullet. They are, however, a tremendous aid for comparison and discovery. In the end, it's going to take your expertise and judgment to seal the deal.

Let's draw a line in the sand. Decision-making is a broad proposition. The "decision" to hire (evaluate and select) a specific employee from a pool of potential employees is completely different from the "decision" to declare the need (create an official paid position) for a new employee to join the team and do a particular job.

If you're losing inventory from your warehouse loading dock, you might use a "fishbone diagram" decision-making help tool to pinpoint the weakness in your organization. An examination of your options might lead you to hire a full-time security guard, stationed inside a booth, on the dock. You would then apply a "needs assessment" help tool to determine the specific duties your yet-to-be-hired security guard would carry out. Finally, you would apply a "profile assessment" help tool to compare the competencies, personality traits, and physical attributes of potential security candidates to determine if they possessed a high probability to carry out the duties specified by the needs assessment. Still, other tools would be used to measure employee attitudes, burnout tendencies, inclined passion factors, and loyalty.

That's a mouthful. But if the duties require the security guard to keep a keen watch, periodically patrol the premises, and interact with drivers and forklift operators, you don't want to hire someone who has lost one eye and been crippled in the war. With a strong commitment to supporting the nation's veterans, you might find another position for the war hero, inside the office, making customer service calls. However, the emotion-free, decision-making help tools will prevent you from offering him the security guard position on the dock.

The point of this scenario is to demonstrate the diversity of decision support software applications. Depending on the challenge you face, all of these tools have the potential to enhance your productivity and identify the most promising solutions at hand. But for our primary objective of identifying a compatible business niche, going forward, we will focus on tools that specialize in profile assessments and market analytics. You need to understand precisely who you are, what skill-set you possess, and which market niche is right for you. Your **"niche fit"** is on the way.

Get Ready!
The Next Chapter Is Huge!

In our next chapter, we will walk through the entire process using a hypothetical selection scenario to nail down your profile and identify a compatible market niche. We'll select several popular decision-making tools to demonstrate the power of these systems and work our way through the maze of options to identify an optimal "niche fit". We are not seeking perfection. In this process, perfection doesn't exist. What we hope to achieve is a systematic approach to problem-solving and decision-making, a playbook, if you will, that will give you the best chance for success, profile by profile, market by market, no matter the product or service you entertain.

Are you ready for this? Indeed you are ... Let's GO!!!

TIME TO LAUNCH

*I*nsight #14   merges the powerful forces of holistic thinking, research analytics, artificial intelligence help tools, and over-50 proprietary experiences into YOUR personal platform of identification and discovery. Without calling upon the services of a $300-an-hour psychoanalyst or digging up **Carl Jung** from the grave, we will attempt to identify the business niche to which your passions, preferences, skill-sets, and competencies suggest you belong.

Let's GO!!!

Even after absorbing the illuminative insights from previous chapters, discovering who you are and your compatibility to a specific industry is a tall order. **All of the dynamics exist in a constant state of flux, including YOU, the marketplace, and the disruptive forces that work relentlessly to impede your progress.** There is no silver bullet. There is no perfect outcome. The process upon which you will embark narrows the margin of error, reduces the distortion of human biases, and points you to green pastures you have the inclination to plow. In the final analysis, however, based on all of the available evidence, the AI robots and fancy algorithms have to acquiesce. You have the final word. **You have to decide what's best for you.**

Let's use three critical steps to nail this selection process to the wall.

STEP 1: IDENTIFY YOU

Who are you, really? Ironically, no matter who we are, we tend to answer this question the same way. Our protective subconscious mind, which strives to keep things simple, positive, and predisposed toward a good night's sleep, tells us we are that familiar face in the mirror. That single reflection is a composite of who we are, the purpose for our existence, and the value we bring to the rest of the world. If all goes well, we bed down, peacefully, justified in our deeds, obligated to recharge our batteries for a brand new day.

The problem with this answer, the entire process for that matter, is that it is based on a lie.

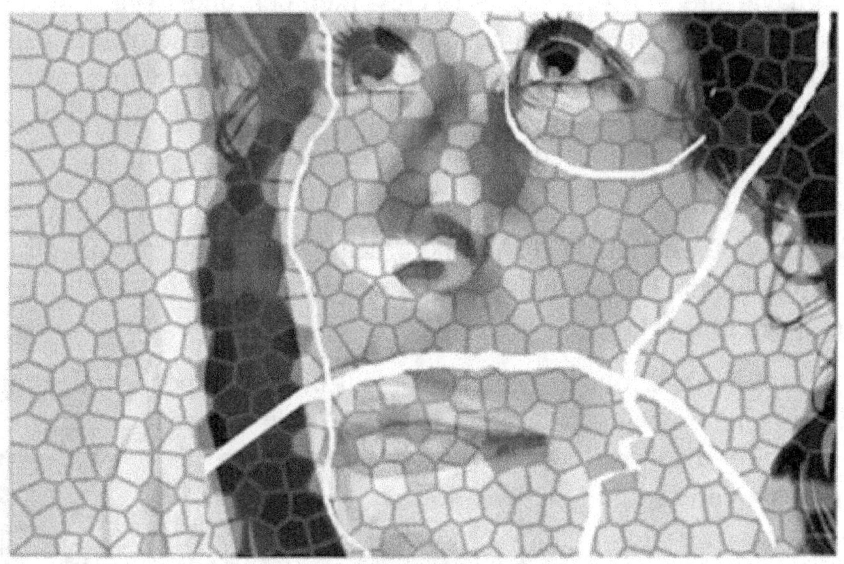

FOR THE SAKE OF YOUR SUCCESS, HAPPINESS, WHOLENESS, AND HEALING, YOUR SUBCONSCIOUS WILL TELL YOU A LIE.

We are not one person. We are a complex coalescence of many fractured pieces that strut and fret their hour upon the stage, and then are heard from no more.

Because this concept is so critical to understanding who you really are, let's crank up the old time machine for one last journey. Let's go back in history to a profound, life-or-death scenario in which you might examine your reactions under fire.

Miracle of the Andes

Back in 1972, a chartered turboprop airplane, carrying the Uruguayan amateur rugby team (5 crew members and 40 passengers) crashed in the Andes Mountains in Argentina. Because of the harsh environment and snow-covered mountains, the white plane, resting in a deep valley, was impossible to find. After eight agonizing days, officials called off all rescue efforts and presumed everyone was dead.

After two months of bitter cold and starvation, only 16 passengers ultimately survived the ordeal. They did so by resorting to cannibalism. **They ate the frozen dead carcasses of other team members and crew.**

When you look in the mirror at that single composite reflection of yourself, do you see a cannibal? And yet, in those months of desperation, can you truly say you would have chosen a slow, starving, painful death over life?

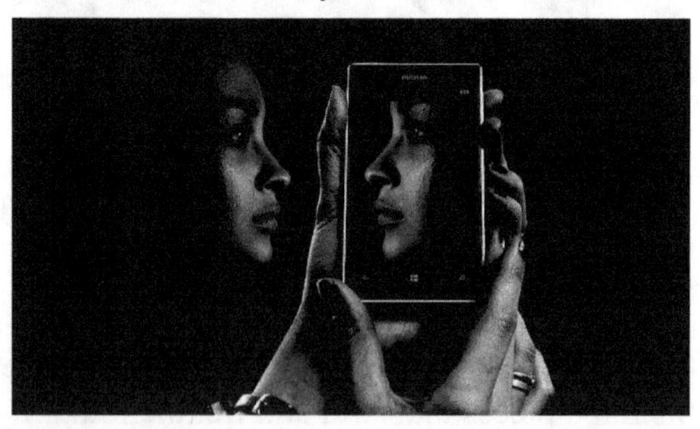

Were you able to answer the question? Or did your subconscious step in and beat you to the punch?

Self-image, that is to say, what we think of ourselves and what we will do or won't do under certain circumstances, is primarily recorded in our brains on a global level, similar to a catchy slogan:

Nike ... "Just Do It";

KFC ... "Finger Lickin' Good";

M&M ... "Melts in Your Mouth, Not in Your Hands";

The U.S. Marine Corps: "The Few. The Proud. The Marines".

When we look in the mirror at our single composite reflection, our brain says:

"The lady's man";

"A caring mother";

"A company go-getter";

"A fighter to the end";

"A decent person";

" A mistreated victim";

"A no-nonsense truth seeker";

"A bad-ass you don't want to mess with";

"A leader chosen by God";

These one-dimensional personal slogans make us think we know who we are. But in reality, we are so much more. Under extreme pressure at work, **"A caring mother"** might get too drunk or pop too many sleeping pills and not be able to get up the next morning to take her young daughter to school. **"A decent person"** might log on to Facebook to bully and belittle a weaker person into suicide. **"A bad-ass you don't want to mess with"** might accidentally spill coffee on Mike Tyson's shirt, get pushed around and cursed out, and in the end, tuck his tail and creep out of the door.

We are not one-and-done monolithic composites. We are complex contextual beings that act or react within the context of our present urgency.

That's a mouthful. We promised to keep things simple. So let's break it down.

We live in multiple dimensions. For the purposes of this discussion, let's focus on the most prominent four:

1. Intellectual dimension: This is our logical, evidence-based dimension. We allow our intellect and rational thinking to guide us through the decision. It doesn't mean we're smarter. It simply means we're fact-based.

2. Physical dimension: This dimension represents both the location of our physical body and the appearance (height, weight, hair color, genitalia) we perceive it to project to others. A big red facial zit before an important departmental meeting might make "A no-nonsense truth seeker" call in sick, although she has no sick days left.

3. Moral dimension: This dimension contains our complex code of ethics, our perception of right and wrong. Although both are legal in most states, a person hosting a New Year's Eve party at his house might allow whiskey, but not marijuana. A company executive might steal funds by falsifying his expense report, but absolutely refuse to litter on the sidewalk.

4. Emotional dimension: This dimension represents our inclination to give or take, to indulge or restrain, to support or resist with no logical or moral justification. We like ole Mike, so we vote for ole Mike, even though ole Mike is immensely unqualified to carry out the duties of the office.

At any given time, the pressure from these dimensions, acting with singularity or in combination, can shatter our composite image in the mirror and make us do things we never thought we'd do.

"I don't know what came over me. Before I realized it...."

"I generally don't take those kinds of chances. But...."

"I want to apologize. I'm really not that kind of person...."

Are you a cannibal? Sitting in your living room by a cozy fireplace, drinking hot chocolate and reading the story of such appalling savagery in the Andes Mountains, your physical dimension allows your moral dimension to move to the forefront. Your subconscious mind secretes hormones soaked in virtue and human decency. It exaggerates your code of self-discipline and then offers up the comforting "NOT ME" reassurance you want to hear.

Over the years, psychiatrists, psychoanalysts, and other mental health experts have struggled to bypass the biases created by the subconscious mind. **Asking the patient a direct question seldom leads to the unmitigated truth.** Not to say there exists an intentional motive to deceive. Rather, the respondent is delivering the truth as he or she perceives it to be.

The eureka moment came when experts **(Please research these names: Carl Jung, Katharine Briggs, Isabel Myers, Raymond Cattell, Marcus Buckingham)** realized perception was the key. No matter how different we appeared to be, as human beings, we consistently perceived the world around us in basically four ways: **sensing, thinking, intuition, and feeling**. Said another way (because nothing in the cognitive realm is absolute) researchers determined that these four processing methods represented the dominant ways most individuals made sense of their world.

1. Sensing ... this method of perception gives priority to what we can see, the tangible "here-and-now". People who rely on this method trust their five senses and see things in concrete and literal terms that enhance practical application. They seek straight talk about the nuts-and-bolts of an issue, no metaphors. They are quickly irritated by esoteric discussions that cannot be proven. They gravitate toward perfection and order.

2. Thinking ... this method of perception is more often impersonal and logic-based, leaning toward activities that rely on systems such as mathematics, computer science, and engineering. Predominant thinkers love to research and extract meaning from the patterns and probability of occurrences. People who perceive through thinking seek order and predictability. Usually, their work takes priority over everything else.

3. Intuition ... is a non-rational method of perception that thrives on inspiration, imagination, and abstract concepts that reveal new possibilities. Intuitive people extract knowledge by reading between the lines and dissecting the true meaning of life through symbols and patterns. This method of perception values insights that reveal themselves spontaneously rather than through the rigid limitations of step-by-step deliberation. Intuitive people are neither surprised nor mistrusting when answers come to them out of the blue.

4. Feeling ... this is an emotionally driven method of perception that gives priority to social relationships and considerations of the heart. Feelers value harmony, social tolerance, and expressions of bonding (art and love stories) that go beyond words. They jump at the chance to support or counsel people experiencing emotional difficulties. Material things are secondary to human development and growth. Feelers often sacrifice their own best interests for the sake of harmony within the group. They express themselves in terms of "I feel this is best" or "I have a feeling this is not going to work out".

Let's say you and your friend, Fred, are standing by the window, looking out at the backyard. A colorful green bird flies in and perches on a limb near the back fence.

You say, *"What a beautiful bird with such vivid colors. Wonder what kind it is?"*

Fred says, *"The kind that needs to get the hell out of here. The Center for Disease Control people have been warning us about these exotic birds spreading that h1n1 bird flu. If I had my grandfather's shotgun, I'd give him a boost back to Hong Kong."*

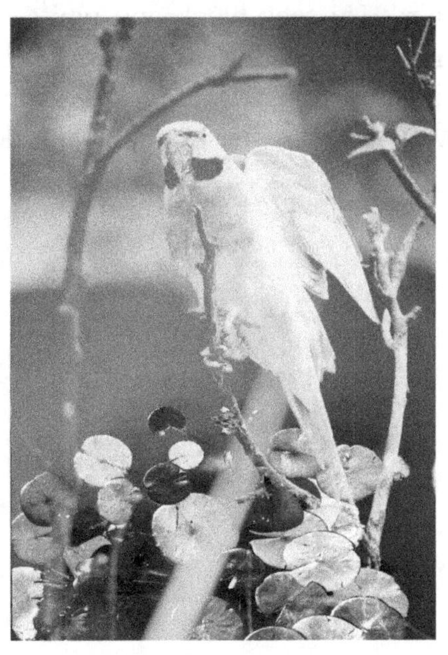

A few minutes later, you hear Fred talking on his cell phone. *"Listen, I'm not trying to throw a wet blanket on your sales pitch. But you're giving me a bunch of fancy words and pie-in-the-sky possibilities. What's the bottom line? How much is it going to cost and how long to install it?"*

When Fred gets off the phone, he turns to you. "I used your bathroom earlier and noticed you didn't have any toilet paper. I need to take a quick dump. Do you have toilet paper in your house ... ANYWHERE?"

When Fred comes out of the bathroom, he tells you about his potential new business. *"I'm thinking about opening a halfway house for non-violent prisoners. The state has allocated a ton of money to relieve the overcrowded prison system. I think I could make a nice piece of change. What do you think?"*

You don't have to think. You already know Fred is going to crash and burn.

Even with the limited knowledge you have about methods of perception, you know that Fred is a sensing type, rough around the edges, operating predominantly out of his five senses (see, hear, smell, taste, touch) Intellectual dimension. He does not see a green bird. He sees black and white medical facts. He does not want to indulge in esoteric discussions. He wants the nuts-and-bolts laid out in simple terms. He is irritated by a lack of order and predictability. ALL bathrooms should have toilet paper, and that's that

To reduce his chances for success even further, he has declared that his only interest in opening the halfway house is profit.

Think about a daycare center, or marriage counseling service, or drug rehab and addiction center, or elder care facility, or halfway house. What words best describe the core values of these types of businesses?

If we asked Fred a direct question about any of these things, his subconscious mind is going to step in to remind him he is a **"decent person" ...** maybe not a sob-face, bleeding-heart teddy bear type. But he wouldn't take advantage of anyone.

With the advent of artificial intelligence AI-based passion assessments and perception profiling, we don't have to ask Fred a direct question. **His subconscious mind doesn't get the chance to step in to rescue him because it doesn't understand the framework of our interrogation.**

What brand of dog food or cat food did you feed your pet when you were growing up? How has your animal nutrition awareness changed? What brand will you feed your pet when you get home?

Your subconscious mind has no way of knowing these are the lead questions to a section on career choices and whether you are a good fit to own a pet store. Unless you're feeding those poor critters bad horse meat that sets off a guilt alarm, you will answer these questions with the unmitigated truth.

If we wanted to detect Fred's level of empathy, caring, and sensibility toward other people, we might include a series of questions about his voting record for the last ten years. If, in their platform, none of the candidates for which he voted mentioned job retraining for returning veterans, or upward mobility, or reduced prescription drug costs and healthcare premiums, or stabilizing social security for retirees, **their priorities represent his priorities.** Empathy for others was not a priority in his voting selection. His subconscious mind has no way of knowing how to protect him. It's busy regurgitating facts about the Constitution and his right to vote.

By no means is Fred out of the entrepreneurial game. He might do very well selling custom pipes to fracking companies drilling for oil. But based on his initial sensing profile and his tendency to operate predominantly, out of the **Intellectual dimension**, his chances of running a successful halfway house are very low.

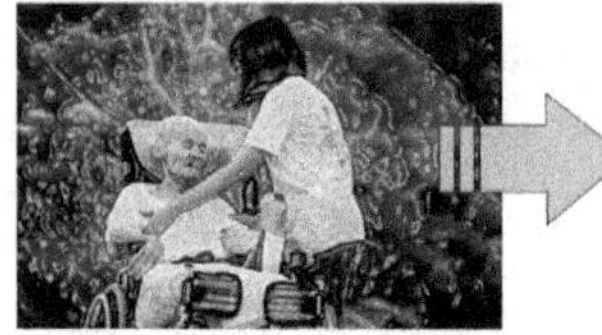

We know about Fred. But what about you?

Armed with a better understanding of how these dimensions and methods of perception circumvent interference by the subconscious mind, what steps do you now take to determine who you really are and what business niche is best for you?

There are many reliable personality assessment options in today's marketplace, fully capable of making an end-run around your subconscious mind. Some are free. Others charge a minimal fee.

Without wading too deeply into the ocean of diverse assessment types and objectives, we can classify these tests into two broad categories: **self-report inventories and projective tests.** Self-report inventories such as the popular Minnesota Multiphasic Personality Inventory (MMPI) require respondents to answer written true-or-false or multiple-choice questions that identify disorders such as depression, hysteria, and paranoia. Projective tests such as

the **Rorschach Inkblot Test** use ambiguous images or other stimuli to uncover unconscious challenges, desires, and fears.

The Myers-Briggs Type Indicator, The Caliper Profile, and StandOut® Strengths Assessment are probably the most popular tests for business and employment sectors. But for the purposes of our ownership discovery process, and because of its simplicity and high level of relevance to over-50 entrepreneurs, we will focus on the findings of the **OVER-50 ENTREPRENEURIAL ASSESSMENT Q9®.**

Relatively new to the marketplace, the OVER-50 ENTREPRENEURIAL ASSESSMENTQ9® uses comprehensive algorithms to evaluate a respondent's passions, skills, experiences, personality traits, and strengths and weaknesses. It distinguishes itself from other personality assessments by identifying characteristics that skew toward **the context of ownership rather than employment**. You're not looking for a job. You're looking to own the whole company. This assessment pays closer attention to the ultimate objective of ownership.

AN IMPRESSIVE VARIETY OF ASSESSMENTS NOW DOMINATE THE INDUSTRY.

- The Caliper Profile

- The Myer-Briggs Type Indicator

- The Hogan Personality Inventory (HPI)

- StandOut® Strengths Assessment

- The DiSC Behavior Inventory

- Minnesota Multiphasic Personality Inventory

- Over-50 Entrepreneurial AssessmentQ9®

- The Birkman Method

- True Colours

- The Eysenck Personality Inventory

- Hogan Motive, Values and Preferences Inventory (MPVI)

- Keirsey Temperament Sorter

- Rorschach Inkblot Test

- WonScore

- 123 Career Test

Let's reach back to an important principle you learned earlier in the book and apply it to this scenario.

You'll remember back in Chapter 2 when we talked about the fallacy of trying to make a meaningful decision by listening to one loud-mouth YouTube influencer? The same principle applies to your selection of assessment options. **One assessment is not enough.** Since many online assessments are free or require a minimal investment to access, it makes good sense to take as many assessment tests as you can. It's similar to getting ten doctors to examine you instead of one. You get a wide range of eyeballs on your problem. If nine out of ten say your tonsils need to come, it's probably a good idea to schedule the operation.

Thorough research is not one precise, indisputable, black and white answer. It's an accumulation of independent findings that point in the same direction. If you're in New York and ask a hundred people how to get to California, most of them will point west. They may recommend different roads or modes of transportation. But the bottom line is you need to head west.

Multiple answers don't have to be identical answers. You look out at your audience. Several people are using their official program to fan their faces. A few have pulled out handkerchieves to wipe their sweaty brows. One man just stood up and took off his coat.

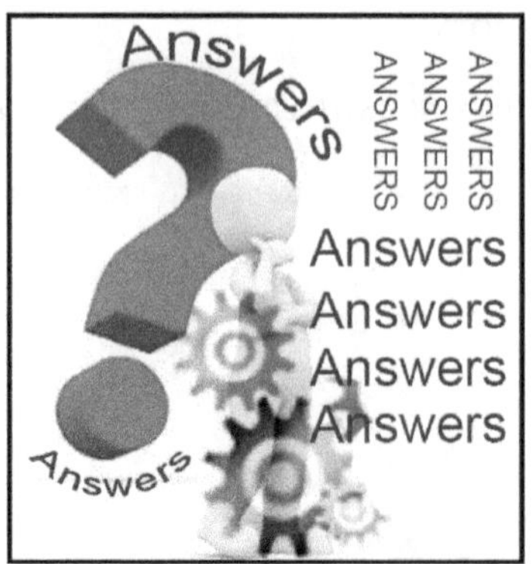

These are not identical answers. But they all point to the same truth. The room is too hot. The anxiety level has heightened. The temperature needs to go down.

Because thousands of people will read this book, take their assessments, and receive their vastly different profile results, there is no way to cover all possibilities. Instead, we will use one simplified, hypothetical Q9 assessment to demonstrate how you should dissect and extrapolate your specific results.

(A) Finish this chapter. Read every word.

(B) Familiarize yourself with the step-by-step discovery process.

(C) Take your series of online assessments. Without paying a psychoanalyst $300 an hour, find out who you really are.

(D) Choose a potential business niche that fits your true passion. Climb into the ring with the SMACKDOWN bruisers to see if your "niche fit" has a fighting chance.

ASSESSMENT PROTOCOL

Set your mind to no less than five assessments. (Yes, five ... unless you would rather take the shortcut and pay a psychoanalyst $300 an hour to tell you what these assessments are going to tell you.) Expect these assessments to be similar in structure, but different in nuances and emphasis. Some will attempt to determine if you're crazy. Starting a business with limited capital, while braving the headwinds of a raging pandemic, we already know the answer. Other assessments will attempt to determine if you are assertive, hopeful, and courageous. Starting a business with limited capital, while braving the headwinds of a raging pandemic, we already know the answer.

For the sake of simplicity, most assessments go out of their way to categorize, summarize, and personalize their results. Earlier in this chapter, we used a similar technique with Fred. You won't forget him or his inclinations. The characteristics become more vivid when associated with a name, color, or character.

Should you decide to take **The Birkman Method** assessment, which focuses on such measurements as communication style and triggers for stress, the nomenclature or system of personality profiles will look like this:

<table>
<tr>
<td>DOER

RED is the Birkman color for people who prefer to make quick decisions and get results. Reds are direct, action-oriented, and give full attention to the task at hand. Reds enjoy building and working with their hands...</td>
<td>COMMUNICATOR

GREEN is the Birkman color for people with a strong desire to communicate and work with people. Every time you see a Green, they are selling, persuading, promoting, motivating, counseling, teaching...</td>
<td>ANALYZER

YELLOW is the Birkman color for people who love working with processes, details, definitions and rules. Yellows enjoy doing careful and detailed calculations, scheduling, record-keeping...</td>
<td>THINKER

BLUE is the Birkman color for the concept and idea person. Blues love innovation, being creative and long-term planning. They enjoy abstract thinking and discovering fresh ways to solve problems...</td>
</tr>
</table>

The Myers–Briggs Type Indicator (MBTI), developed by Isabel Briggs Myers and her mother Katharine Briggs during the Second World War, is probably the most well-known assessment in the industry. Based in part on Carl Jung's Psychological Types theories, it attempts to measure differing psychological preferences in the way people perceive the world and make decisions.

Results are assigned to four categories: [introversion vs extraversion], [sensing vs intuition], [thinking vs feeling], [judging vs perceiving]. Clinical researchers take one letter from each category to produce a four-letter test result, such as "ISTJ" or "ENFP".

Here is an example:

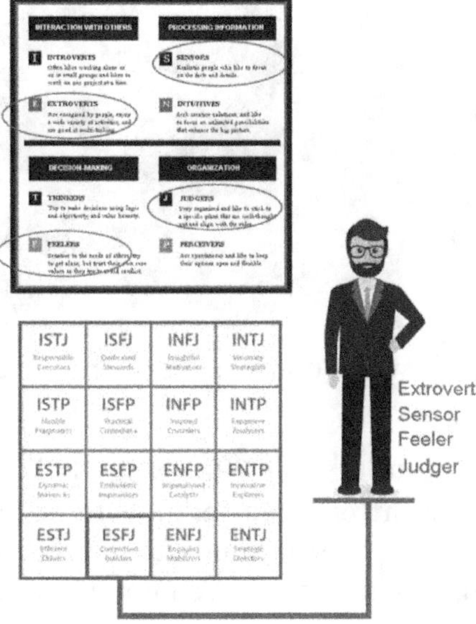

The **Myers–Briggs Type Indicator (MBTI)** offers sixteen different combinations of personality profiles. You might have excellent people skills and love to sell. But if you're careless with details and numbers, the assessment will steer you away from opening up a used car lot or pursuing a career in finance. Millions of people have taken the test and discovered characteristics about themselves they had not previously understood. It's definitely worth your time.

During this home stretch, we will draw most of our inspiration from profiling examples created by the **OVER-50 ENTREPRENEURIAL ASSESSMENTQ9®.** It is similar in structure to the other previously mentioned assessments, but skews heavily toward business ownership.

For instance, some assessments were originally designed to provide career guidance and organizational compatibility keys. They ask respondents the standard questions like, **"describe your ideal supervisor" or "how do you plan to fit into our glorious corporation" or "where do you see yourself in five years?"**

For (over-50) you, these types of questions are a waste of your time. YOU will be the ideal supervisor. YOU will own the company. And if things go poorly, five years from now, if they 

want to have a follow-up conversation, they can find you in the local cemetery.

What the OVER-50 ENTREPRENEURIAL ASSESSMENTQ9® does is prioritize your **entrepreneurial objectives**, query the values that are most important at this stage in your life, and super-charge your lift-off down your short runway to success. You don't have time to fool around with matters relating to corporate bureaucracy and who should get the parking spot closest to the door. You need every ounce of entrepreneur insight you can get.

The OVER-50 ENTREPRENEURIAL ASSESSMENTQ9® offers six consolidated profiles to capture your passions, preferences, and style of decision-making. In this context, the word decision-making is just a simplified way of identifying the manner in which you "perceive" your world. If you perceive everything in black and white (like Fred), you're not going to be a very good art gallery owner. The Q9 test focuses on these kinds of ownership compatibility issues.

Here is one thing to remember about all assessments. If you answer honestly, the results reflect YOU. But YOU are not the same YOU every day of the week. You are influenced by outside drivers or stimuli. Time, environment, and circumstances alter your lens of perception. The test might ask, **"Do you consider yourself to be hopeful or optimistic?"**

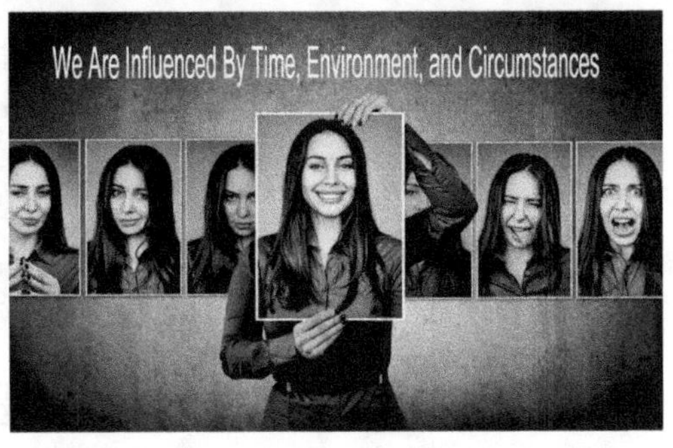

Your answer might be one thing today. But the next day, when you find a note from your fiancé stating he's breaking off the engagement and moving back to London with his old girlfriend, your answer might change to something else.

Try to take your assessments without disruptive cataclysms hanging over your head. Give your core processing unit time to resurface. Life is full of peaks and valleys. Take a deep breath and allow the many fragments of YOU to fall back into place.

Let's look at the six profiles offered by the OVER-50 ENTREPRENEURIAL ASSESSMENTQ9®:

"We need solutions. There's a better way. Let's get it done, no excuses, no sobbing over spilled milk."

COMMANDER///CRUSADERS are intelligent, ambitious, and highly focused on the task at hand. They value facts, logic, and concrete data over emotional responses and intuitive (feeler) decision-making. They speak clearly and directly, and expect the same exchanges of verbal and written clarity from others around them. Their analytical minds possess an instinctive ability to understand complex ideas and theories. This ability to break down complexities is most valuable in their quest to improve the world around them. They study the past to identify patterns they can apply to the present to change the future. The future and its infinite possibilities is where their minds are most engaged.

Their greatest weakness is their lack of emotional intelligence. They find it difficult to work with emotionally driven people or people who try to use guilt to gain favor or manipulate perception. Passive-aggressive behavior is not only a waste of their time, but insulting to their desire to fix what's wrong. Because of their instinctive ability to recognize flaws and find solutions, the emotional impact of discarding someone else's idea and concentrating on a more proficient way of getting things done often creates resentment by collaborators rather than praise (JFK vs the Joint Chiefs).

We need to place an asterisk here.****

In reality, there are two types of COMMANDER/// CRUSADERS. We will refer to the second type as COMMANDER ///CRUSADERS (E). An "E" type is basically the same, but has sought specific training to heighten his or her emotional (E) sensitivity. These "E" types have come to recognize the downside of operating, predominantly, out of their (get out of my way) Intellectual dimension.

These evolved Bill Gates types have compensated for their natural tendency to create emotional friction in the work environment by adding a sensitivity alarm to their normal interactions. They have opened up to learning more effective "people" techniques. With this new human matrix in their arsenal, they offend less and inspire more, which contributes to the enhanced proficiency they coveted all along.

Intelligent
Systematic
Intelligent
Ambitious
Self-confident
Futuristic
Systematic
Judgmental
Facts/Logic First
Demands Loyalty
Seeks Closure
Knows
Patterns
Emotional Deficit
Charismatic
Strategic
Innovator
Verbal Expertise

"We're not competing. We're in this together. Let's support each other and leave no one behind."

SUPPORTER ///ENABLERS (SEs) are, by nature, perpetual supporters and nurturers. Their caretaking instincts direct them to put others first. They are generous with their time and possessions, and share without being asked. They appear almost clairvoyant in their ability to detect disharmony and mental stress in others. This is due to their keen observation of social signals ... body language, facial expressions, and voice inflections ... of everyone in the room. The refrigerator is constantly being refilled on their watch. They see the empty corners and know when supplies are running low.

Because they are feelers, their perceptions and ideas are determined by intuition which may or may not be a valid basis for understanding. They draw conclusions through the relationships they have with people in their group or tribe. Rather than read a research report about population preferences, they prefer to observe the direct interactions of those around them to reach a conclusion. They desire to see and feel the answers that go beyond graphs, charts, and statistics on the page. With this method of decision-making, confirmation bias often creeps in to support their wishful thinking for a better world. They see hope where others do not, and offer encouragement in the darkest of times. They see connections and broken links very clearly. But to avoid intimidating others, they have learned over time to conceal their vivid comprehension of inconsistencies and flaws.

No matter the assignment or obligation, SEs tend to over deliver. If they promise to bring a cake to the party, they are going to bring ice cream too. This trait is driven by a twofold compulsion. SEs need to be validated by others. The positive emotional exchange energizes them with a sense of purpose and fulfillment. Secondly, SEs harbor a strong aversion to disappointing anyone else. They remember people facts like birthdays and anniversaries because, to overlook or forget things that are important to others, is an unforgivable offense by anyone claiming to care genuinely for the people around them.

At the core of their desire to promote harmony and cooperation is their worldview of connectivity. They look at the world through a web of external linkage that affects everyone, everywhere. If they help a single person in society, the tiniest gesture has a domino effect, helping society as a whole, and ultimately, finding its way back to them. Karma, as some call it, is an old belief, passed down through the ages and indicative of the SEs' attachment to old things. You would expect to find a grandfather clock in their home before you would a fancy new computer. For them, older things have meaning and capture the human side of our existence.

Entrepreneurs who fit this profile are often labeled as "soft bosses". They hate to confront employees, even when these employees have demonstrated negligence and justify a reprimand or dismissal. On their subconscious level, the act symbolizes the replacement of harmony with potential conflict. SEs need strong general managers who can compensate for these personality-driven weaknesses.

"I love what I do. I take great pride in what I do. And I can't do something halfway, three-quarters, nine-tenths. If I'm going to do something, I go all the way." — Tom Cruise

STRUCTURED///OVERSEERS are firm, decisive, organized, and thrive in a world of scheduled, predictable activities. They are frank, though not always tactful, and can be critical without always knowing how they affect other people. They possess a strong work ethic, are willing to make sacrifices to accomplish a stated goal, and strive to always be right. Because of their dedication, they tend to have unreasonable expectations of others who share responsibility for completing a task.

These Dick Cheney/Madeleine Albright types seek to preserve tradition and observe rules. They take deadlines very seriously and are easily unraveled by team members who lack punctuality, disrespect authority, and operate outside the established framework of procedures to accomplish a given task. The rules are there for a reason. One broken rule can set off a costly chain reaction.

STRUCTURED///OVERSEERS quickly identify inconsistencies and are willing to verbalize their findings in unmitigated terms. This is because they live in a world of black and white and do not easily read between the lines, nor desire to communicate through nuances or symbolic language. This often results in team members perceiving them as insensitive and overly critical. Their true feelings of care and empathy seldom rise above the noise of conflict.

They criticize but have difficulty receiving criticism from others. This is because they perceive it as an unjustified attack upon their hard work and commitment to excellence. They are there in the heat of the battle when one else is around. They expect people to see their heart and know their intent. This is a hidden

Hardworking
Assertive
Rigid
Organized
Confident
Analytical
Outspoken
Curious
Direct/Frank
Thick-skinned
Competitive
Goal-oriented
Impersonal
Perfectionist
Controlling
Determined
Intense
Responsible

frustration that **STRUCTURED///OVERSEERS** seldom express, even to their small circle of friends.

When it comes to friends and relationships, STRUCTURED ///OVERSEERS define love as being synonymous with agreement and support. This narrow definition limits the number of individuals allowed into their friendship circle, in that, their personalities are nourished by recognition and appreciation, not challenges to their rigid beliefs.

Because of their deep-rooted value system and finely tuned perception of morality, STRUCTURED///OVERSEERS desire deep, philosophical conversations. They see more shallow forms of social interaction as a waste of time. They are usually voracious readers and want to share their knowledge and get feedback from other intellectual minds. The most rewarding aspect of this exercise is finding shared values and like-minded individuals that validate their opinions and beliefs.

As business owners, they are generally clock-watchers who equate timeliness to a worker's dedication to the company. Sometimes, especially among young millennial workers, this rigid approach is perceived as unnecessary and petty. These workers prefer a more flexible environment, and quickly move on.

"I'm a problem-solver. I let my work do the talking."

TECHNICAL///CRAFTSMAN

Charles Darwin and Albert Einstein are well-known examples of the TECHNICAL///CRAFTSMAN profile. They are easygoing, non-confrontational, no-nonsense, awkwardly social individuals with complex personalities and a natural gift for problem-solving.

Their secret for success is not easily unraveled. Because they are highly skilled operators of mechanical and technical tools, an outside observer might label them computer nerds or home gadget gurus on steroids. In fact, their highly inquisitive minds are working much harder than their greasy hands, employing theoretical and abstract possibilities to figure out the real world. TECHNICAL ///CRAFTSMEN are not limited by tradition or protocol or past solutions that so-called experts have endorsed. They are independent thinkers who seek out-of-the-box solutions that change the whole game.

Because they are intensely driven innovators, they do not like rigid rules. Try going in to tell Bill Gates he needs to take an early lunch. They tend to apply their own logical litmus test to a 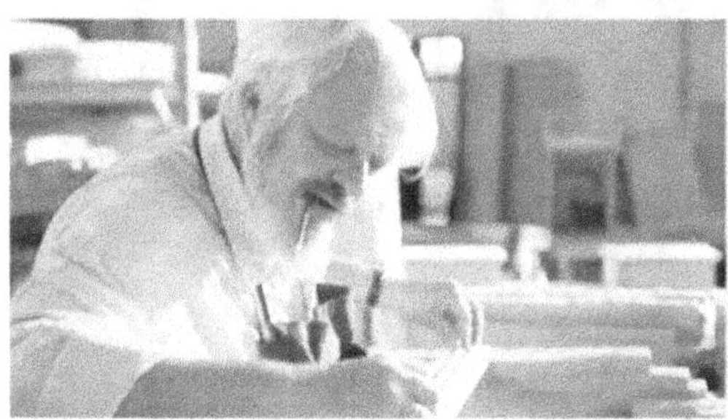 rule or procedure, and if the underlying premise doesn't make sense, they simply disregard it. They are adept problem-solvers who want to cut to the chase, find the solution, and not be inhibited by bureaucracy or BS. And if, in the eyes of their managers, their superior contribution doesn't justify their self-exemption from petty rule, they simply move on.

TECHNICAL///CRAFTSMEN almost always lack soft skills and seldom appreciate the importance of social interaction. They prefer objects, hardware, and systems over people. They hold a curious soft-spot in their hearts for robots and AI. They may not be loners. But their circle of friends is invariably small, and most often, limited to like-minded adventurers in the technical, scientific, experimentation world.

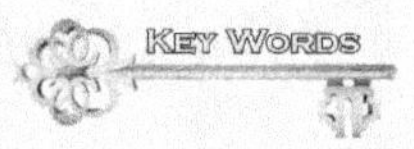

Adaptable
Technical
Logical
Analytical
Unemotional
Problem-solver
Self-reliant
Hands-on
Thorough
Private
Independent
Flexible
Impersonal
Handy
Objective

"I love being in the spotlight and watching others enjoy my gift of entertainment. No problems, no conflicts, or I'll be on my way."

PERFORMER ///PROMOTER

Ronald Reagan, Magic Johnson, Vince McMahon, and Oprah Winfrey are well-known examples of the PERFORMER ///PROMOTER (PPs) profile. They are fun-loving, outgoing, adventurous individuals who love people and have a way of making them love back. They are entertainers by nature, usually the life of the party, with an arsenal of experiences to share, and a warm, receptive ear, eager to take in the unique experiences of others.

PPs are primarily guided by their heightened senses (Extraverted Sensing) which allow them to operate in the moment, in real time, with the rest of the world. They seldom overlook a shift in the mood of the crowd or the subtleties of body language and voice inflections by key players in the room. To say they rely, exclusively, upon their five senses to extract reality from their surrounding world would be an understatement. PPs amplify

their awareness of reality by adding to their arsenal a keenly intuitive sense of time and payoff. They know exactly when the Calvary should come riding in to save the day.

This unique, spontaneous ability to improvise in real time serves as a critical component in shaping their personality. PPs thrive on harmonious interaction with others without the predictability of a plan. They are highly stimulated, living on the edge, giving and receiving instant gratification, and shielded from the uncertainty of the future. No one can hurt them. In these crowd-pleasing, communal moments of ecstasy, no one really wants to hurt them. They seek to preserve this harmonious existence at (almost) any cost.

Spontaneous
Outgoing
Risk-taking
Thick-skinned
Enthusiastic
Assertive
Sensation-loving
Highly sociable
Persuasive
Gregarious
Lively
Informal
Creative
Flexible

There is a downside to this behavior. The premium value placed on "right now" can lead to overindulgence in sensual pleasures and a tendency to avoid the future altogether. PPs dread planning, or doing taxes, or saving money for a rainy day, money that could go to a shiny new Rolex or Louis Vuitton Limited Edition designer bag ... RIGHT NOW. **Desiring to keep their options open, and paranoid of what the future might bring, they procrastinate about future decisions, no matter how inconsequential they might be.**

PERFORMER///PROMOTERS are easily bored by long-term relationships. The excitement, energy, and emotional rush of a new, unpredictable, right-now thing becomes bogged down in the mundane effort to preserve the old thing that the new thing has become. A dozen red roses on Valentine's Day were just fine two years ago. But now, he's walking through the door with the same roses on the same day from the same store with the same goofy smile on his face. Borrrrring!!!

Eventually, there is a crossover in priorities that seduces PPs to sacrifice their inner convictions for a more conventional return ... marriage, children, a paid mortgage. These sacrifices, however, must produce a strong counter-balance in happiness to suppress the PPs deep-seated urge for visceral experience with no future strings attached. Without heavy doses of spontaneity and highly sensual intervention, the divorce lawyers almost always win this fight. The PPs' subconscious mind exaggerates the long-lost sensual experiences still waiting on the mountaintop. The PP crosses back over in search of the illusive life he or she has sacrificially pushed aside.

We need to place another asterisk here.****

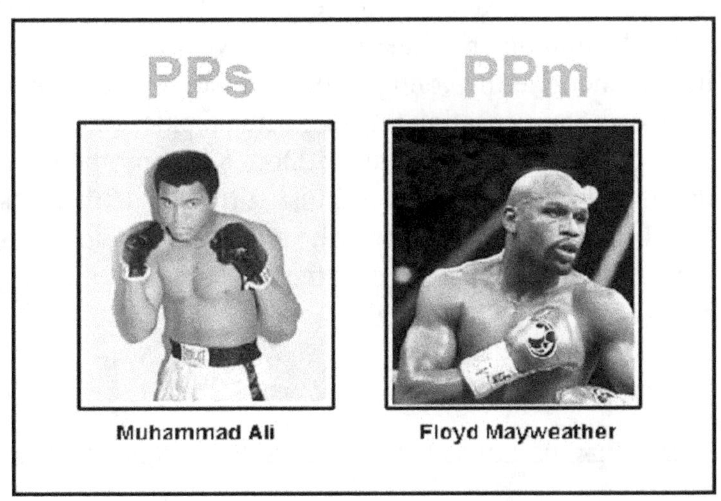

As in the case of the COMMANDER /// CRUSADER, there are two types of **PERFORMER /// PROMOTERS.** We will refer to the second type as **PERFORMER///PROMOTERS** (PPm). With the "M" type **(manager type),** you should think of Oprah Winfrey or Martha Stewart. They are basically the same visceral experimenters and commanders of the spotlight as PPs. However, these PPm personalities such as film director, producer, and actor Ronald

Ronald William Howard

William Howard operate predominantly out of their Intellectual dimension. They are more analytical, more attuned to future payoffs than the emotional rewards of "right now". They seek outside financial advisors, personal trainers, and other forms of restraint to rain in their reckless indulgences. Jay Leno owns 169 cars and 117 motorbikes. MC Hammer burned through $78 million in three years. Someone has to be there to prevent these natural instincts from taking over.

Nothing here should rule out **PERFORMER/// PROMOTERS** as capable entrepreneurs. They are pragmatic, realistic, quick-thinking risk-takers who have the ability to draw people in and energize the contributions of everyone on board. The key to success is compensating for their often reckless extravagance. As over-50 owners who operate as Don King promoters rather than Muhammad Ali fighters, they must surround themselves with level-headed, consciences enablers who stick to plans and watch the bottom line. A PPs that relies on the "feeling" method of perception.

"What would the world be like if everyone decided to do their part, to do the right thing. Dream big. Change the world."

CREATIVE///DREAMER

Pablo Picasso, Eleanor Roosevelt, Steven Spielberg, Martin Luther King Jr, John Lennon, and Wolfgang Mozart are well-known examples of the CREATIVE///DREAMER (CD) profile. **They are highly creative individuals with passionate ideals about a better life, a better world, and a better coexistence among all human beings, no matter their background, status, culture or ethnicity.** They are free-thinkers with an inclination to live and let live. They process information through their senses and rely less on hard data, and more on how they feel inside (Introverted feeling), that is to say, how the options line up with their personal convictions.

They are inspired by unusual patterns and aesthetically pleasing colors, and seek out beauty in their surroundings. If they cannot find it, they will create it, right down to the spacing of cookie dough on a baking sheet before it goes into the oven. They seldom forgo an opportunity to express their creative nature because birthing new ideas and concepts is their way of offering an alternative to the corrupted ways of old and striking a blow against man's inhumanity to mankind.

They are great pet owners and have trouble killing a spider on the wall. They prefer not to eat meat because they have difficulty disassociating the sense of guilt that accompanies the animal's death. They apologize for the rudeness of others, even though they did not take part in the inhospitable conduct.

CDs dream big because their yearning for free expression places no limitations on human potential and possibilities. They see the human experience as being so much more than human. They see and feel our connection with each other as part of an even greater connection with the universe.

Introspective
Idealistic
Caring
Empathetic
Sensitive
Private
Selfless
Abstract
Gentle
Future-focused
Peace-loving
Encouraging
Committed
Purposeful
Intuitive
Passionate
Values-oriented

Over-50 CDs probably took part in some kind of protest march in their lifetime, because sitting around, doing nothing was not an option their convictions would allow. In their many private moments, they spend a great deal of time thinking about the ways individuals could make a difference if they commit themselves to a worthwhile purpose or goal. This is important because, without a compelling purpose, CDs are reluctant to participate, resent being bullied or coerced into "group think", and will ultimately pull away from the noise and madness of the crowd.

As long as the task does not go against their inner convictions, CDs are generally quiet and cooperative. Because they listen well, they make good counselors and therapists. **They help others bring out their true feelings,** but are quite reluctant to share their own. This is a learned defensive mechanism, developed over time, after realizing expressing their big dreams and deep convictions puts them at odds with the rest of the world. Most people are afraid to dream.

In addition, stakeholders demand more than dreams. They want logic and rationale to justify potential projects. Because of the CDs' esoteric, free-thinking nature, **they dread being pulled into any universe cluttered with logic and facts.** When asked to explain their ideas in the context of logistics and hard evidence, they tend to stumble.

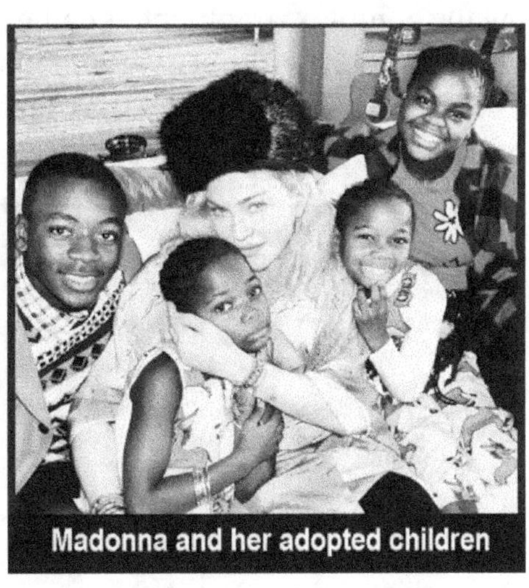

Because **CREATIVE///DREAMERS** (such as bestselling author J. K. Rowling) possess superior creative skills, they can change an entire industry. As entrepreneurs, their gift is the product. They surround themselves with branding and marketing experts, financial advisors, and legal counsel. They succeed because the team succeeds. The need for these CDs to spend time alone is never an issue because there is always someone out in the forefront, pushing the envelope.

As an over-50 entrepreneur, you still have that unique creative spark in your DNA. Though, many years of corporate bureaucracy may have watered it down, it never totally dies. You still ask deep questions. The bold ideas still come to you. You simply have to muster the courage to act on them.

DREAM BIG!!!

STEP 2: USE YOUR ENLIGHTENED IDENTITY TO FINALIZE YOUR GOLDEN CIRCLE.

We talked about three critical steps to nail this selection process to the wall. **The first step is to "identify you".** Your protective subconscious mind, which strives to keep things simple, positive, and predisposed toward a good night's sleep, presents you with that familiar face in the mirror. But now, you know better. You know the complex, fragmented being you really are. **Once you have completed your online assessments, you will begin to unravel the hidden building blocks that foster your uniqueness and give value to your place in the cosmos.**

After fifty-plus years, if there's one thing you should know, it is that you are different and wonderfully made, and never intended to be a duplicate of anyone else.

Remember to follow this chapter's step-by-step logistics. Read the entire chapter, paying close attention to the painstaking research applied to each potential option. The designated SUPPORTER/// ENABLER profile example leaves no stone unturned. In your personal market quest, you shouldn't either. Complete your online assessments. Then come back to this chapter with a fully enlightened profile, really to take on the SMACKDOWN bruisers.

Meet Kristine, Dallas, Texas

To construct our master example, the one you will follow once you have your personal assessment results in hand, we'll need to do a bit of improvising. We will borrow one of the **OVER-50 ENTREPRENEURIAL ASSESSMENTQ9®** assessment profiles, add some work history, and move forward from there.

For the purposes of our example, and to keep things simple, let's use the **SUPPORTER///ENABLER** profile. It would be advisable to go back to review the entire profile. But to keep things moving along, we will summarize the basic traits and keywords associated with this personality type. With our hypothetical work history attached to the profile, we can begin our *(what we like / what we do well) Golden Circle* match.

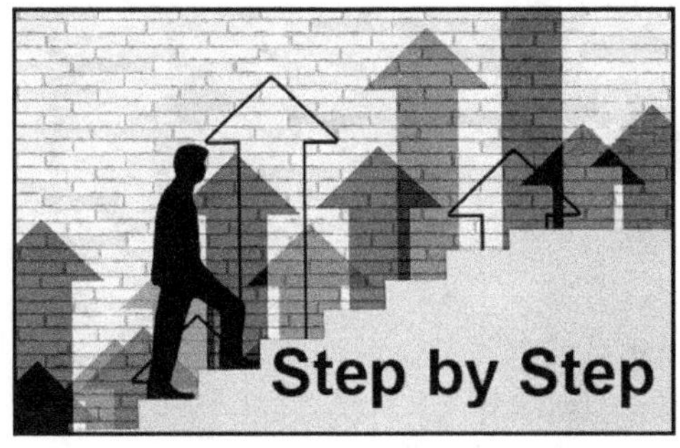

Don't overthink the process. You're identifying YOU, selecting a compatible business niche, testing the viability of that niche against the six highly disruptive market forces, and finally, deciding without bias or sentimental attachment, whether to go forward or start your search all over again.

BASIC TRAITS OF KRISTINE'S SUPPORTER/// ENABLER PROFILE

♦ Instinctive caretaker and nurturer that puts other people first.

♦ Generous with her most prized possessions.

♦ The ability to detect disharmony and mental stress in others.

♦ Keen observation of social signals such as body language, facial expressions, and voice inflections.

♦ To avoid intimidating others, has learned to conceal her vivid comprehension of inconsistencies and flaws.

♦ Very pragmatic and will do what it takes to get the job done.

♦ Rather than read a research report, she prefers to observe the direct interactions of those around her to reach a conclusion.

♦ Sees hope where others don't, and offers encouragement in the darkest of times.

♦ Receives a sense of purpose and fulfillment by over-delivering on all promises and assignments.

Nurturing
Selfless
Observant
Service-oriented
Kind
Humorous
Sensitive
Traditional
Loyal
Protective
Disciplined
Empathetic
Compassionate
Responsible
Responsive

♦ Harbors a strong aversion to disappointing anyone else.

♦ Learns best when the subject matter is related to or focused on people.

♦ Believes the tiniest gesture has a domino effect, helping society as a whole.

♦ Often find herself in the role of motivating and counseling.

♦ Hates to confront employees, even when employees have demonstrated negligence and justify a reprimand or dismissal.

♦ Needs a strong general manager who can compensate for personality-driven weaknesses.

WORK HISTORY OVERVIEW

Dentist Office Receptionist

Nurse Assistant

Medical Records Clerk

Licensed Practical Nurses (LPNs)

Clinical Nurse Lead Supervisor

As you can see, we added Kristine's basic work history. She has spent most of her life in the medical industry, which fits quite well with her nurturing, service-oriented profile. **Even if,** over the years, she had deviated a few times from the beaten path to work as a pizza cook or real estate broker or transportation dispatcher,

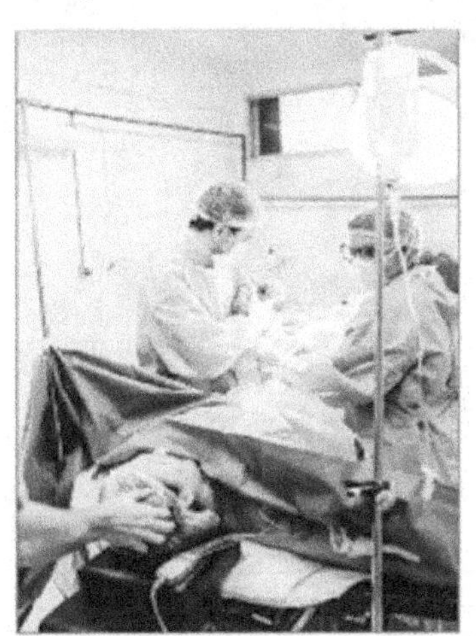

her core competencies are still in the medical field.

When you look at "your" work history and "your" assessment results, the two may not be a perfect match. **Because, in those early years, you were a bit adventurous and unfulfilled, and nothing synchronized with your innermost convictions, you may have jumped around from industry to industry, profession to profession**. This is not unusual for an entrepreneur trying to find a place in which he or she might happily work for someone else. It's possible to find a needle in a haystack, but highly improbable. There aren't that many companies like Google or Apple, looking for team members with entrepreneurial instincts. Better you shut up and follow instructions.

The good thing is that all of your diverse experiences are about to pay off. As you embark upon your entrepreneurial journey, you will find that all of the dots line up. All of the previous experiences will contribute to your success in their own unique way.

With the critical components in place, let's set up Kristine's *Golden Circle* and see what happens.

KRISTINE'S GOLDEN CIRCLE

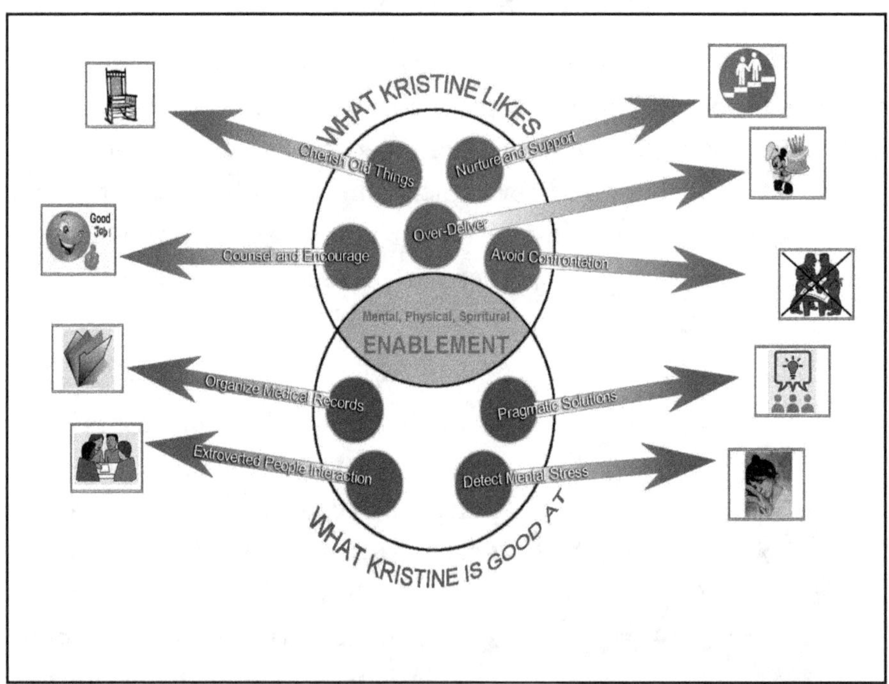

MENTAL, PHYSICAL, SPIRITUAL ENABLEMENT

According to all of the assessment results and cumulative profile data, Kristine should pursue an entrepreneurial career in the field of mental, physical, and spiritual enablement. This latitude of choices may appear broad at first. But in reality, the targeted cluster of options is nothing less than pure gold.

 ...

Let's stop right here and give our brain a breather. We've covered a lot of ground. Nothing we've covered or plan to cover is overwhelming.

Think of it this way. We have to identify the plane, confirm the credentials and experience of the pilot, designate a specific runway, make sure there are no mean-spirited bruisers dumping trash and debris on the runway to impede our takeoff ... and then blast off into the wild blue yonder!

Kristine is our test pilot. Her *Golden Circle* has revealed her "likes" and what she "naturally" does well. Her online assessments have confirmed her personality type. **She is at her best when helping and supporting others.** Her work experience reflects the same inclinations.

Now it's time for her to choose a niche, get past the bruisers, and launch her business.

Understand. At this stage in the process, the SMACKDOWN bruisers are on paper, NOT in a live 1985 New Coke market test, draining her cash. We are testing with decision-making tools and sophisticated algorithms, NOT hard-earned cash. She will use the knowledge from previous chapters to assign probabilities for success or failure. The bruisers will try to stop her before she jumps into the market like most poorly-mentored, research-LESS rookies and goes broke.

Got It? Less GO!!!

Knowledge is pure gold...

Let's say you recently purchased a brand new white Toyota Camry. In the last few weeks, you have seen at least 20 white Camry's zipping down the highway. Did everyone go out and buy a white Camry when you did?

Obviously not. According to the laws of probability, there has been no increase in the number of white Camry's around you. You just hadn't noticed before. Psychologists call this the **Baader-Meinhof phenomenon, more commonly, the frequency illusion.** Now that your brain has associated you with your new car, it will alert you when it sees another white Camry, even if it's a different year and model number (Le vs XLe).

When you declare your intentions to start a new business, it appears the entire world is listening. You begin to receive business opportunities in the mail. Salespeople call you out of the blue, offering to help you become financially independent through ownership of your own franchise or multi-level sales team. Your LinkedIn box fills up with entrepreneurial offers. Every YouTube guru from here to China interrupts your video viewing with a free class about making millions, owning your own revolutionary, ten-step online business. Just one more seat left.

This is the Baader-Meinhof phenomenon at its best. If you have not done your assessments; if you don't know who you are and where your greatest potential for success lies, you might easily dive down one of these incompatible rabbit holes, wasting time and money on dreams that will never be fulfilled.

The same holds true with friends and relatives. Once you publicly declare your intentions to start a new business, your friends will separate into two groups. The first group will spend a great deal of time trying to discourage you from embarking upon such a risky, costly, potentially embarrassing journey. The second group will spend a great deal of time offering ownership suggestions, and in some cases, setting you up with contacts that have made millions in one industry or another.

Both groups care about you and mean no disrespect. But if you've done your self-assessments and know the direction in which you should head, it doesn't really matter if local trucking companies are making millions, or Chick-fil-A franchises are accepting applications in your area, or solar panel

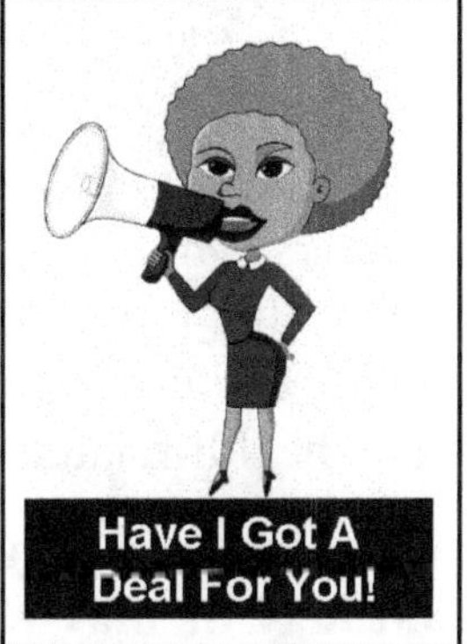

distribution is bursting through the roof. You know what you are made of. You know where you belong. **The limited vantage point upon which their suggestions are based is sincere, but driven (almost exclusively) by profit potential.** YOU see the full picture ... your passions, your personality traits, your strengths and weakness, your core employment competencies developed over many years. You see YOUR light at the end of the tunnel. You are NOT an unmentored research-LESS rookie. You're holding pure gold.

Let's walk through Kristine's Golden Circle to understand the fundamentals of her profile recommendations.

1. She loves people. (Extroverted feeling) (Emotional dimension). This is huge, the entryway to a number of "people-oriented" opportunities to which Fred will not have privy. Kristine not only loves being around people, but possesses an instinctive inclination to nurture them and put them first. She developed her initial people skills as a receptionist at a large dentist office ... lots of traffic, lots of irritated customers, lots of face-to-face crisis management. Her soothing personality made her an excellent fit for the position. She carried forward those skills throughout her career.

2. She is keenly attuned to social signals such as body language, facial expressions, and voice inflections (Intuitive sensing). She has the ability to detect disharmony and mental stress in others. This is a key attribute among counselors, psychoanalysts, and health professionals in general. Her many years in nursing solidified these valuable skills that are key social competencies in many health-related venues.

3. She is very flexible and can engineer pragmatic solutions that may or may not be in the procedure manual. As a Clinical Nurse Supervisor for so many years, she learned to compensate for the long hours and shortage of personnel, especially during the evening shifts. Sometimes, she would allow her nurses to take a nap for a couple of hours to recharge their batteries. Meanwhile, she would make the rounds for them. They were still on the clock, asleep. For two hours, she was both a supervisor and a replacement nurse, carrying out their duties. Unlike other supervisors, she NEVER had an open shift. People were always willing to come in and work for her (crawl out of bed on their day off if necessary) because they knew she had their backs.

Consider the **STRUCTURED///OVERSEER** in this position. **"A rule is a rule.** Either come to work, ready to work. Or don't come in at all."

If you think about it, the **STRUCTURED///OVERSEER** would end up working the entire shift short-handed, by himself, because no one would be willing to help him out. HOWEVER, the integrity of the rules (the most important thing to him) would remain in place. Rules are there for a reason.

Kristine is "people-savvy" and knows how to create unconventional options to get things done.

4. She is good with records and numbers. Her years as a Medical Records Clerk enhanced her knowledge of record-keeping and systems organization. In addition, she learned that precise measurements of patient medications and timetables associated with all treatments could mean the difference between life and death. Computers are not her first love. But she can aptly navigate the processing software for medical coding and government billing.

5. No matter the promise or assignment, she has a tendency to over-deliver. Actually, it is a deeply ingrained need to over-deliver. This is good in any business, but especially in people-oriented business services in which the customer's perception of quality service is based on suppliers going the extra mile. She does not want to disappoint people because their happiness energizes her as a human being. This is a self-governing, self-correcting attribute that needs no supervision. No matter the business, this is very, very advantageous for an entrepreneur to possess.

6. She is a stickler for old things. This means she places a great deal of value on older people. As the disproportionately large population of Baby Boomers fades into retirement, the need for eldercare and related products and services grows exponentially. Kristine has both the background, mental aptitude, and personality traits to provide critical services for an expanding, underserved medical market.

We could go on. Many of Kristine's lifelong experiences advocate this "enablement" pathway. This could easily have been a **TECHNICAL///CRAFTSMAN** that loves computers and has been writing code since he was 15, or a **PERFORMER///PROMOTER** that has appeared on stage most of his or her life and now wants to discover new talent to manage and promote. When you bring all of the components together, as we have with Kristine's ownership profile, you begin to see clear patterns and connections, a roadmap forward, pass all of the distractions, to a business niche that's right for YOU.

Self-made millionaire and serial entrepreneur Marcus Lemonis once said,

"If you don't love what you do, then you shouldn't do it."

What he's talking about is the fallacy of relying on money motivation, exclusively. It's a short road to misery. The lure of profit won't get you out of bed each morning. To face the ups and downs of an entrepreneurial lifestyle, you need a sense of engagement and purpose that connects with your very soul.

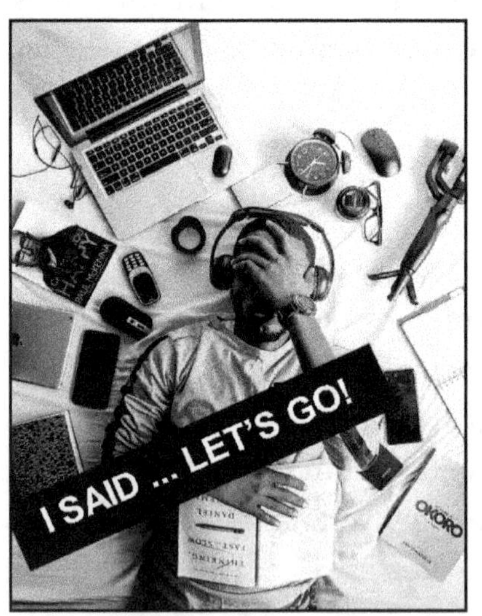

Back in the 70s, the O'Jay's released a hit song entitled **"Livin for the Weekend."** The lyrics resonated with many people who were simply enduring the workweek to make it to the weekend. It was on the weekend, away from the misery of their current job, that they discovered the best version of themselves.

Your business will be no different, perhaps, even amplified in misery, considering the tremendous ownership responsibilities you'll have to endure. Digging in for the sake of profit won't get you there. You're going to crash and burn.

Now that we have a firm handle on Kristine's connection, let's move to the final stage. Let's select an actual business that gives our eager, unselfish, pragmatic, solution-creating SUPPORTER/// ENABLERS a fighting chance for success.

STEP 3: ENTER THE RING WITH YOUR GOLDEN CIRCLE BUSINESS NICHE SELECTION IN HAND. STUMP THE HELL OUT OF THE HIGHLY DISRUPTIVE SMACKDOWN BRUISERS.

In Chapters 3-8, we introduced the six highly disruptive SMACKDOWN opponents that will either enhance your chances for success, or drive your business into the ground.

Let's choose a business that matches Kristine's "enablement" profile, and then climb into the ring with these bruisers to see how things turn out.

Many businesses come to mind ... **from Eldercare to medical supply distribution to In-home therapy to Drug Treatment/Rehabilitation Centers.** But for the purposes of this example, let's keep things simple. Let's focus on one potential opportunity:

Orthotics / Prosthetics Supply Rep

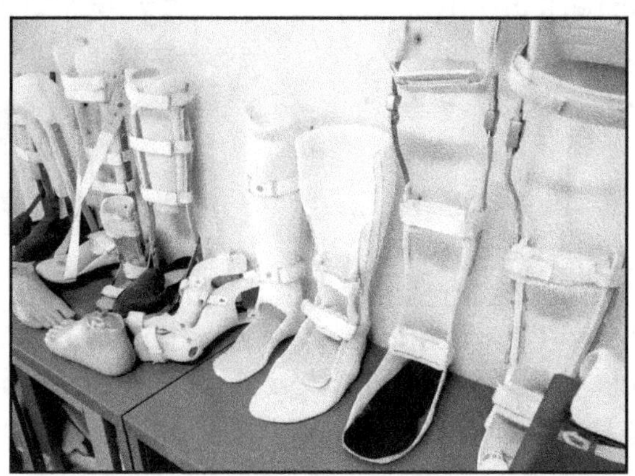

You will remember this entrepreneurial opportunity from Chapter 11. According to The World Health Organization, a Prosthetist / Orthotist is a healthcare professional who provides specialized treatment for patients who need added support for body parts that have been weakened by injury or disease, or by disorders of the nerves, muscles, and bones. An orthotist works under a doctor's orders to design, fabricate, and fit custom-designed bracing to help each patient's mobility and independence. The major difference between orthotics and prosthetics is that, while an orthotic device is used to enhance a person's limb, a prosthetic device is used to replace a limb entirely.

See if you can say the word "Enablement" without seeing Kristine's face, well, her personality profile. She loves to enable others, to move them from where they are, to where they need to be. This is enablement in the purest sense.

She's worked in the medical field, taking orders from physicians, conforming to strict medical specifications and formulas.

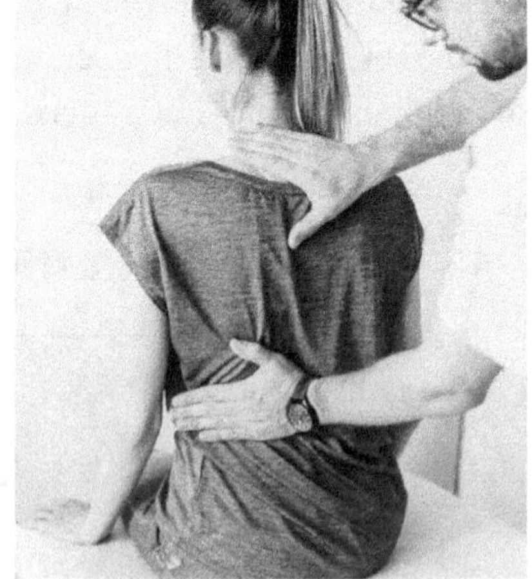

She has a sincere desire to nurture, to protect, to encourage, and to over-delivery on any assignment of which she takes ownership. She loves old things, which can be extrapolated to mean she is comfortable with things and people who are less than perfect, physically or emotionally destabilized, cracked, broken, or fragmented on any level.

Kristine will have to be certified by the American Board for Certification in Orthotics, Prosthetics and Pedorthics or the Board for Orthotist/Prosthetist Certification. After passing the brutal Licensed Practical Nurses (LPNs) examination and earning other clinical certifications, getting certified in Orthotics should be a piece of cake.

Your SMACKDOWN Opponents...

How does this entrepreneurial opportunity fair against our highly disruptive, FRIEND OR FOE SMACKDOWN Opponents? Will these data-driven bruisers agree with Kristine's proposed "niche fit", or stomp her selection into the ground?

Let's walk with Kristine through all six face-offs, one-by-one, just as you will do in your selection process. Let's see if she can start her supply rep business, or whether she needs to go back to the drawing board.

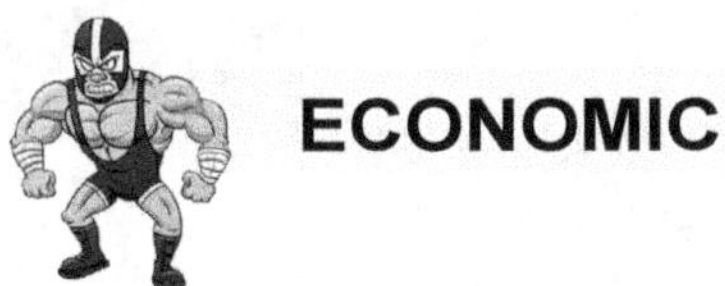

ECONOMIC

We have four basic questions. However, depending on your industry, you may ask many more.

1. What is the primary barrier to entry?

For Kristine, the barrier ratio is a perfect 10/10. Unlike the nuclear plant industry in which only a few highly technical, highly connected, well-financed players may compete, Kristine's only major barrier is certification. Having said that, not every Tom, Dick, or Harry has the skills to get certified. This is not as simple as going down to City Hall to get a health permit to open a fruit stand. Competitors in the Orthotist/Prosthetist industry need "technical" credentials. Not everyone can pass the test. There is a wall to keep most people out, a wall over which Kristine can easily make the leap.

Secondly, the financial outlay to get started is not prohibitive. Working out of her garage, roughly $250,000 to cover 24 months of personal expenses (mortgage, food, utilities, etc) plus business materials and small equipment will allow her to get started. We'll discuss startup capital a bit later.

2. Who's controlling the market?

Stated another way, how many well-known, well-financed, dominant players monopolize the available business? Would you really want to start a cable company to go against Comcast and AT&T? Would you really want to invest in a search company going head-to-head with Google and Bing? In this case, with the exception of maybe Boston Scientific and Stryker Corp., the Orthotics, Prosthetics, and Pedorthics markets are fragmented with several small-to-medium size competitors. For Kristine, the ideal situation would be to rep these larger companies and their products as she perfects her own private niche.

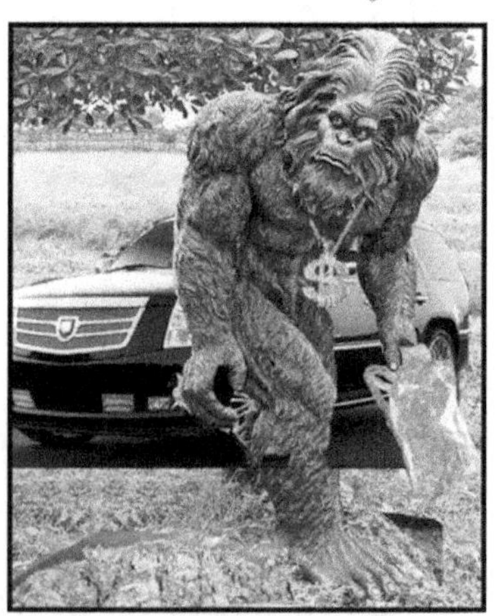

Maintaining a healthy sense of realism, acknowledging several mid-size boutique shops with solid reputations, and territorial reps with which to compete, Kristine's competitive ratio would NOT be a perfect 10/10, but more like a 6/10, which still gives her a fighting chance. She is not going into a brand new virgin market. There are competitors (other reps/ other product innovators) waiting. However, the dynamics of the independent rep system will allow her to compete without going head-to-head with the dominant suppliers.

Think about the legal sale of marijuana. Its growing popularity has changed the United States' perception of the plant from associated criminal activity and dangerous mental inhibitions to a natural health remedy.

In the 2020 elections, New Jersey, Arizona, South Dakota, and Montana became the newest states to legalize marijuana. This addition raised the total number of states with recreational cannabis use from 11 to 15.

You could open a store and become a certified distributor for the big boys in California, Illinois, Michigan, Nevada, Washington and so on, while developing your own private brand. **The lesson here corresponds to the strategic (Safe Island) alliance contracts discussed in Chapter 9.** You enter the market as their distribution partner, not their competitor.

3. What is the expected return on investment?

In Chapter 3, we talked extensively about **Profit Maximization and Shareholder Value Maximization.** Both want to grow the company and increase earnings. Both want the stock price to be an attractive lure for current and future investors. Thus, in the context of this question, we are NOT referring to profit numbers that go into QuickBooks. We are more interested in profit objectives, opportunities, and wiggle room. So let's reframe the question. **Can this business generate enough revenue to meet Kristine's stated objectives as a startup during these early years of trial, error, and experimentation?**

Let's take a look at industry performance in recent years, based on data from a reputable tracker of industry trends and comparative analysis: Stock Analysis on Net.

*SOURCE: Stock Analysis on Net (NYSE:SYK)	Dec 31, 2019	Dec 31, 2018
Example Financial Data - Stryker Corp.		
Gross profit	9,696	8,938
Net sales	14,884	13,601
Profitability Ratio		
Gross profit margin[1]	**65.14%**	**65.72%**

Gross Profit Margins

Industry Leaders

Becton, Dickinson & Co.	47.94%	45.44%
Boston Scientific Corp.	70.98%	71.37%
Danaher Corp.	55.74%	55.83%
Edwards Lifesciences Corp.	74.37%	74.77%
Intuitive Surgical Inc.	69.45%	69.92%
Medtronic PLC	70.04%	69.77%
Thermo Fisher Scientific Inc.	44.35%	44.57%
UnitedHealth Group Inc.	23.19%	23.33%

Based on: 10-K (filing date: 2020-02-06), 10-K (filing date: 2019-02-07), 10-K (filing date: 2018-02-08), 10-K (filing date: 2017-02-09)

In this diagram, we have selected one high-profile leader that offers a general benchmark for the entire pack. Stryker Corp's performance is indicative of the rest of the industry with huge gross profit margins. In this case, the company has reported a hefty 65.72% gross profit in December of 2018 and 65.14% in December of 2019. In other words, these large gross profit margins are no one-year fluke. Boston Scientific is reporting a whopping 70.98%.

Holy, moly, guacamole, McGillicuddy!!!

This is incredible! It certainly beats the 2% markup for which grocery stores scramble to stay afloat. Even Apple, the richest company in the world, which charges an arm and a leg for its products, operates on an average gross margin of 64%. Although the more realistic "operating" margins for this industry range between 18% to 25%, that still offers respectable wiggle room for Kristine to make a decent profit. In this line of business, you are able to charge an arm and a leg and a hip and a joint.

It's important to understand why Kristine should not be preoccupied with the net "operating" profit these companies present to the IRS. **Net operating income is the figure left over after the accountants and tax gurus have picked the bones of the annual operation completely dry.** All of the first-class plane tickets and luxury hotel rooms and lobster dinners at key management pep rallies and executive retreats have left a pitiful skeleton for the Internal Revenue to scavenge. The true worth of the company is hidden behind tons of legal tax breaks and write-offs.

Kristine will be operating out of her garage, the same way Apple and Amazon started out, with a scrupulous eye on savings. Until she reaches the same economics of scale, she won't expect to achieve Stryker's 65.14% gross margin. But even if she does half of that (33%) her first few years, she will be well within the minimum most industries require for sustainability. She has control over the product sectors (general surgery, cardiovascular, bio-surgical, endomechanical, and electrophysiology and vision products) she distributes. The ability to test and pivot from sector to sector is almost unlimited.

In the specialty areas of joint reconstruction, trauma, craniomaxillofacial, spinal surgery, and sports medicine, innovative suppliers are creating new AI-driven products each day. This is a bonus strategic advantage for Kristine. It means no one has a monopoly on knowledge. No one has had time to become an entrenched expert on the latest technology. This gives her company a chance to get in and fight for business on equal footing with everyone else.

4. How much capital to get started?

No battle with the disruptive economic bruisers would be complete without discussing startup capital. The beauty of this niche is you don't need a prohibitive amount. You need good credit, a good bank, and a 24-month round of capital that covers "TWENTY-FOUR MONTHS OF ZERO INCOME. It's going to take time to identify

the most profitable niches, the most popular product lines, and paying customers that are willing to take a chance on a startup.

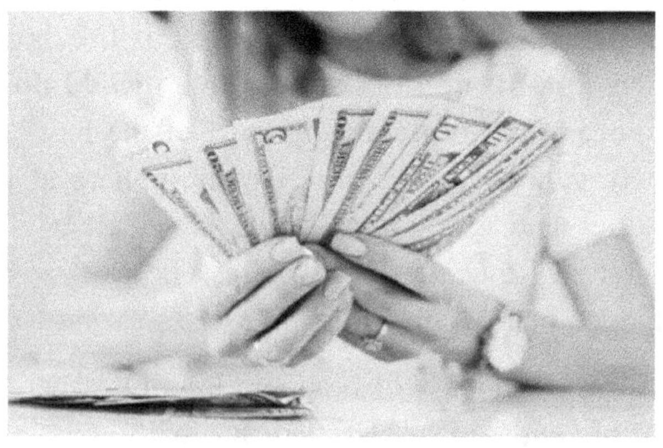

Kristine would do well to set her sights on $250,000 cold cash in the bank, a few credit cards like the Chase Freedom Card and a list of disposable extravagances like the BMW car note and annual Carnival Cruise that she can exchange for back-up cash in the cookie jar. She's going to have to pay accountants, lawyers, insurance brokers, web developers, certification fees, and some kind of customer lead generation company to get her business off the ground. She may outsource the work for a while. But if she plans to build her own unique brand of enablement devices, she is going to have to bring in a full-time technician with experience. The garage will eliminate the cost of office space. But the monthly house mortgage, food, utilities, and other expenses go on.

Being a successful entrepreneur is not easy. But handled with due diligence and a willingness to sacrifice for the long haul, it holds the potential to be the most rewarding adventure Kristine has ever had.

Good News! We have stomped the highly disruptive, money-hungry, economic bruisers into the ground. It's time to move on to round two. Next up is the tricky, razzle-dazzle footwork of demographics. Let's see if Kristine can carve out a promising future before they contaminate it with complex statistical datasets of doom and gloom.

Your SMACKDOWN Opponents...

DEMOGRAPHIC

We have three basic questions.

1. What is the customer profile?

There are three answers to this question. It all depends on the narrow or expanded focus Kristine uses to position her company.

A. There are large international suppliers that need local reps.

B. There are physicians and physical therapists that need special devices for their patients.

C. There are direct patient inquiries from savvy, proactive patients who are not satisfied with their current provider and seek a unique solution that people who do not have Kristine's strong empathy have not bothered to explore.

These three groups will provide payments, partially or fully subsidized by the federal government, based on the patient's insurance provider, state medical policies, and the specific beneficiary restrictions that apply to the condition or injury.

For Kristine, neither of these potential customer levels is out of reach, that is to say, beyond her scope of project management. If, on the other hand, she were selling nuclear rods to nuclear scientists at a nuclear plant, she would require a technical intermediary.

In addition, Kristine has extensive experience in medical records and government medical codes. She can position her devices in compliance with accepted government electronic payment protocols.

2. According to the demographics, is the market growing, stagnant, or in decline?

There is more to this question than meets the eye. We can clearly see that sales volume for the industry's major player is increasing year after year. But the deeper question is, do these figures depend on a demographic profile in decline? Reaching back to our earlier example, if we sold paper checks, sales might be good for now. But the demographic profile of elderly users is dying out. Our core customer is disappearing. It won't be long before our services are no longer needed.

For Kristine, the answer to this question is twofold. The device market is national and the service market is regional. Both markets are declining in one segment and increasing in another segment, all at the same time.

With the official end to the Iraq and Afghanistan Wars, **the number of wounded soldiers coming home with damaged or missing limbs is declining.** As far back as late 2001, this

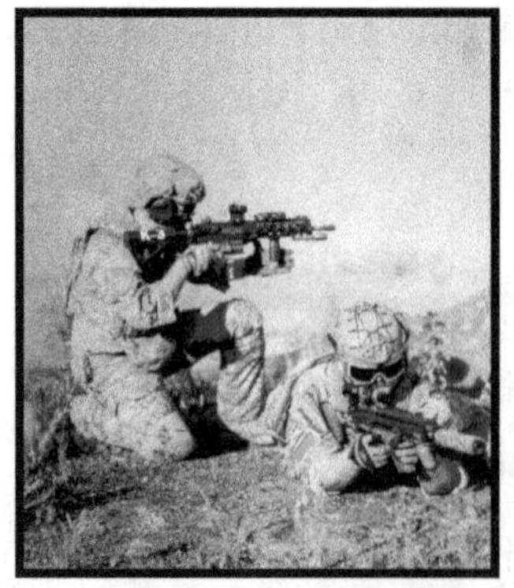

profile of some 980,000 young military men and women, needing replacement parts and enabling devices, was the mainstay of the industry's innovation impetus and R&D spending. However, the surge in older Baby Boomers with multiple levels of health deterioration, bone and joint failures, cancer-driven amputations and other surgeries, mostly caused by Peripheral Vascular Disease and Diabetes, has skyrocketed. The new patient profile is taking precedence over the old.

The World Health Organization estimates that 30 million people need prosthetic and orthotic devices — yet more than 75% of developing countries do not have a prosthetics and orthotics training program in place. This market is virtually untapped.

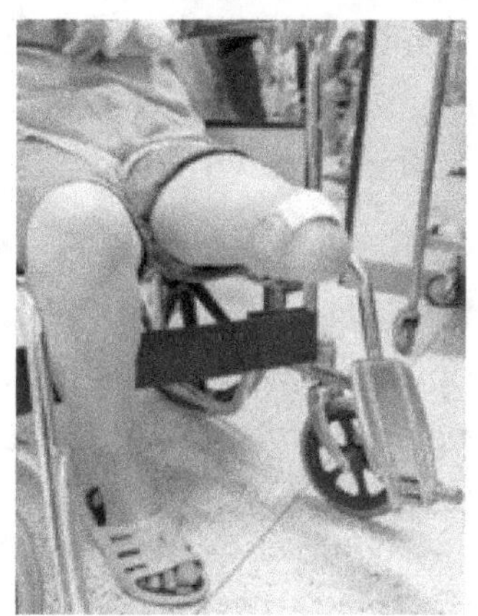

The over-populated generation of Baby Boomers represents 68% of all amputations. Add to it the freak accidents involving motorcycles and lawn mows, childbirth deformities, extreme sports venues, and the increased influx of international patients not able to find prosthetic and orthotic solutions in their own countries, you can expect a growing need for these critical services for decades to come.

3. Is any stratification of age, gender, race, or ethnicity driving the market?

This demographic profile question is important in the context of access and frequency. If you intended to open a Soul Food restaurant, you wouldn't pick a town like Scottsdale, Arizona, where the African-American population is 1.7%. Your prime customer, who has the highest potential to value access and buy with frequency, is just not there.

With Kristine's Orthotics/Prosthetics business, we know that age has a disproportionate impact on the market. **Older Baby Boomers are driving the majority of amputations.** For the sake of access and frequency, she would want to be in or near a city that had an aging population sufficient to support her products and services. We will explore this in detail when we enter the ring with the highly disruptive physical bruisers.

Fortunately, the other demographic categories, gender, race, and ethnicity, will not have an impact upon her business. We can move on.

One thing before we move on. The World Health Organization estimates that 75% of developing countries do not have a prosthetics and orthotics training program in place. When it comes to emerging market opportunities, this is big. Many large corporations report that, in the previous five years, over 50% of their growth has come from outside the United States.

Kristine should keep an open mind. There are 60 plus counties outside the United States in which English is the official language. With the internet, setting up partnerships in some of these untapped markets could provide substantial revenue.

The Demographic bruiser is no sweat. Let's move on.

MOVE ON!

Your SMACKDOWN Opponents...

TECHNOLOGICAL

We know technology plays a huge role in this market. We have three questions to gauge its impact upon Kristine's Orthotics/ Prosthetics business.

1. Are the industry's rapid technological advances helpful or harmful to Kristine's business?

Let's use some big words ... **POSTERIOR OCCIPITOCERVICAL – UPPER THORACIC RECONSTRUCTION and IMPLANTABLE CARDIOVERTER DEFIBRILLATORS (ICDS) and THORATRAK MICS RETRACTOR.**

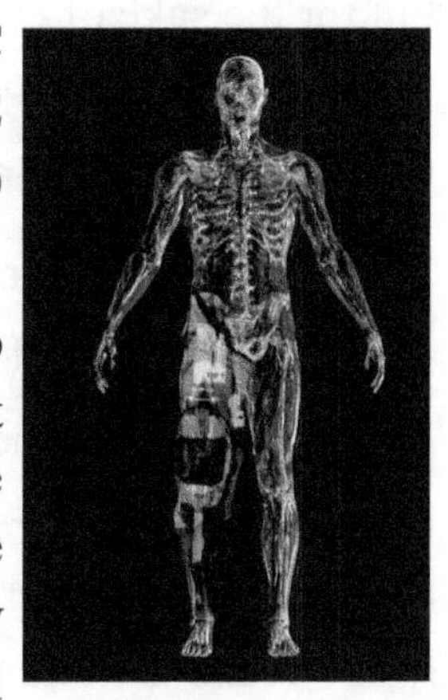

By 2023, these big words will add up to a \$410 billion medical device and implant market. Paired with these big words are mind-boggling spikes in innovation that were literally science fiction a decade ago. New generation aerospace laser-based 3D medical printing, myoelectric arms, lower extremity rotationplasty, hybrid robotic exoskeletons, direct AI brain interfaces, electronic feet that store energy, and complex microprocessor implants that enable biological systems of movement of the joints, tendons, bones, and muscles.

Each week, some new phase of innovation disrupts the marketplace and makes last week's products obsolete. With industry consolidation, new (anti-competitive) strategic partnerships, stringent government regulations, and mandates to cut costs, the pressure to remain viable while addressing unmet patient needs is unrelenting. To keep up really means to keep ahead, plowing millions into R&D, and amassing enough capital to pivot on a dime.

Ironically, this is the ideal environment for Kristine's business to prosper. New businesses are able to come into the chaotic marketplace to take advantage of new opportunities with new companies launching new products and seeking new distribution allies wherever they can find them. A level playing field welcomes any newcomer willing to dig in and learn the new technology and come up with innovative ways to perfect its usage.

In these situations, the pendulum swings toward people who really care about the end-user, that is to say, technicians who have an eye for comfort and customization, not for the sake of money, but for the sake of enabling the patient. Faced with the dynamics of these "people priorities", Kristine will do well.

2. Has the new technology made end-users safe and happy? Has it improved their quality of life?

Stated another way, will Kristine be forced to embrace pre-packaged devices and therapies that end-users don't like, don't need, and threaten their well-being?

This is more a question about Kristine than the industry. It will be a question about you and the compatibility of your industry, once you finish your assessments and get back to this phase of the selection process. When you look at your end-users, you may have to decide whether your liquor store business is enabling alcoholics, or whether your drug rehabilitation center is really helping patients if they keep falling off the wagon and coming back.

We are aware of Kristine's personality profile results. She cares about the people around her and doesn't like to disappoint. As the new kid on the block, will she be able to rep devices and therapies that meet her **(always over-deliver)** standards?

The answer is yes, although it's not a given yes. Invariably, as in the aerospace, cell phone, and computer industries in which rapid innovation occurs, **some products explode, or contaminate, or wreak havoc upon the existing grid. Some products simply suck.**

♦ In 2009, Medtronic had to recall approximately 60,000 potentially defective tubes associated with its MiniMed Paradigm insulin pumps used by diabetics to receive insulin.

♦ In 2010, because of persistent metal alloy problems, DePuy had to recall its defective ASR XL Acetabular hip replacement and ASR hip resurfacing systems. Lawsuits ultimately resulted in DePuy's agreement to a $2.5 billion settlement.

♦ In 2001, after authorities in Spain reported ten patients had died while or shortly after undergoing kidney dialysis using the Baxter dialysis filter, Chicago-based Baxter International recalled its A, AF, and AX series dialysis filters. It cost the company roughly $300,000 per family for the 50 plus patients that died.

♦ Merck paid $4.85 billion to settle its Vioxx arthritis drug lawsuits.

♦ Orthofix Inc., a Texas-based manufacturer of medical devices, paid the United States Government $34,234,263 to settle allegations tied to the company's sale of bone growth stimulator devices. The company also agreed to plead guilty to felony of obstruction of a federal audit, and to pay an additional $7,765,737 criminal fine.

♦ In the largest knee replacement lawsuit settlement, Sulzer Medica paid $1 billion to settle 4,000 hip and knee implant cases.

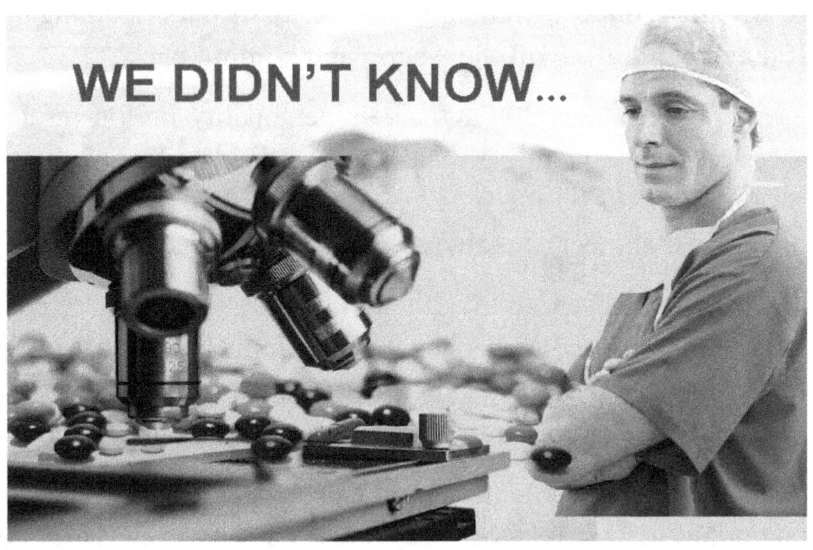

This is just the tip of the iceberg. As these new products roll out with Food and Drug Administration approval, people assume they are safe. But in many instances, they are not safe. By the time the manufacturer recalls the defective drug or medical device, patients may have suffered severe injuries, or even death.

Think about the many COVID-19 vaccines developed at breakneck speed. Years from now, no one will be surprised when the lawsuits pile up because, through human error or manufacturer defects, so many people end up injured or dead.

With over 190,000 different devices on the U.S. market, there are many marketing rep opportunities directly or indirectly associated with this niche:

♦ Medical devices

♦ Medical equipment

♦ Pharmaceuticals

♦ Biotechnology

Regardless of Kristine's chosen specialization, nothing is guaranteed. A good company might make a bad device. An effective device might take years to show its harmful effects. A bureaucratic, over-worked government watchdog such as the FDA might give a passing mark to a device, therapy, or medication that never should have been released to the public in the first place.

Kristine will exert due diligence and carry the necessary bonding and insurance liability coverage. But in the end, the rewards of this niche cannot be separated from the risks. Her end-user will benefit. But she cannot guarantee the impact of these benefits over the long haul.

3. Will the rapidly changing technology require a steep learning curve or costly training?

Depending on Kristine's chosen specialization, the training could run from a few weeks to a year. The cost would average around $15,000 - $20,000, not bad for a projected income of $175,000 per year.

For example, some curriculums offer hands-on medical device training in the areas of the spine, lower and upper extremities, head trauma, and sports medicine. Others specialize in manufacturing materials and sterilization processes. Still, other courses focus on the huge $12 billion a year product quality assurance aspect of the medical device lifecycle.

There is an extreme shortage of skilled medical device quality assurance professionals and consultants. A 20-hour web-based ISO course would run about $400. A three-day seminar on sports injury devices would run $1200. Other courses such as Regulatory Requirements for Software Validation and Integrating Risk Management into Medical Product Lifecycles would cost roughly $2400 for certification.

No matter her specialization, some technical training will be required. The whole point of any training is to enhance her level of entrepreneurial savvy. She is NOT trying to go to work for anyone's company. She is trying to develop the core knowledge base to run her own.

This training phase won't be a piece of cake. But because of her many years in the medical field, using medical devices and adhering to stringent measurements and patient wellness protocols, the transition to representing manufacturer's devices and therapies, and ultimately, developing her own unique brand, is well within reach.

We won't get a clean victory against the highly disruptive technology bruiser. Still, Kristine's inability to control long-term risk variables of specific medical products is not enough to end her quest. Early on, we established that finding a **perfect niche** was unattainable.

MOVE ON!

In this category, we'll take our "break-even" draw and move on.

Your SMACKDOWN Opponents...

POLITICAL

In this section, we will use government and politics interchangeably. The government (multiple bodies of government) set policies. The politics by large corporations and lobbyists to influence these policies is thick and inseparable, and often represents the vested interests on which the final bill is crafted. We ask three questions to determine whether this category is Kristine's friend or foe.

1. Which government bodies regulate the Orthotics/ Prosthetics business?

The short answer is everybody...

Because of high-profile injuries and deaths caused by defective or malfunctioning medical devices, the industry has come under increased scrutiny from inspectors, regulators, and policymakers throughout the world. Regulatory compliance has become more complicated. Product releases face a more rigorous journey to market.

Medical devices, therapies, and new technologies are subject to complex regulations and strict enforcement by the US Food and Drug Administration, US Department of Justice, Department of Health and Human Services, Office of the Inspector General, Environmental Protection Agency, United States Patent and Trademark Office, and roughly twenty other non-governmental authorities and associations.

State regulators have gotten into the act. **California's Proposition 65, The Safe Drinking Water and Toxic Enforcement Act** requires businesses to inform individuals of potential exposure to certain chemicals that may cause cancer, birth defects, or reproductive complications. Raw materials used in the creation of a medical device must be approved as an individual component and in combination with other components (chemical reaction) before the device as a

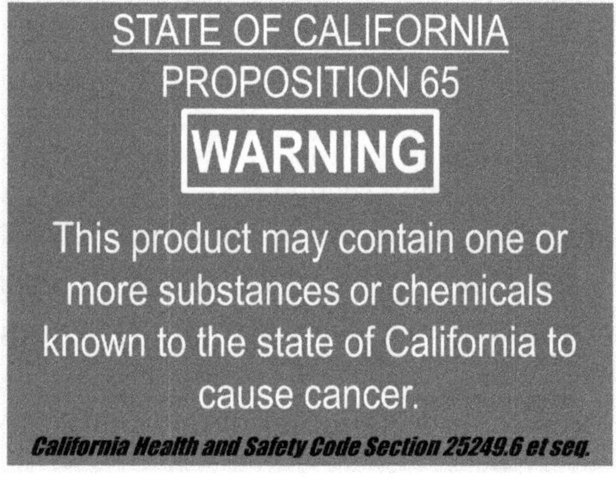

completed whole can go to market in that state.

The European Parliament and Council on medical devices ratified new MDR laws requiring more trials and stricter device safety compliance. So have many other countries throughout the world.

Despite all of these new regulations, the market is vibrant and growing at an exponential rate. For one reason, the average gross markup is still very attractive. And, with continued product innovation, the customer base continues to expand.

For the most part, Kristine will not be affected by these stricter regulations, at least, not until she introduces her own brand. As we go through this section, we will explore this aspect in more detail.

2. Are all of these regulations really necessary?

History would suggest they are. Without them, we can be reasonably sure many more injuries and deaths would have occurred.

Like any other large industry such as food supplies, the airlines, and oil & gas, the lure of profits corrupt some irresponsible players. Self-regulation is sufficient for some, but not for all.

Government intervention saves lives. Would food distributors voluntarily spend extra money to double-seal their products and put expiration dates on the labels? Would airlines install expensive wind shear detectors on all of their commercial planes? Would oil & gas companies voluntarily report a spill, or resist the expediency

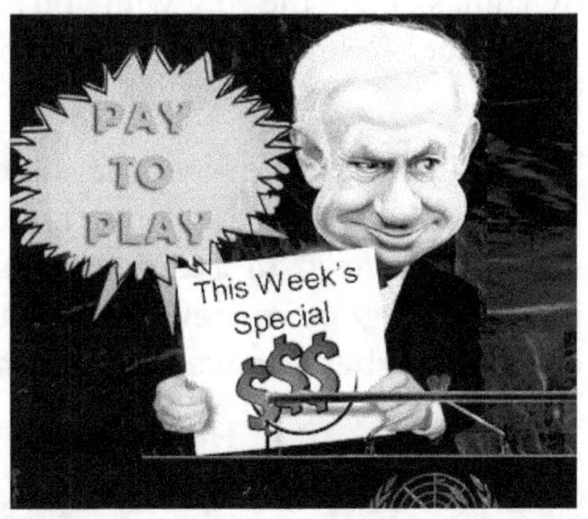

of dumping toxins in a nearby stream used for drinking water?

We know the answer. **But the answer gobbles up profits from the bottom line.** To act responsibly comes with a price. Someone has to pay.

Medical device companies have invested tons of time, money, and human capital into R&D, compliance programs, and cutting-edge technology. They have also spent billions to influence Congressmen, regulators, hospitals, and doctors, luring them across the line with exorbitant consulting fees, research grants, travel perks, and speaking fees. According to the U.S. Justice Department, **Olympus Corp.,** the largest U.S. distributor of endoscopes, misled patients and defrauded federal health care programs by providing physicians "powerful" financial inducements that turned them into "salesmen". Other device companies have been fined for bribing physicians, outright, and paying for false studies.

Lobbying records show the top four spinal-cord stimulator manufacturers spent more than $22 million combined since 2017 to obtain favorable legislation for the industry. Some laws contained extraordinary exemptions. In these cases, product safety was pushed to the back row.

Invariably, the age-old question of regulations vs free market dynamics enters the ring with you and tries to steal the whole round. How much is too much regulation, and how free should the free market be?

In these situations, the intent is to strike a balance between the two. As Ohio's Lt. Governor Jon Husted put it, **"Laws and regulations need to keep people safe and healthy, but we can't have our regulations ever standing in the way of innovation . . . especially when innovation can improve people's lives."**

The whole point of this discussion is to emphasize the importance of industry perspective. You need to understand the BIG picture before you jump in. **The computer security and privacy market has the same disruptive government dynamics.** Regulators are clamping down on undisclosed digital snooping and subliminal coercion. You need to know where your industry is headed before you commit to a niche that inhibits product innovation. In this niche, legislative headwinds are increasing each year. However, technology is moving so quickly, the regulations can barely keep up.

In Kristine's case, these costly, complex, protracted battles of product compliance will be fought by the larger companies which she will represent as an independent distributor. In the initial stages of her business, this tug of war between regulations and the free market will not be a major concern.

3. What can Kristine do to make sure her small business is not negatively impacted by government regulations?

The short answer is to comply with the law. This may seem simple. But you can go to any federal prison to find a high-level company executive who will tell you how difficult it really is. Firestone Tire executives knew their defective Wilderness AT tires were killing people, but kept right on selling them. Cigarette executives knew their products were linked to five different types of cancer, but kept right on selling them. BP's Deepwater Horizon drilling executives got cozy with federal inspectors, cut corners with safety procedures, blew up the whole rig, killed a bunch of workers, and caused the largest accidental marine oil spill in the world.

Let's face it. Shortcuts are tempting, profitable, and addictive. The Bernie Madoff's of the world will tell you the first one was so easy, they couldn't stop.

To stay in compliance with the law, Kristine will have to know the law. With so many new state, federal, and international regulations rolling out each year, this won't be easy. She will have to make a commitment to ongoing re-education and training. She will need to

establish a formal relationship with an attorney that specializes in the Orthotics/Prosthetics industry. She will have to join industry associations and attend seminars that keep her abreast of the latest FDA compliance regulations and pending legislation.

There is an unspoken upside to this investment of time and money, that is to say, beyond avoiding fines and staying out of prison. The more knowledgeable she becomes, the greater the opportunity to expand her services to the more lucrative "consulting" arena, helping other small distributors and manufacturers to adopt industry best practices and maintain compliance for their own operation.

As mentioned earlier, there is an extreme shortage of expert medical compliance professionals. If Kristine becomes knowledgeable and "certified" in just one key area, such as reporting adverse events involving medical devices, she can easily double her revenue each year.

Good News! We have stomped the highly disruptive, back-slapping, political wheeler-dealers and restrictive government regulators into the ground. It is time to move on to round five. Next up are the ethical dynamics of **social consciousness**. Let's see

if Kristine's new business is an eyesore to the rest of the world.

MOVE ON!

Your SMACKDOWN Opponents...

SOCIAL

Two questions help us determine whether the social category is Kristine's friend or foe. What are the critical dynamics that drive the industry? And is her profile compatible?

1. What are the social dynamics of the industry?

As it turns out, this is an easy one; no protestors for cleaner air or advocates against child labor, clamoring outside her gates. Everyone wants victims of health diseases, catastrophic injuries, and age deterioration to improve. The greatest social pushback comes, not from the traditionally judgmental outside world, but from the chaotic inside world of the patients, themselves.

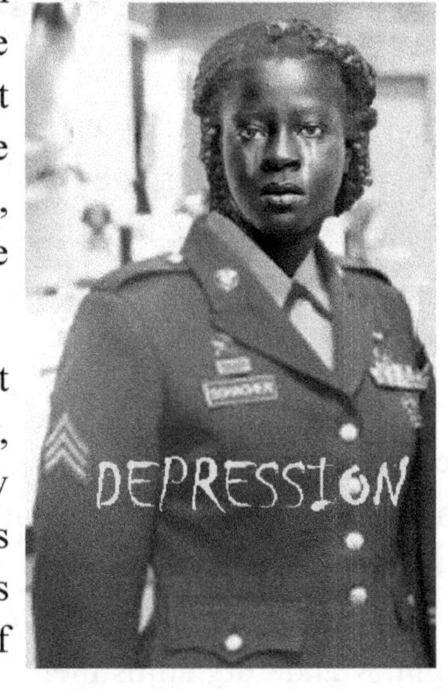

According to the Department of Veterans Affairs, each day, approximately 17 U.S. military veterans die by suicide. This rate is almost two times that of nonveterans after adjusting for the demographics of age, race, and sex. Roughly, 325 active-duty soldiers, sailors, airmen, and Marines died by suicide in 2018, up by 40 reported deaths in 2017.

The reasons - **insomnia, depression, anxiety, sexual victimization, complications with aging, substance abuse, etc.** - are varied and complex, and far beyond the scope of this chapter. Add the stress of coping with missing limbs, constant pain, and a growing sense of dependency on others, and you get an explosive fermentation of ingredients, poised for self-destruction.

Since the Iraq and Afghanistan Wars, this group of military veterans has represented a sizable chunk of those patients needing services and procedures related to orthotics and prosthetics. Thus, mental stability plays a huge role in the success rate for enabling these patients back to their hopeful, purposeful place in society.

Let's put it this way. With all of its futuristic, AI space-age features, a new robotic arm won't work if the patient doesn't have the mental stamina and determination to make it work. **These patients must see a ray of hope in their seemingly dismal future.** They must identify a purpose, "a legitimate, ennobling reason" to join the fight. Mandatory adjustments to housing and transportation services, social transitions, and stringent, painful hours of rehabilitation represent very high mountains to climb. What is the use in climbing if nothing is waiting on the other side?

There are public officials who run on a platform of lower taxes and budget constraints, and advocate closing veteran facilities and re-defining high profile terms like Post-traumatic stress disorder (PTSD) so fewer patients are eligible for government assistance. Indeed, these are uncompassionate, opportunistic enemies of rehabilitation. But, for the most part, the real battle is within the patient. The psychological reaction of an amputee is not only the visual loss of the limb, but the loss of independence, self-esteem, career, and relationships as well.

The real core of the enablement process is to restore hope and purpose and visions of an alternate universe that makes life worth living. What person (profile) do we know that would relish the challenge? Who has the medical experience, competency mix, and personality traits to save the day?

Take the time to re-examine Kristine's overwhelming compatibility to this niche, and in doing so, highlight your own compatibility questions when YOU take center stage. Your connection to the unmet needs of your market should be equally as strong.

2. Is Kristine compatible with the social dynamics of the industry?

If you've studied the results of Kristine's profile assessment, you already know the answer. She is EXACTLY what the industry needs.

By her very nature, she is a perpetual supporter and nurturer who loves to enable others, to move them from where they are to where they need to be. She has a sincere desire to protect, encourage, and over-delivery on any assignment of which

she takes ownership. She loves old things and will do well with Baby Boomers, the second customer profile for this industry. **She has the ability to detect disharmony and mental stress in others.** She will be able to address patient anxieties and product customization details that other product reps and orthotics/prosthetics specialists won't even see.

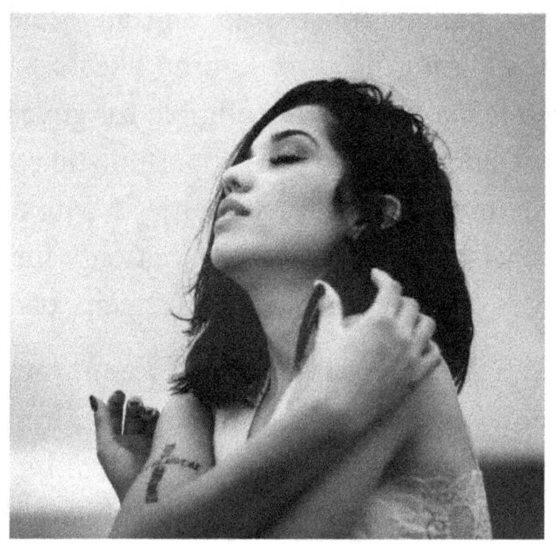

We can move on. We have stomped the highly disruptive social consciousness of mankind into the ground. Next up is the final bruiser, the question of physical location. Let's see if Kristine's new business can find a place to call home.

MOVE ON!

Your SMACKDOWN Opponents...

PHYSICAL

In many industries such as shipbuilding, ski lodging, winemaking, and Hollywood prop supplies, physical location can be the difference between success and failure. You need to be there, up close and personal, to have a fighting chance.

Let's examine the impact that physical location will have on Kristine's business.

1. Does physical location have the potential to hurt or enhance Kristine's Orthotics/Prosthetics business?

We define physical location as the address (city, state, nation) at which a business conducts its primary operation. McDonald's is all over the world. But if you purchase a McDonald's franchise, your focus is the local address from which you service customers and generate profit.

Regardless of your business niche, location has (to a greater or lesser degree) some impact on your ultimate success. It might be the high price of rent, or the ability to attract superior talent, or the ability to play golf with key decision-makers each week. Location has the potential to give you the edge, or place you at a disadvantage that stifles your ability to compete.

Here are seven location drivers that could affect your bottom line:

♦ High real estate costs that force you to charge more for your services.

♦ Podunk/crime-ridden/culturally deprived cities to which top industry talent refuses to relocate.

♦ Highly taxed/highly regulated states and regions that inhibit operations and stifle innovation.

♦ Accessibility to key (raw) products, services, and shipping options.

♦ Accessibility to key decision-makers. Agents representing movie stars and Broadway actors live in Hollywood and New York. They are not closing mega-million-dollar deals from Pine Bluff, Arkansas.

♦ Level of established competition, crowding the market, providing the same or similar products and services.

♦ Weather hazards such as hurricanes, earthquakes, and volcanoes, as well as coastal cities on the global warming hit list.

When it comes to Kristine's business, location is a factor. **She needs to be located near major trauma centers where patients,**

physicians and Orthotics/Prosthetics specialists make decisions about enablement therapies and procedures.

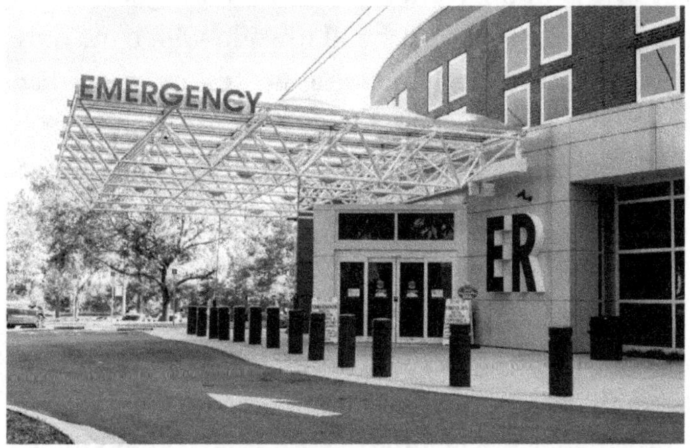

Here are the top ten Medical Centers in the United States:

♦ Walter Reed National Military Medical Center in Bethesda, Maryland.

♦ Johns Hopkins Hospital in Baltimore, Maryland.

♦ Texas Medical Center in Houston, Texas.

♦ Stanford University Medical Center in Palo Alto, California.

♦ Ronald Reagan UCLA Medical Center in Los Angeles, California.

♦ Massachusetts General Hospital in Boston, Massachusetts.

♦ New York-Presbyterian Hospital in New York, New York.

♦ University of Pittsburgh Medical Center in Pittsburgh, Pennsylvania.

♦ Phoenix Healthcare Cluster in Phoenix, Arizona.

♦ Washington University Medical Center in St. Louis, Missouri.

Volume is important. It wouldn't make good business sense for Kristine to set up shop in a small town in which the only medical facility is a veterinary clinic, nursing horses and cows back to life. Her business needs to be located within reasonable proximity to ongoing enablement, research, and rehabilitation activities. She needs to visit, observe, and identify the unmet needs at various facilities. She needs to get to know the people working on the front lines.

Kristine's extroverted personality and love for people will open doors to which most competitors will not have privy. At some point, she will begin to see patterns (opportunities) in various orthotics/prosthetics procedures that offer new, more effective ways to nurture and support patients on a personal level. This is a strategic advantage, and indicative of intuitive feeler personality types who see "people" details that others do not see.

2. Does location have a direct impact on revenue?

Unfortunately, the answer is yes. Some states pay more than others for the same services. This inequity is not an oversight, but rather, the results of heavy lobbying by the insurance industry.

The Military Health System (MHS) within the United States Department of Defense provides health care to active duty, reserve, and retired military personnel and their families. The coverage is governed by arbitrary constraints.

According to the Affordable Care Act (ACA), all insurance plans legally cover ten categories of "Essential Health Benefits," including rehabilitative services and devices. So do all states taking part in the Medicaid expansion plan. However, federal law does not specify how much these plans have to cover. This allows state Medicaid plans to **arbitrarily cut corners and create exemptions to reduce benefits that might be available in another state.**

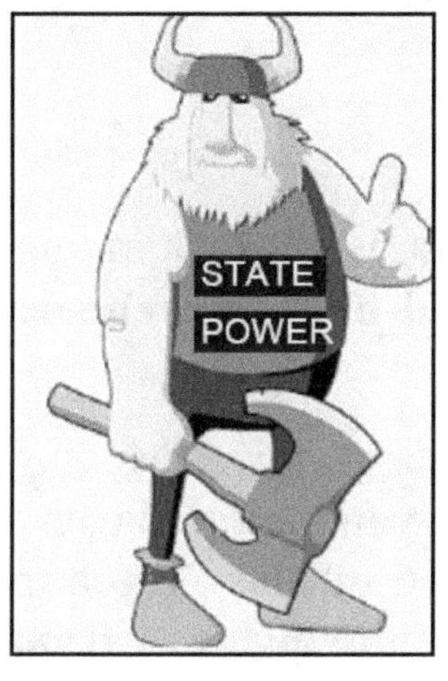

To some extent, all states cover orthotics and prosthetics as a Medicaid benefit. **But the maximum coverages vary from state to state.** Florida's program covers only one prosthetic per lifetime. Utah allows coverage of one prosthetic every five years. Some states are very stingy in their coverage of more advanced devices, such as myoelectric prosthetic arms, although these arms have proven to be efficient and reliable for over a decade.

If third-party insurance payers refuse to approve the industry's cutting edge technology, and patients cannot afford the additional out-of-pocket expense, patients lose out. They must forgo new and improved enablement devices that could enhance their chances for a full recovery. These realities find their way back to budget constraints and the nuances of current legislation. The insurance companies have well-paid lobbyists. The military personnel, returning from the Iraq and Afghanistan Wars, do not.

If Kristine is currently living in South Dakota, Utah, or Montana, she'll probably have to relocate. Fortunately, there are a number of thriving medical

centers throughout the United States that would welcome her expertise. Research is key, for her and for you. Choose a location that will give your business a fighting chance.

Let's deal with the major, nightmarish, life-changing decision that may be staring many would-be entrepreneurs in the face.

Relocation is an exquisite way of saying *moving*. Moving is the abbreviation for *moving away*. If your knees haven't buckled and your dry throat hasn't choked off the oxygen to your lungs, you can finish the phrase with **"moving away from friends, family, and the comfort zone you've worked so hard over the years to create".**

The CEO of Coke or Pepsi or General Motors will tell you how difficult it was to spend two years away from his or her family, heading up the operation in **Argentina or South Africa**. The Brigadier General over the Joint Chiefs will tell you how challenging it was, being assigned to **twelve different air bases in twenty years.** The top Hollywood movie stars will tell you how disorienting it was to shoot **three different movies in three different countries in three years.**

In the pursuit of a successful entrepreneurial career, moving is a wildcard you play, or don't play, but never take off the table. Otherwise, you limit your possibilities for the sake of maintaining the (crumbling) status quo. In the context of this decision, you have to ask yourself a question: **How is the status quo looking right now?**

If the answer is unfavorable, or unfulfilling as a measurement of your true purpose in life, the next question is: **Is my greatest potential for fixing the problem here, in my current location, or somewhere else?**

This is not easy. But, at least, you know how to frame the question(s). Many of the auto industry workers in Saginaw, Michigan, who lost their jobs to automation and artificial intelligence, are still in Saginaw. They traded their $30 an hour assembly-line job for an $11 an hour delivery truck job in a dying town with no hope of recovery. They made a conscious decision to cling to the (crumbling) status quo.

Kristinc is in Dallas. So, with hundreds of medical facilities in her area, all is well. But what about you? After evaluating your potential business niches, you'll have to decide if all is well in your current location, or whether your future prosperity beckons you to another time and place.

Stomping our **physical location** adversary into the ground came with a bit of emotional soul-searching and recalibration of long-term priorities. Nevertheless, in Kristine's case, we emerged from the ring with a win. Now, we move to the awards ceremony to tally our score and determine if our business niche survived the intense combat against the six highly disruptive forces blocking our entrepreneurial dreams.

MOVE ON!

This is BIG!!! If you're Kristine, you can stop, take a deep breath, and then exhale with jubilation. You've identified a business niche that's compatible with your unique personality and gives you a fighting chance. Your *Golden Circle* selection has survived.

These are the results you always hope for, but don't always achieve. Sometimes, a business niche has so many strikes against it, you have to acknowledge the harsh realities of failure and let it go. Do you really want to sell cancer cigarettes, or open up a sugar diabetes donut shop, or start a neighborhood gym where everyone is running and jumping and lifting ... and breathing out massive clouds of a new strain of COVID-19, with an untested vaccine, months, maybe, years away?

I don't think so. Sometimes the odds are just too overwhelming. You have to move on to higher ground.

The extensive research, due diligence, holistic thinking, and decision-making tools have all collaborated to reach this point. Kristine's business niche is not perfect. But it's a go! ... Let's GO!!!

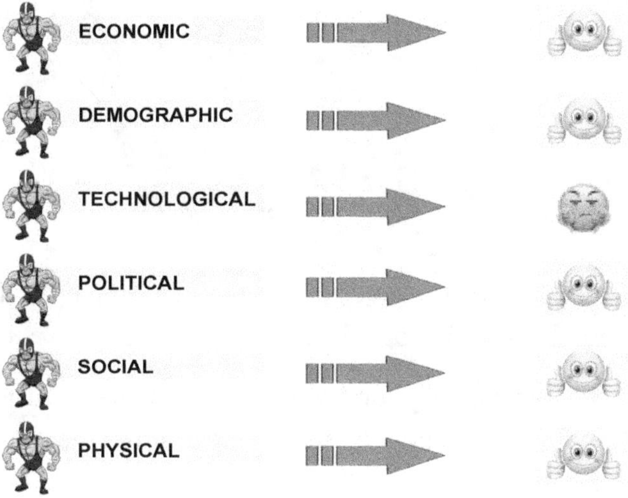

This comprehensive example, **the example YOU will follow in constructing your own entrepreneurial path forward,** demonstrates the step-by-step procedure for selecting your business niche:

(A) Finish this chapter. Read every word.

(B) Familiarize yourself with the step-by-step discovery process.

(C) Take your series of online assessments. Without paying a psychoanalyst $300 an hour, find out who you really are.

(D) Choose a potential business niche that fits your true passion. Climb into the ring with the SMACKDOWN bruisers to see if your "niche fit" has a fighting chance.

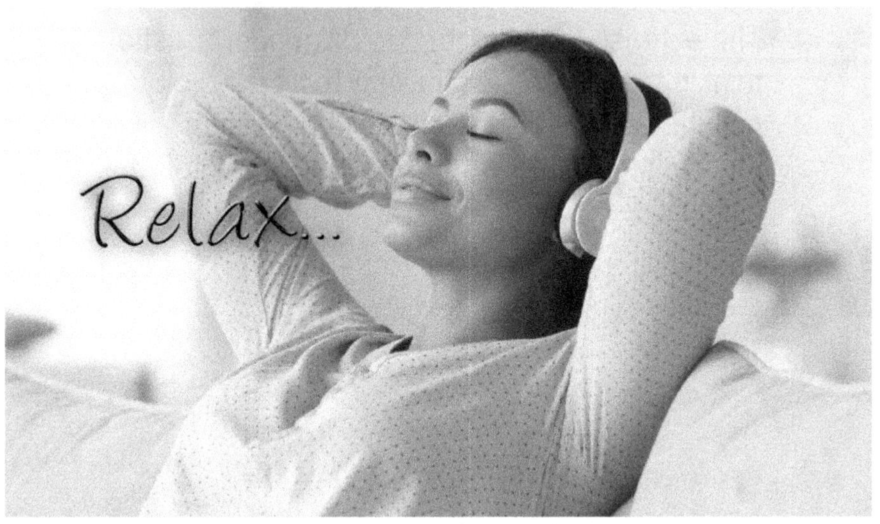

Now breathe! You're over the hump. You have the formula for the atom bomb tucked neatly inside your briefcase.

After you've taken your online assessments, return to this chapter with your assessment results and follow the previously mentioned steps.

LIST OF ONLINE ASSESSMENTS> https://bit.ly/39i63JY

Hopefully, the process has been simple and straightforward, a promise we made at the very beginning of this journey ... not to mention you've saved yourself a ton of money and made the big research companies cry. **This is a game-changer, a life-changer. You want to get it right**

In Chapter 15, we close out with a brief discussion of **"nit-picky details"**. Don't fret that your head is bursting with new knowledge and an irrepressible yearning to move forward. Try to make room for a few more tiny nuggets of wisdom, and then we're done.

NITPICKY DETAILS

*I*nsight #15   closes out with a meticulous eye on details. Think of your mother, looking under your bed to see where the piles of dirty clothes, smelly sneakers, and candy wrappers have gone.   She'll end up telling you what you already know: ***Cutting corners and taking unnecessary risks will come back to bite you.*** She'll tell you this before the rats and the roaches move in.

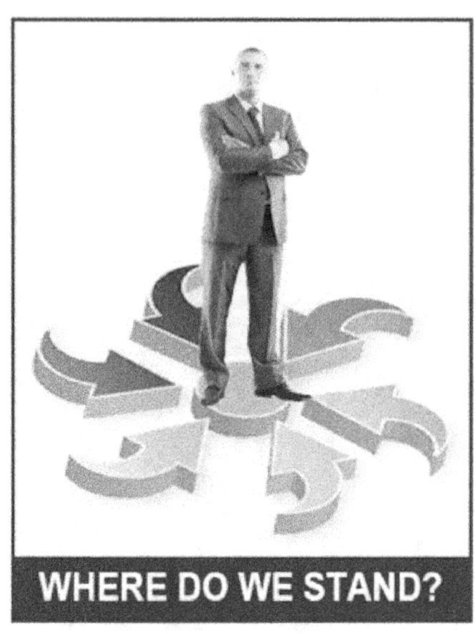

In our quest to identify a compatible business niche, we are loaded for bear. **We have the formula, the steps, the tools, the patterns of thinking, the historical perspective of other entrepreneurial successes and failures, and most importantly, the clinical keys to liberate ourselves from the restrictive biases of our subconscious mind.**

The only thing left is a brief discussion of some nitpicky details. We refer to them as "nitpicky" because most business books and entrepreneurial websites don't consider them important enough to mention. With so many other critical aspects of starting a business garnering our attention, we tend to overlook these cautionary reminders … well, overlook them until they slip up behind us and bite us in the rear end.

You may go to the Small Business Administration (SBA) website to review the ten basic steps for starting a business, such as: conduct market research, write your business plan, fund your business, pick your business location and so on. **Our discussion of nitpicky details offers ten steps you should NEVER take so that your fledgling business will remain focused, healthy, and moving toward your ultimate goals of longevity and profitably.**

 ...

We're closing out very soon. It would be expedient to revisit a basic premise we introduced in earlier chapters. Here is the premise: **THERE IS NO SILVER BULLET.** There is no perfect outcome. The process upon which we embarked in Chapter 1 narrows the margin of error, reduces the distortion of human biases, redefines and re-focuses your research techniques, and points you to green pastures you have the inclination to plow. These ten nitpicky prohibitions warn you to stay away from certain risky habits and inclinations.

You might follow the expert guidance and resist the temptation to take unnecessary risks ... and still go out of business. A new vaccine-resistant strain of COVID-19 might come along and close your new store or restaurant. A careless person might slip down while visiting your premises and sue you for all of the operating capital in your bank account. A big China conglomerate might re-engineer your patented device and start selling it for half the price. A new clinical study might link your product to cancer. Another war might break out and force the government to buy up a scarce Iridium-type raw material you need to manufacture your best-selling product.

There are no guarantees. As an entrepreneur, you should not look for guarantees. You are in the business of **OPPORTUNITIES AND PROBABILITIES.** Using historical research data to understand why certain business propositions succeeded or failed, you are an explorer with powerful Cliff Notes and AI-driven profile maps in your back pocket, searching out opportunities to which YOU are compatible, and betting on the probability for their success.

With your clear mission in mind, hedge your bets, cut your losses, and stay away from risky, reckless, nitpicky mistakes that can change the dynamics of your business and destroy all that you have worked so hard to achieve.

Nitpicky Mistakes

Here are the ten most costly nitpicky mistakes. Avoid these temptations. Explore all of the alternative options available. Stay out of the cracks.

1. Don't hire your neighbors, friends, or relatives to be your bookkeeper or CPA.

There are many reasons for this prohibition, beyond the potential loss of privacy. The most damaging one is this group's emotional, unsolicited advice. In most instances, they haven't read any business books, or taken any assessments, or learned to extrapolate the research tea leaves that facilitate your understanding of highly disruptive environmental forces and future dynamics of the marketplace. What they possess is a caring, protective spirit that wants the best for you and your family.

When times are bad and the future looks bleak, they feel an obligation to give you their best advice. Invariably, their best advice is to cut your losses, throw in the towel, and see if you can find a real job.

Every time you see a FedEx truck, an iconic reminder of the vast Federal Express network, delivering 1.2 billion packages in 220 countries, you should conjure visions of the company's early day when founder and CEO Frederick Smith found himself drowning in debt and on the brink of bankruptcy.

With all of his investment sources dried up, Smith took the company's last $5,000 and flew out to Las Vegas. With a few lucky blackjack hands, he turned the $5,000 into $27,000, just enough to pay fuel costs and finance another week of operations. That critical additional week in business led to additional financing. The rest is history.

How many friends or relatives would look at your dwindling books and negative cash flow, and tell you to fly out to Las Vegas? They would beg you to come to your senses and throw in the towel.

Whether you end up broke, or miraculously resurrected from the grave, you don't need their protective instincts plotting your course forward. You need the bold inspiration of people saying, *"YES, we can get to the moon. We just need to figure out how."*

---

2. Don't hire your adult children to help you start the business.

If you're a parent, you never get those early images of your child out of your mind. From diaper years to college graduation, it's your job to protect, nurture, and prepare them for the real world. You spend twenty-plus uninterrupted years doing just that.

When they finally grow up, a sense of loss creeps in. You have to make a deliberate, heart-wrenching effort to let them go. The unspoken reality is that you never let them go, not completely. That innate mother hen/ father hen sense of responsibility follows you to the grave.

This is bad for business ... your business if you hire them. You still see them as dependent little children, when all they've done in their latter years is try to escape your dominance, leave the nest, and fly free from your control.

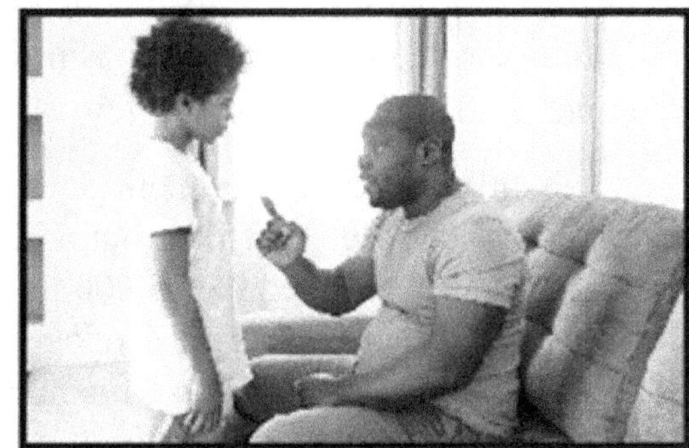

Conflict between CEO parents and employee children is inevitable. Every disagreement is amplified. Every action can be construed as a "personal" insult or betrayal. How dare your son be late, knowing the seriousness of the business venture, currently on

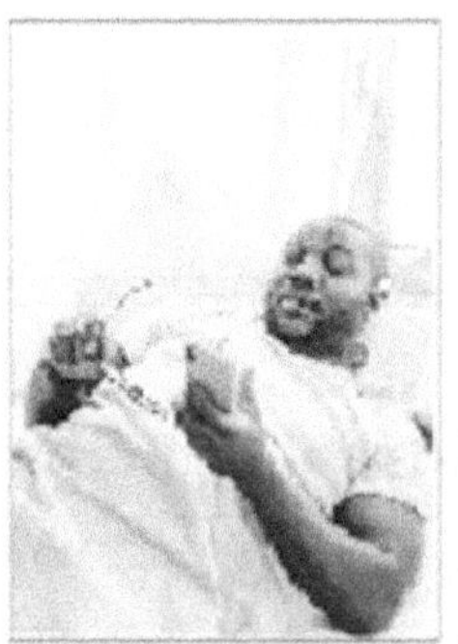

"My father keeps calling. I told him I don't work on Fridays."

"Dress code??? MY look is MY business."

"Yes, I quit. My Mom's got too many stupid rules."

the table. How dare her own father not understand that when her menstrual cycle comes, his daughter, only daughter, whose recurring medical problems should be no surprise, is probably going to miss a few days.

These company conflicts work their way into holiday and weekend family gatherings. The son doesn't want to talk about a mistake he made at the office, so he doesn't bring his family over to mom and dad's house at all. The daughter has started dating the UPS delivery guy and doesn't want to hear another negative comment about her low aspirations and their dismal future together.

Starting a business is stressful. Studies show children who observe their fathers under constant psychological pressure often experience a sense of (reciprocal) emotional instability. In addition to these internal family conflicts, other company employees often express resentment for any perks or recognition awarded to family members, even if the recognition is warranted. The whole company is watching and waiting to see the ugly hand of nepotism shower its unscrupulous favoritism upon "daddy's little girl".

There will come a time ... years after the company is well established ... that a parent may bring his son or daughter into the business without a major upheaval. This time usually corresponds to the parent's retirement plans and a mutual readiness by the son or daughter to rescue the old Barnaby Jones frontline fighters from their labor. As perceived by the child, the act is noble.

The exchange is fluid and purposeful. The transfer of ownership is mutually beneficial to all parties and replaces the long-standing authoritarian relationship with one of caring and respect.

3. Whether married or single, don't ignore the laws regarding sexual harassment.

For most men, this is a no-brainer. Over fifty, you are especially susceptible. Working late hours, sharing the stress of the journey, ordering in a few pizzas and beer to celebrate the rare victories, someone is going to cross the line. You don't need 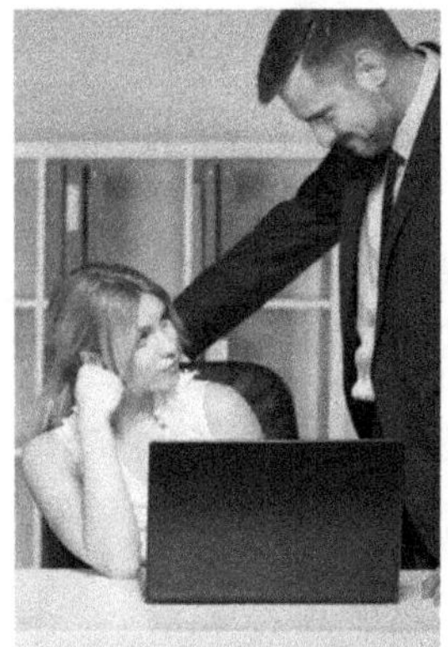 an ongoing distraction that keeps your mind fractured. Even with all of your brain cells working in harmony, you're going to make mistakes. Don't overload the system with forbidden fantasies, popping in and out of your head.

Keep your business life and personal life separate. Thoroughly familiarize yourself with the federal and local laws applying to sexual harassment, hostile workplace environments, and overtime abuse. Otherwise, by the time you finish paying court settlements and legal fees, you might have just enough money left to send in your vehicle deposit fee and start driving a cab.

---

4. Don't be afraid to go into debt.

This aspect of the business is difficult for long-time wage-earners who have been taught to work hard, save often, and minimize their debt load. Drowning in debt implies you're a poor financial manager and have somehow over-extended your spending beyond your income. Your grandfather, father, accounting professors, corporate bosses, and grumpy old taxman have all told you the same thing...

"Live within your means."

Your subconscious will NOT like this. But we must replace an old comfortable lie with a new, uneasy truth. Columbus did not discover America. There are more than eight planets in our universe. There were no weapons of mass destruction in Iraq. **AND ... unless Uncle Floyd left you a secret stash in his mattress, you will have to go into debt.**

Yahoo operated for ten years on billions in borrowed funds before turning a profit. After operating in the red for nine years, **Amazon** finally turned a profit in 2003. The **ESPN** all-sports network was founded in 1978. It didn't turn a profit until the mid-80s, and stayed afloat, largely because of a desperation bailout by **Anheuser-Busch.** Founded in 2009, **Pinterest** went public with a whopping IOP of $12.7 billion, and is still operating in the red. The **United States Government** is $24 trillion in debt, and that's before the COVID-19 pandemic.

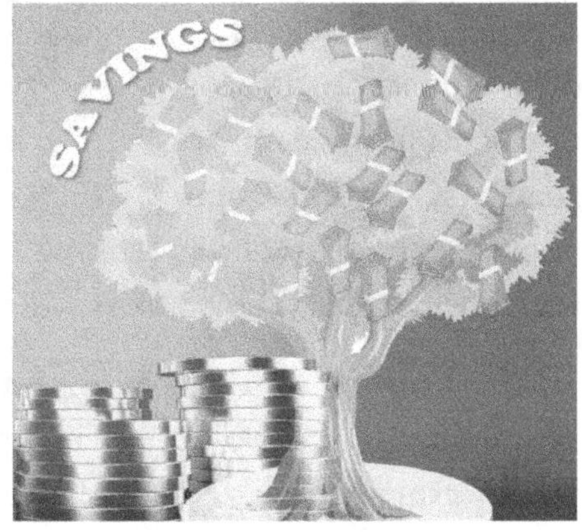

The beautiful, predictable wage-earner's universe is really a bubble inside the chaotic world of finance. Leave the bubble and you're in for a bumpy ride. You might make millions, or you might go broke. Either way, you're going to have to finance the ride.

The biggest reason startups go under is a lack of capital. You have a vision. You see the Promised Land. But you don't have enough money to get there. Surveys show that roughly 55% of new entrepreneurs expect to turn a profit the first year. This is an unlikely scenario. Optimism must be balanced with practicality. When you present a potential investor with this rosy projection of a miracle money tree, he knows you don't know what you're doing. He's going to turn you down.

Try to anticipate your financial needs. A business plan will help. But no plan can fully anticipate the precise ebb and flow of an ever-evolving marketplace. Disruptors come out of nowhere. You need a sufficient financial cushion to hang on. Either, your trusting family members, or a good bank that will probably require a 35% debt-to-income ratio, or a crowdfunding website such as Kickstarter, or a

venture capitalist who is looking for a radical, game-changing idea, are your best funding sources.

Finally, don't take anyone's money if you don't believe. Tip-toeing out of the bubble is a sure-fire way to go under. Spend wisely. But spend like you believe.

---

5. Don't base your business model on flashing and asking.

As you may recall, in an earlier chapter, we examined the negative impact of team members refusing to take "operational ownership" in your company's projects. Owners of a project, event, business, or social movement understand the full ramifications of the project's existence and readily embrace obstacles associated with its ultimate outcome.

There are times when employees refuse to take ownership in a project because the official owner of the company is flashing and asking. He is flashing his wealth and elite lifestyle, while asking everyone else to sacrifice, to accept the scarcity of the moment and dig in for the long haul.

Think about a scenario in which the CEO arrives on Monday morning in his new Mercedes-Benz; Tuesday, he drives his big, gas-guzzling Lincoln Navigator; Wednesday, he rides in on his

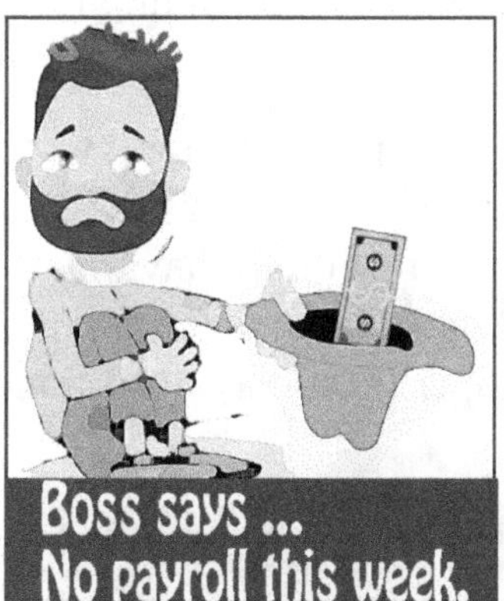

MTT Turbine Superbike motorcycle. At the weekly meeting, while punching numbers into his brand new $1500 iPhone MAX, he explains why salaries will have to be cut and people will have to be laid off.

If you're this CEO, you're going to lose good people. Those you don't lose, you'll alienate beyond an acceptable level of productivity.

Expect high turnover, a lack of respect, and ultimately, a company full of yes-men/women who have few other career options.

Even if you are that selfish, it would be advisable not to show it. True leaders "lead" through times of victory and sacrifice. Leave those expensive trinkets at home until you can pay everyone to go out to get their own trinkets. Use some emotional intelligence, or you will be out of business very soon.

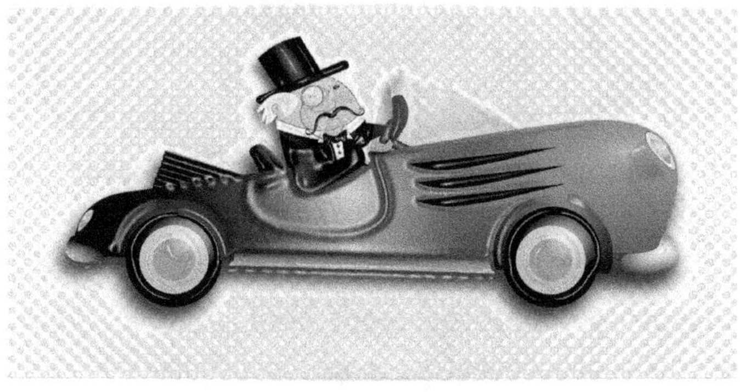

6. Don't box yourself in with the old, familiar business models you experienced during your wage-earner years.

You can't grow your business alone. To develop meaningful traction in your chosen niche, and move from the inefficiency of jumping from desk to desk, wearing a different hat each hour, you'll need to assemble a team.

Depending on your industry and specialization, your team may look completely different from those of your previous employers. The brick-and-mortar dinosaurs of old may have had a front office receptionist, a mailroom clerk, an IT manager, a CPA, and a room full of smooth-talking salespeople. You may need none of those people.

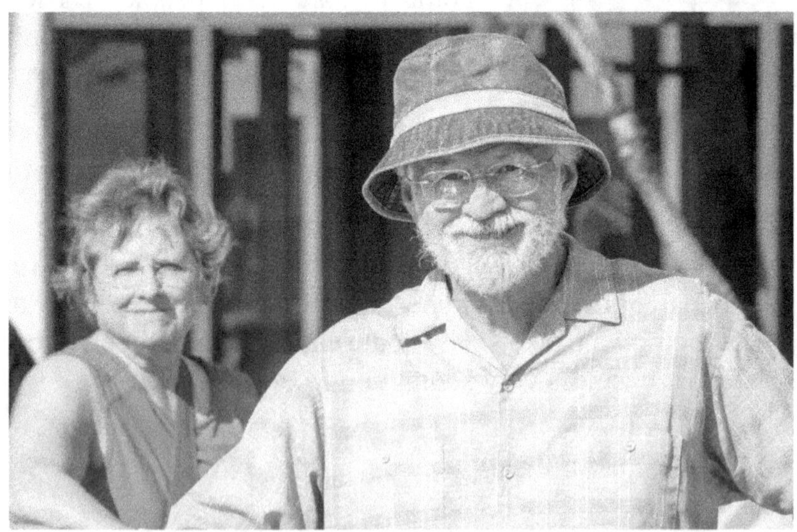

For the startup entrepreneur, the creation of a team is based almost exclusively on functionality. What functions (tasks) do you need to get done, and who do you need to do them?

Think of a small husband and wife custom home remodeling business generating a million dollars a year. They work out of their garage, taking on minor projects that don't require complex architecture or high-level city and county permits. They over-deliver on each job, maintain an exemplary 5-star rating, and get most of their business by word-of-mouth.

They don't need a front office receptionist, or mailroom clerk, or room of sweet-tongued salespeople. Their in-coming calls are answered by a live virtual assistant company capable of transferring the calls to their cell phones, as if sitting in an office next to them.

Their cloud-based emails come directly to their home computers, mobile tablets and cell phones. They work closely with highly seasoned carpenters, plumbers, painters, cabinetmakers, and other independent contractors that are deeply loyal to them, primarily, because of their unique bonus 

system which pays more than the industry's standard rate.

There is no need to hire a full-time CPA. The couple pays an accounting firm to keep their books, file their quarterly reports, and end-of-year taxes.

You get the picture. The couple's team is almost 100% external. They pay with company checks and write off their vendor expenses through a system of 1099s.

Let's take a step back to look at personalities. If an owner is overwhelmingly focused on profit, this system won't work. He's going to lean on his vendors and keep as much revenue as possible. He will not implement a performance bonus that pays more than the current industry rate. He will not develop the same loyalty (ownership of the project) and will tolerate inefficiencies based on turnover and time spent searching for new vendors.

If an owner is accustomed to the top-down, tight-control management model, this system still won't work. Unless he's in total control, that is to say, observing the work, the time spent on lunch breaks away from the work, the

pace in which the nails are driven into the wall, the order in which each room is painted, he will not be completely happy with the arrangement. As with the **STRUCTURED///OVERSEER**, a firm, methodical owner will be most comfortable with employees that clock in and demonstrate commitment and accountability on every level. For these types of owners, the end project result is only part of the equation. The manner of execution is just as important.

What's the bottom line?

The bottom line is "fit". A business model that brings in a million dollars for the couple down the street might not work for you at all. Study your assessments. Analyze your company's core functionality. Choose a model that fits YOUR specific needs.

7. Don't ever talk to your team members in a tone that you wouldn't use with your grandmother.

He's passed on. So out of respect and admiration, people refer to **Steve Jobs** in heavenly whispers. He was a brilliant visionary. But let's face it. The old iPhone guru was also a tyrant. Many times, he spoke to team members as though they were roaches beneath his feet.

There is no justification for this manner of Machiavellian conduct. Einstein was a lot smarter. Warren Buffett was just as famous, more successful, and had a lot more cash in the bank. Neither found it necessary to treat their coworkers with disrespect. You shouldn't either.

First, it's wrong on so many emotional and sociological levels. Secondly, with such negative intensity, the brain rclcascs so many harmful hormones into your system, this type of conduct WILL lead to some form of sickness.

Thirdly, if you haven't already noticed, we live in a crazy world. It's not unusual for a disgruntled employee to return to the job site with an ak47 and kill everyone in sight. The project is looking good.

But people are too dead to see it through.

A good rule of thumb is to never talk to your team members in a tone that you wouldn't use with your grandmother. Be civil ... be kind ... stay alive.

8. Don't impose job-related social attendance and external gatherings on team members.

You've read a few misguided articles on building trust and camaraderie among team members. Some of these articles advocate a social function each quarter, away from the job site. People can let down their hair and get to know each other outside the formal constraints of the work environment.

The advice is well-intended, but a bit outdated. People no longer view these functions as social. Studies show Generation X and Millennials value their private time. A job function is just that ... a job, an unwanted interruption of their preferred private activities.

Company parties can backfire and lead to reductions in future raises and promotions.

They're smart enough to know that letting their hair down with people from work can have consequences, sometimes influencing the outcome of raises and promotions. They prefer to choose their social friends and "hair-down" moments. They don't need your help.

If you plan a work-related social event, it's best to emphasize the "unimportance" of attendance, no hard feelings if they have other things to do. The most effective way to get people to come to these gatherings is to have a great time and give away a bunch of "stuff" that people in attendance rave about at work. Ten $50 free gift cards get a lot of press around the water cooler. A free car wash for thirty days is another big winner.

COVID-19 will eventually diminish. People will start to venture out. But don't turn these well-intended gatherings into a burden. Your very talented web designer may be a **CREATIVE/// DREAMER** who cherishes her private time. Different generations and personalities appreciate different things. Give your team members a choice.

Invite, don't demand. Nothing in your invitation should imply potential repercussion for team members who choose not to participate.

9. Don't hide from bill collectors at the expense of your employees.

This one should be in red letters.

During those early years, unless you have a huge mattress inheritance from Uncle Joe, expenses will exceed income. You won't be able to pay all of your bills. One of the most damaging responses, and perhaps, quickest way to lose the respect of those who look to you for leadership, is to force your team members to take the heat.

The irate calls are going to come in. It's not the job of your loyal soldiers to dodge bullets while you hide in the bunker. Take the calls, explain your situation. Believe it or not, the bill collectors want you to succeed so they can get paid. Try to buy some time. But whatever you do, don't put your people in the line of fire.

Lone ago, while calling on a client, I saw a hot check for $322, written by a multi-millionaire. Over the years, my client had saved the check as a reminder of the multi- millionaire-to-be's darkest hours and how he had handled himself with such character and integrity. The multi-millionaire-to-be called my client every few weeks to let him know he hadn't forgotten, and that the money was coming. Perhaps, he had a list of creditors he called on designated days. Fighting through a rough patch, it was quite unlikely he had only one outstanding debt.

A few months later, when he finally paid off the debt, he thanked my client for his patience and told him to just throw the check away.

My client didn't throw it away. (A few years into our long friend/client relationship, he showed it to me.) It served as a reminder that not every entrepreneur was callous or sleazy. Years later, when the multi-millionaire ran for (and won) Mayor, my client wrote a check for $3,220 to his campaign, **ten times the amount of the transaction years ago**. That little symbolic check was, no doubt, lost in the millions of dollars sent in by other big-time contributors. But to my client, it was a lasting tribute to one man's integrity that he would take to his grave.

Take care of your people. Protect them from the fire. In the end, they will trust your leadership ten times over, and follow you wherever you go.

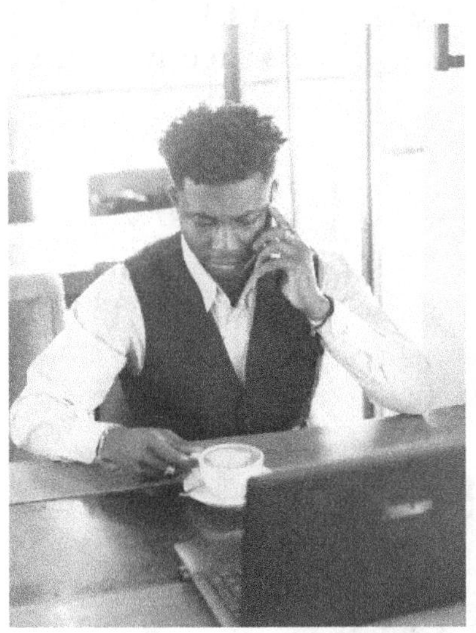

"Yes, I'll take the call. Patch it through."

10. Don't ask for advice if you never plan to use it.

Although you may not have mentors or consultants, you probably have unofficial advisors, friends, and relatives you trust and sometimes call upon to unravel the great mysteries of life.

There is a common misconception about asking others for their opinion. The person asking for help considers the advice optional, that is to say, an option among many other options to either select or discard. This is true, but only up to a certain numerical threshold. **At some point, the advisor's subconscious mind, which remembers everything, calculates the number of options discarded versus the number of options presented.** You asked for help twenty times, but discard nineteen of the suggestions your advisor placed on the table.

When you peel back all of the layers, the advisor's subconscious mind counts these as rejections, even worse, a declaration of unspoken mistrust. The advisor perceives his or her labor to be fruitless. Whatever thought and/or research that went into formulating the opinion is re-classified as wasted time. In response to your next request, your advisor will simply brush aside your crisis. "You'll figure it out."

Don't ask for help until you have exhausted your own list of options. If you genuinely value your advisor's input, then, from time to time, try his or her solutions. If none of them work, you know you have the wrong advisor.

Stop asking for advice you never plan to use.

You have your DOs from the SBA and your DON'Ts from the Over-50 Entrepreneurial Treasure Chest.

Now, let's close this thing out.

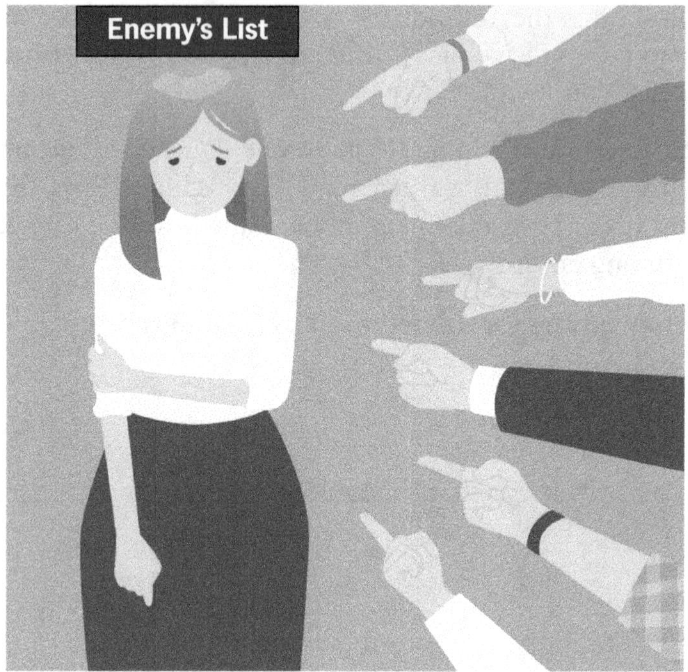

You may have forgotten. There is still one stone left unturned. We can't close out without getting your spouse off the enemy's list.

Whether we like it or not, spouses are co-adventurers on this entrepreneurial journey. Each spouse is different. But they all have one thing in common, and that is the desire for financial security.

In a precarious, uncertain, ever-evolving universe, the easiest way to arouse her already heightened anxiety is to mess with the small measure of predictability presumptuously in place. The security of a steady paycheck, insurance policy, declining mortgage, and modest savings that didn't go bone dry during the toxic derivative meltdown are monumental pieces to the security puzzle. She knows the age-related medical expenses are coming. She sees the evening news featuring COVID-19 catastrophic financial events, Enron meltdowns, pensions going belly-up, and Bernie Madoff cracks in the system that leave hard-working families, living under the bridge.

And now, with big dreams, a restless mind, and a faded birth certificate issued during the Vietnam War, you plan to put everything up for grabs.

Can you understand the deep, visceral fears you have awakened? Can you see why she is fighting you all the way?

Corresponding to thousands of years of evolution and hereditary keys to survival, your spouse's response has been hard-wired into her DNA.

Clinical studies show that almost all species - insects, animals, and humans alike - fight much harder to protect property than acquire it. The brain operates on a very elaborate system of ownership, partially based on sight (mirror likeness), touch, proximity, and difficulty to acquire.

Competitors for property invariably assume one of two roles. **Either they are owners or intruders.**

Without saying it, perhaps, without even knowing it, your spouse instinctively sees you as an intruder. Her brain releases "ferocious" hormones to protect what she owns ... what you both own, but what you apparently fail to value to the same precious, indispensable degree as she.

The easiest thing to do is to give her a condescending pat on the noggin and tell her she doesn't understand. The complex world of capitalism is over her head. One day, she'll thank you for your keen insight into evolving business opportunities of which most people are not aware. One day, she'll taste the fruits of your (entrepreneurial) prosperity and see the light.

This is the ABSOLUTE worst thing you could do. Besides insulting her intelligence, you are opting for the cowardly way out, leaving her to bear the brunt of fear and uncertainty you both should be openly sharing together.

Let's face it. You both are fearful, and rightly so. These are uncharted waters that could lead to blue skies or stormy seas. The sharks are waiting. They don't care that you have put in your faithful years with the corporate bureaucracy, or COVID-19 has set your employment prospects adrift. They'll gobble you up, anyway.

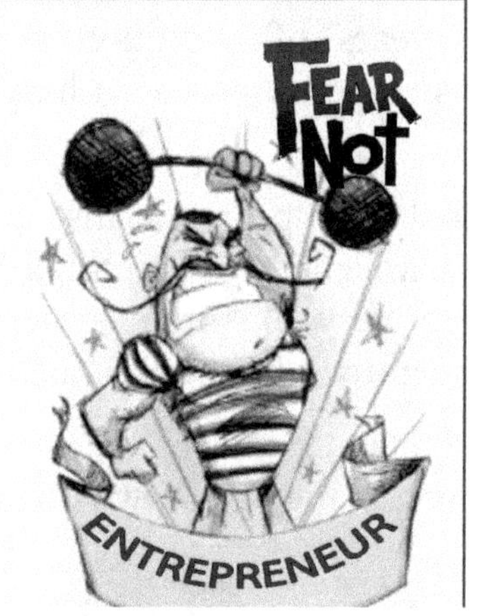

You have the right to be afraid. What you don't have is the right to assume a deceptive, macho identity that leaves your spouse with the impression something is wrong with her, that her protective instincts are off-base, that she needs to seek counseling for her lack of courage and faith.

The key to resolving this conflict is communications. You have an obligation to share your TOTAL vision with all of its grandiose potential and catastrophic high risks, the upsides and downsides ... even the sides you simply cannot see. You have to climb aboard the enemy's list to walk her down from the enemy's list.

You have to let her know you're both in it together, fearful, aging, and uncertain of what an entrepreneurial future will bring.

You share the same objective, to protect the things you own, the things you have accumulated together. But to protect these things means to face certain harsh realities ... the disruption of the employment marketplace, the diminishing social safety net, the new normal created by a worldwide pandemic, the relentless march of time that empowers the new generation and discards the old. You can sit idly by and watch your hard-earned fortunes flow down the drain. Or, you can fly out to Las Vegas and place your $5,000 FedEx chips on the line.

There is a certain level of misery and purposelessness that accompanies the inaction of sitting idly by, waiting for the vultures to move in. You have to make a choice. You "both" have to make the same choice. All humans are neurologically programmed to answer questions that are critical to them. Ask her this question ... **"In five years, where do you see us if we do nothing?"**

This may be strong medicine. But there will come a day, perhaps, many days, when the sky is falling and everything is going wrong. On those hell-bent days, you will need her voice of encouragement, her reinforcement of your shared decision, your shared belief. You won't get it if you chose to pat her on the noggin. You'll swim with the sharks ... all alone.

You're in it together ... got it?

Welllllll...

This ends our journey, at least, this phase. Go back to Chapter 14 with your assessment results, walk through the process, and make us all proud. You can do this. You can become the entrepreneur you always wanted to be.

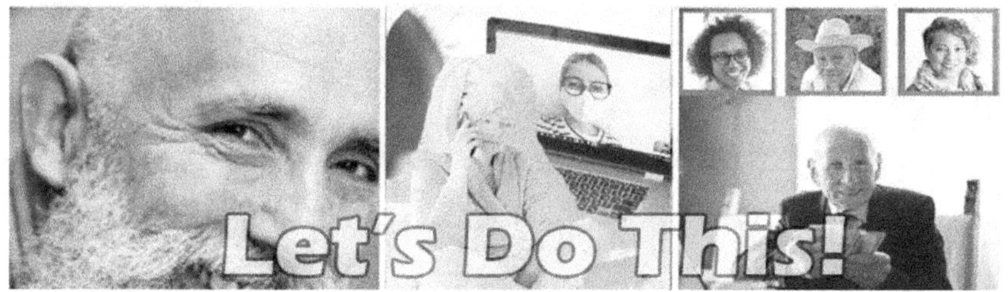

GOOD LUCK!!!!

- Leander Jackie Grogan -

Over50enterprises.com